# Classroom Management for Elementary Teachers

**Ninth Edition**

# Classroom Management for Elementary Teachers

## Carolyn M. Evertson
*Peabody College, Vanderbilt University*

## Edmund T. Emmer
*University of Texas, Austin*

Boston  Columbus  Indianapolis  New York  San Francisco  Upper Saddle River
Amsterdam  Cape Town  Dubai  London  Madrid  Milan  Munich  Paris  Montreal  Toronto
Delhi  Mexico City  São Paulo  Sydney  Hong Kong  Seoul  Singapore  Taipei  Tokyo

**Vice President and Editorial Director:** Jeffery W. Johnston
**Vice President and Publisher:** Kevin Davis
**Editorial Assistant:** Lauren Carlson
**Vice President, Director of Marketing:** Margaret Waples
**Marketing Manager:** Joanna Sabella
**Senior Managing Editor:** Pamela D. Bennett
**Senior Project Manager:** Mary M. Irvin
**Senior Operations Supervisor:** Matt Ottenweller
**Senior Art Director:** Diane Lorenzo
**Cover Designer:** Jason Moore
**Cover Art:** © Ted Horowitz/Corbis
**Project Coordination and Composition:** Aptara®, Inc.
**Printer/Binder:** Courier/Westford
**Cover Printer:** Courier/Westforrd
**Text Font:** Sabon

**Photo Credits:** Morgan Lane Photography/Shutterstock.com, p. 1; © H. Mark Weidman
Photography/Alamy, pp. 11, 102; © Dennis MacDonald/Alamy, p. 29; michaeljung/Shutterstock.
com, p. 51; iStockphoto.com/Christopher Futcher, p. 69; Monkey Business Images/Shutterstock.
com, p. 126; Katy McDonnell/Thinkstock, p. 146; Jaimie Duplass/Shutterstock.com, p. 163;
iStockphoto.com/Terry J Alcorn, p. 185; © Jim West/Alamy, p. 211.

Credits and acknowledgments for materials borrowed from other sources and reproduced, with permission, in this textbook appear on appropriate page within text.

Every effort has been made to provide accurate and current Internet information in this book. However, the Internet and information posted on it are constantly changing, so it is inevitable that some of the Internet addresses listed in this textbook will change.

**Library of Congress Cataloging-in-Publication Data**

Evertson, Carolyn M.
  Classroom management for elementary teachers/Carolyn M. Evertson, Edmund T. Emmer.—9th ed.
    p. cm.
  Includes bibliographical references and index.
  ISBN-13: 978-0-13-269326-4
  ISBN-10: 0-13-269326-7
  1. Classroom management. 2. Education, Elementary. I. Emmer, Edmund T. II. Title.
  LB3013.C528 2013
  372.1102'4—dc23
                                                                    2011033210

10 9 8 7 6 5 4 3 2 1

**PEARSON**

ISBN 10:     0-13-269326-7
ISBN 13: 978-0-13-269326-4

# BRIEF CONTENTS

# CONTENTS

# PREFACE

This book is intended as a guide for establishing and maintaining a comprehensive classroom management plan. Doing so will take some time and effort initially, but it will pay you large dividends later in the year because your students will be more engaged and cooperative. A good management plan will also leave you more time to teach, and it will provide your students with a better climate for learning.

You may have heard simple nostrums for becoming a good teacher: "Don't smile until Christmas," or "Treat all students the same," or "Be well prepared in your subject, and the rest will take care of itself." The trouble with such aphorisms is that they offer easy prescriptions for complex tasks, and their oversimplification creates an expectation that a classroom full of children or adolescents can be managed with good intentions but without a lot of thought about organizing and managing behavior. Neglecting to do a good job of organizing and managing the classroom—including space, behavior, and activities—means your teaching suffers the consequences. Unfortunately, so do the students.

The basis for this book grew out of an extensive program of research conducted by the authors over several decades. During the course of our research, we observed and conducted research in many hundreds of classrooms in a variety of schools to learn what skills, approaches, and strategies are necessary to manage classrooms effectively. We have also benefited from the research and writing of many other classroom researchers. A good summary of the research base for classroom management can be found in *Handbook of Classroom Management: Research, Practice, and Contemporary Issues* (Evertson & Weinstein, 2006). *Classroom Management for Elementary Teachers* (and its companion, *Classroom Management for Middle and High School Teachers*) represents our attempt to distill this accumulated body of research and scholarship into a usable guide for teachers. We hope you will find it helpful as you develop your own classroom management plan.

## New to This Edition

This edition contains several changes and additions:

- An updated introductory chapter sets the stage for learning about classroom management.
- New vignettes and response prompts for many chapters will stimulate discussion and deepen knowledge.
- Summaries have been added to draw together the concepts presented in each chapter.
- New chapter activities, along with new and updated readings, encourage students to process the ideas and extend their knowledge.

- Increased attention is given to the multiple ways technology affects classroom management (e.g., the increased use of technology for communication, etc.)
- Introductions are provided to response to intervention (RTI) and positive behavioral interventions and supports (PBIS).
- Research and further reading materials have been updated and added.
- Readers are given opportunities to respond to and interact over the vignettes.
- The Appendix has been expanded to include potential activity responses for Chapters 1 through 11.

## Acknowledgments

We extend our gratitude and appreciation to Inge R. Poole, Ph.D., Peabody College, Vanderbilt University, for her insightful suggestions and classroom examples; to Andrea Flower, Ph.D., University of Texas, Austin, for her insights and comments on managing special groups; and to Mary Claire Gerwels, Ph.D., University of Texas, Austin, for her many helpful suggestions on contemporary technology use in the classroom.

We thank the reviewers of our manuscript for their insights and comments: Terrell Brown, University of Central Missouri; Judith M. Geary, University of Michigan–Dearborn; Jean Roth Hawk, Bridgewater College; Kathleen Morris Kortz, SUNY–Potsdam; and Eleanor Wilson, University of Virginia.

## CHAPTER 1

# Introduction to Classroom Management

Classroom management is a broad concept that encompasses the set of behaviors and strategies that teachers use to guide student behavior in the classroom. Its goals include fostering student engagement and securing cooperation so that teaching and learning can occur. Classroom management has both planning and interactive aspects. Planning aspects include such tasks as organizing the physical space of the classroom, identifying expectations for student behavior, developing incentives to encourage desirable behavior, arranging consequences to discourage inappropriate behavior, and organizing instructional activities to promote student involvement and engagement. Classroom management also includes a very interactive, real-time set of teacher behaviors and strategies, including monitoring and interacting with students, providing support and feedback, intervening to redirect student behavior, and working with students to stimulate interest, involvement, and cooperation.

The many hours of our lives that we have spent as students have given the classroom environment a very familiar feel, so much so that it may not seem that it would take much effort to make the transition from student to teacher. But taking responsibility for teaching a group of 25 or more children is a very different task than being a student in a classroom. As students, we observe teachers without being privy to the decisions that teachers make or to the planning that has gone into their teaching. Students enter an environment that has been arranged, participate in designed activities, and interact with or observe peers and teachers without getting "behind the scene." For example, we probably observed teachers dealing with students who behaved inappropriately in the classroom. As students, we didn't usually think about alternate strategies for managing such behavior or what factors need to be considered when deciding what to do. One of the goals of this book is to provide insights into this behind-the-scenes world, so that you're better prepared for your work as a teacher.

Many skills, attributes, and actions contribute to making a great teacher. The ability to design lessons that stimulate student interest and promote learning is certainly high on everyone's list. Another important quality is establishing a connection with students, so that they feel supported and motivated to learn. A great teacher also needs good communication skills in order to be able to work with diverse groups of students and their parents. To this list of important competencies, we would add classroom management ability, not only because of its importance in fostering desirable student behavior, but also because it facilitates the other desirable teacher traits and skills. And all these desirable teaching traits then improve the general behavior of students and thus contribute to classroom management.

# ■ Classrooms Are Complex Places

It is also important to learn about classroom management in order to simplify a complex environment. The idea that classrooms may be complicated workplaces has been recognized for a long time (Jackson, 1968) and is a persistent view (Brophy, 2006; Doyle, 1986, 2006). These observers and researchers have noted that classrooms have multiple actors with different agendas, that teachers have to plan for several activities, and that they have to make multiple, often rapid decisions. Events happen quickly and inexorably, giving teachers a limited amount of time to address students' needs and concerns. Moreover, much of what the teacher and students say and do is public, so everyone is constantly aware of and potentially reactive to events. To complicate matters further, teachers don't have a lot of time to think about what they're doing during an activity; things just happen too quickly for much on-the-spot reflection.

Teachers develop a variety of strategies to help time slow down during teaching and to reduce the demand on their processing abilities. For example, teachers organize the classroom environment to facilitate activities and to prevent problems. They develop and install routines and procedures to guide their own and students' behaviors. They invite cooperation and encourage students to take responsibility for their actions, transferring some of the onus for managing behavior to the students themselves. Teachers endeavor to be consistent in how they respond to students so that students learn what to expect from the teacher and so that the teacher doesn't have to mull over every action and decision. Teachers plan activities to engage students, and teachers use their personal capital to influence students to follow classroom rules and procedures. All of these teacher actions promote order and regularity, freeing up the teacher to focus on instruction and help students learn.

# ■ Learning About Classroom Management

You have probably had the experience of trying to apply a new set of skills in a natural setting. Ideally, you were allowed gradually to acclimate to the new setting with a limited set of tasks. As your skills improved, you were given opportunities to apply the skills in more complex settings with greater demands. For example, when you first learned to drive a car, you weren't expected to drive on an unfamiliar road at high speeds during rush hour. Rather, you were (or should have been!) provided opportunities to encounter different driving situations and develop more-or-less automatic responses to simple aspects of driving, so that as time went on, you could attend to the more complex aspects of the task.

Learning to teach isn't the same as learning to drive, of course, but they do share some common features. Initially you need help focusing on the basic features of the task. With time and practice, some of these basics become automatic, and you can react better to more complex aspects. As you progress, you integrate the skills, the task appears less effortful, and you become more expert.

Reading a book on classroom management will provide you with information about the basic features of classroom management and a more integrated and complete perspective on the topic. But reading is not sufficient to become proficient. You need to apply the ideas in field settings whenever you observe in a classroom, assist a teacher, participate as an intern or student teacher, or reflect on your own work as a teacher. If you are conscientious about applying the ideas to actual teaching situations, you will soon begin to think like an experienced classroom manager, and you will be well on your way to becoming a great teacher.

To illustrate key ideas and to make the content in this book concrete, we'll present short vignettes based on actual classrooms (we've changed some inconsequential features in order to maintain confidentiality). We'll begin by presenting two vignettes of teachers that illustrate a variety of management concepts and how they influence classroom behaviors. The vignettes will also show how good and poor practices can compound their effects over time. As you read these vignettes, try to imagine yourself as the teacher, and reflect on what you would like to add to or avoid in your own teaching practice.

**Vignette 1.** Ms. Johnson's fourth-grade classroom has 26 students seated at 6 round or circular tables, 4 or 5 to a table. A computer station is located at the front of the room, near the teacher's desk. A science center and a book display cart are prominent features at the back of the room. Several decorated bulletin boards display student work and assignment lists. Another bulletin board lists classroom rules and has a chart with character education concepts and skills. Ms. Johnson began the year by developing the rules through discussion with the children, but she rarely refers to them any more. Similarly, although she intended to emphasize the importance of students practicing character traits such as trustworthiness, integrity, and doing one's personal best, the press of covering the curriculum and getting students ready to take the statewide assessment has caused her to scale back this aspect of her management plan, to the detriment of overall student behavior. Some problems are evident during several observations of the class:

- During a reading activity, while the teacher works with several students in the group instructional area, many students who are supposed to be working independently instead move around and talk. Several times Ms. Johnson interrupts her work with the group to tell students to remain at their desks and to resume work.
- On several occasions, there are long transitions between activities while the teacher searches for materials. During these times, students are in "dead time," and the teacher has difficulty getting their attention to begin the next activity.
- When students work in groups, persistent arguments occur that reduce the level of cooperation among group members. Ms. Johnson sends students to "time out" or takes points off a behavior record for the students when the noise level becomes bothersome, but this doesn't help the students resolve the problem.
- During a lesson on writing equivalent fractions, Ms. Johnson notices that students' attention is waning. She claps her hands, expecting that students will respond, but few do.
- She then provides students with a worksheet for problem solving and asks students to work in pairs. After 10 minutes, it's obvious that many pairs aren't able to make progress because the students don't know the steps needed to solve the problems. Ms. Johnson reteaches the lesson, but students run out of time to complete the work when the lunch period begins.
- When two students return noisily from the bathroom, other students laugh and call out to them. The teacher shushes them, but the two students dawdle on their way to their seats, visiting other students and clowning around.

**Discussion** A number of problems are evident in this class. Students need to be more engaged during lessons and during individual or group work activities. There is too much downtime and not enough productive time. Students seem not to understand what behaviors are expected during lessons or other activities, or if they know what is expected, they have little stake in following those expectations. Although she feels affection for the children and sincerely wants to provide a warm and supportive classroom climate, Ms. Johnson finds that she is constantly nagging the children about their behavior. This has led to several confrontations with some of the less cooperative children and has made Ms. Johnson feel more on guard. The general disorder that interferes with her activities, moreover, has frustrated and annoyed Ms. Johnson and blunted her effect while working with the children, some of whom now describe her as "mean." Some of the steps that could have been taken to avoid this deteriorating situation would be to place more emphasis on teaching desirable behavior from the start, make sure that students buy in to its importance, be consistent throughout the year in reinforcing the use of the system, and use a more positive tone. She could identify efficient procedures to manage different activities and make sure that students understand those procedures. She also needs to better prepare herself and her lessons to avoid wasted time and to maximize student learning of content.

**Vignette 2.** When students enter Ms. Carter's third-grade classroom, they find a welcoming, well-organized physical setting. Student desks (flat-top) are arranged in six groups of four or five, while off to the sides and corners of the room are the teacher's desk and areas for students to meet individually or in a group with the teacher, work at computer stations, and obtain materials from bookcases and other storage areas. A media cart with a projector, computer, and other equipment is located at the front of the classroom. On a bulletin board at the front are five laminated signs labeled with the names of common activities (Class Discussion, Independent Work, Small Groups) and behavior modes (Silent Work, Classroom Voices), along with movable check marks that Ms. Carter uses to cue students regarding expectations for the current class activity. Bulletin boards and walls have a variety of displays: a list of five guidelines for behavior, pictures of the students along with information each has written to share with classmates, a display featuring occupations (this month features paramedics and EMTs), and several pictures and charts with math, science, and other content topics.

Ms. Carter spent time and effort at the beginning of the school year to gradually teach students desirable behavior, using a variety of methods that included class discussions, explanations, feedback to students, praise and encouragement, and consistent application of her class rules and procedures. She emphasized the importance of all students working together with her to create "our" classroom community, one that supported each student's effort and success. Although occasional reminders are still needed to maintain her system, students have settled into the routines, and Ms. Carter has had less need to review her classroom system as the year has progressed. Observations of Ms. Carter and her students reveal a smooth-running class whose students are productively engaged.

- During a reading activity, students in pairs take turns reading to partners. Individual students come to the teacher's desk and read to her, while students who finish their pair's reading switch to an independent reading assignment. Although a few students occasionally take a few seconds "break" before resuming their work, there are no interruptions of other students who continue to work.

- At the end of the reading activity, Ms. Carter writes "Activity 3" on the whiteboard. This is a cue for students to work in groups on different activities that are listed on a chart. Six activities are listed, one for each group (each group eventually rotates through all the activities). One student goes from each group to retrieve the instructions and materials needed for the activity from the materials center. Activities include a money-counting task with a worksheet and play money, a computer-based activity, a vocabulary review, and a science activity on determining magnetic objects. As students work on the activities in groups, Classroom Voices is the behavior mode. Ms. Carter monitors the groups, answering questions and making suggestions. When one of the groups has a disagreement, she asks the group members to work out a solution that is acceptable to all of them.

- Ms. Carter signals the transition to the next activity by announcing, "Stop and give me five." As most students raise their hands, Ms. Carter directs students to clean up their activity areas and get ready for the next activity.

- Later in the day, students are working individually on arithmetic problems as the teacher finishes some administrative work at her desk. Several students have a three-sided piece of cardboard on their desks, making an "office" to minimize distractions during the independent work time. The teacher announces, "The timer is about to go off. Show me that you know what to do." Students put their materials away. The teacher has students switch pencils, as the groups' materials managers retrieve red pencils from their group materials box.

- During the checking activity that comes next, the teacher and class review the answers and problem-solving process. Ms. Carter calls on many students, praises frequently with reasons ("Good, you identified the coins and what they were each worth"), and asks students about their strategies for solving the problems.

- After the checking activity, Ms. Carter leads the class in a lesson on counting by 10, 100, and 1,000. After oral practice, students work individually: "Pencils in your hands, ready to go." On the overhead Ms. Carter writes, "Start on 500. Count by 10s." Students begin writing. After a while, she says, "Turn to a partner, check your work."

- On several occasions during the day, the teacher praises the whole class for how well they have been working together. She mentions how they have accepted responsibility for getting work done on time, listened to other students without interrupting, and shown respect for themselves and others.

**Discussion** Students are engaged and participate actively in Ms. Carter's class for many reasons. She uses a variety of well-planned activities, with procedures that are clearly understood by students. She obviously took the time to think through the procedures that were needed to manage her activities, and she communicated those procedures to her students. For example, students were taught to respond to signals that Ms. Carter uses to capture and redirect student attention. This also helps her manage transitions between activities. Because students know what procedures to follow, Ms. Carter can use a variety of activities and formats in her class without needing a lot of time to explain to students what they are supposed to be doing. Inappropriate behaviors are rare and are handled promptly. Because there is less inappropriate behavior, there is less opportunity for activities to get off track; this, in turn, helps maintain momentum in the lessons. It also reduces the number of models for undesirable behavior; also, Ms. Carter's feedback to students keeps the focus on desired behavior. The clarity with which procedures and routines are understood and practiced allows the teacher to monitor students' behavior, and the lower frequency of departures from the norm makes it easier to deal consistently with problems when they do occur.

# ■ Classroom Management's Connections to Other Facets of Teaching

Good classroom management is not an end in itself. It's important because it establishes conditions that enable students to learn better and because poor classroom management creates conditions that interfere with desirable educational outcomes. A substantial body of evidence on the relationship of good classroom management to student learning has accumulated over several decades of research. It demonstrates that good classroom management consistently predicts desirable student outcomes (see reviews by Hattie, 2009; Wang, Haertel, & Walberg, 1993). It is a subject, therefore, that deserves our careful attention.

We also think that it's important to be thoughtful about how management skills are applied. Although an orderly classroom with on-task students is desirable, we don't advocate a rigid, inflexible approach to implementing a plan. If a procedure doesn't work, it will need to be modified; if a student doesn't respond well to some intervention, then a new one must be found. Insisting on appropriate behavior is important, but sometimes a "my way or the highway" attitude won't work, and we have to back off and give a student some time to settle down and regroup. The emphasis should be on cooperation, not just on compliance.

Working effectively with children requires awareness of their motivations and interests. Researchers of student motivation have emphasized the need for teachers to create classroom systems that satisfy needs for autonomy, competence, and relatedness (Reeve, 2006; Ryan & Deci, 2000). Management strategies that are consistent with this motivational emphasis include providing students with opportunities to make choices, discussing the rationale behind a rule, giving students more responsibility, encouraging self-regulation, providing feedback that recognizes growth in skills and competencies, de-emphasizing comparisons among students, and using activities that promote student collaboration. It will be important to take motivation into account when designing your management system.

Developing good relationships with students is another significant corollary to effective classroom management practices. Research has shown that the connections students feel toward school are a significant factor in keeping students motivated (Battistich, Solomon, Watson, & Schaps, 1997; Pianta, 2006) and excelling academically (Hattie, 2009). There is, moreover, a reciprocal relationship: Teacher support of students tends to elicit student engagement and motivation, and students who show higher engagement tend to receive more teacher support (Skinner & Belmont, 1993). Thus, while teachers need to work at building positive relationships with students, they need to be conscious of the tendency to favor those students who are most engaged. Teachers also need to manage "boundaries" in the development of their relationships; teachers should be supportive adults, not buddies or pals.

Good classroom management provides a structure within which students can participate in learning activities and make progress in their development of knowledge and mastery of important skills. As teachers provide the structure, they need to be aware of student interests and take them into account in their lessons and assignments. Often students are not intrinsically interested in many of the topics and objectives in the curriculum (Brophy, 2009; Renninger, 2009). Lesson content, activities, and assignments that appeal to the age- and grade-level interests of the students will be more likely to engage them and will make classroom management easier. Similarly, having a well-managed classroom will make teaching easier, and it will give a teacher confidence to try out different activities and approaches that may appeal to student interests. In other words, just as with other teaching competencies, developing interesting lessons and establishing good classroom management serve complementary purposes and enhance each other.

The content of this book is organized to reflect how teachers experience classroom management. Prior to the beginning of classes, teachers prepare their classrooms and plan their management system's key features, including expectations for behavior, classroom routines and procedures, consequences, physical layout of the classroom, and major academic activities. During the first weeks of the year, teachers establish their classroom systems and help students learn appropriate behavior. As the year progresses, teachers work with students and respond to issues and problems, support student learning, and maintain a positive climate. Chapters 2, 3, and 4 provide details of the features of the classroom environment that must be planned ahead of time so that you are ready for the students when they arrive on the first day. Chapter 5 covers essential features of the first days of school, when you implement your system, and Chapters 6 and 7 address important concepts and skills that you will need to use as you engage students during academic activities.

Chapters 8 and 9 take up the topics of maintaining appropriate behavior and communicating effectively. The emphasis is on maintaining a positive climate and good communication skills. Chapter 10 describes an array of strategies for responding to inappropriate and disruptive behavior if the preventive strategies and simpler approaches from the earlier chapters are insufficient. The final chapter considers the management of behavior arising from individual differences among students. Its position as the last chapter doesn't imply that it is the last thing that teachers consider; rather, the preceding chapters also apply to the management of individual differences, but this chapter adds some specific information pertinent to particular conditions or differences.

## ■ Chapter Summary

Classroom management includes both preventive as well as interactive aspects; that is, teachers organize the classroom environment and prepare their students for appropriate behavior, and teachers must also interact constructively with students and respond as needed to refocus and redirect their behavior. Teaching is a complex task that requires continuing reflection and learning in order to progress from a student role to the teacher role. Two vignettes illustrated some of the dimensions of classroom management and problems that can result from poor management practices. Good classroom management has mutually supporting relationships with the effective teaching of content, the development of healthy student–teacher relationships, good communication, and a positive classroom climate.

## ■ Further Reading

Le Maistre, C., & Paré, A. (2010). Whatever it takes: How beginning teachers learn to survive. *Teaching and Teacher Education, 26,* 559–564.

*In this essay, the authors discuss the common problems faced by novice teachers in comparison to novices in three other fields. The differences that novice teachers experience can be significant challenges. The authors suggest that experienced teachers mentor newcomers to help them understand how to "satisfice" (Simon, 1957).*

McNally, J., I'Anson, J., Whewell, C., & Wilson, G. (2005). "They think that swearing is okay": First lessons in behaviour management. *Journal of Education for Teaching, 3(3),* 169–185.

*This article discusses the challenges beginning teachers (i.e., student teachers) encounter with behavior problems. The authors include quotes concerning new teachers' common struggles, coping reactions, and sense making of their experiences.*

# ■ Suggested Activities

1. Reflect on the vignettes of Ms. Johnson and Ms. Carter presented in this chapter. What are some important differences between their approaches to managing activities and students? How might students in these classrooms react to these differences over the course of a semester or year? What effects on students' learning, motivation, and attitudes might occur, and why?

2. Jot down some details of a classroom situation you remember as a student (e.g., field trip, daily activity, student misbehavior). With a partner, discuss what additional aspects may have been involved from the point of view of the teacher.

3. Describe a former teacher whom you felt had great classroom management. What are some of the skills and strategies that were important to the teacher's success?

---

**MyEducationLab**

Now go to www.myeducationlab.com to:

■ Take a Quiz to test your mastery of chapter objectives.
■ Study chapter content with an individualized Study Plan.
■ Deepen your understanding of particular concepts and principles with Classroom Management Simulations.
■ Apply what you have learned in the chapter to your work with children in Building Teaching Skills exercises.

# CHAPTER 2

# Organizing Your Classroom and Materials

Arranging the physical setting for teaching is a logical starting point for classroom management because it is a task that all teachers face before school begins. Many teachers find it easier to plan other aspects of classroom management once they know how the physical features of the classroom will be organized.

The number of things to consider in arranging the typical elementary school classroom is amazing! Of course, there is furniture—the teacher's and the students' desks, bookcases, filing cabinets, chairs, and a table or two. There also may be electronic equipment such as a projector, computer, CD/DVD player, and television. Visual aids such as bulletin boards must be prepared, charts and maps displayed, and storage for materials provided. Finally, teachers bring personal touches to a classroom—perhaps plants, an aquarium, or cages for pets. When you arrange these features, you must make many decisions. How should desks be arranged? Where should your desk be? Where are the electrical outlets and Internet access lines? Where will groups meet with you and work? What areas of the room will you use for presentations? How will you and the students obtain materials and supplies?

In this chapter we discuss how to plan a room arrangement that supports your teaching. You will learn five keys to room arrangement and read numerous suggestions for managing space in your classroom. You will be asked to analyze two room arrangements. This chapter concludes with a checklist for your classroom.

# For Reflection

Before you begin to arrange your classroom, think about the following questions. The answers will help you decide what physical features need special attention. Before you look at your classroom, think about the kinds of learning you would most like to see there:

- What are your main types of instructional activities (e.g., small groups, whole-class discussions, teacher presentations, student presentations, individual assignments, group projects)? What physical arrangements will best support these activities?
- Will students be making extensive use of equipment (e.g., microscopes, computers) or materials (e.g., science or math manipulatives)? Will these be shared among individuals or groups?
- Does your class include students with special needs that must be considered?
- Where are the areas of potential distraction (e.g., high traffic, animals, group centers)? Which children will need screening or distance from these areas?
- How much movement around the room will be necessary during the day? What areas of the room will be involved? Will students get their own materials, or will you have them distributed?
- Will students need access to references, research tools, or trade books?
- How flexible or permanent will the arrangement be? Will you have to change it during a single day, for each new unit, or will it stay the same for months? Do you share your classroom with any other teachers?

Your room arrangement also affects how smoothly the day can proceed. For example, if areas for storing materials are poorly placed, bottlenecks may occur when students get or return supplies, which could slow down the activities or delay getting them started. The location for your meetings with individuals and small groups must be chosen carefully; otherwise you may have difficulty watching the rest of the class. The positioning of desks is important because a poor arrangement may interfere with visibility of instructional areas, increase distractions during instruction, or make it difficult for you and your students to move around the room.

Your room arrangement communicates to students how you expect them to participate in your class, and your philosophy of teaching and learning will influence how you arrange your classroom. Desks arranged in groups imply that interaction and collaboration among students are expected for at least some activities. Desks in rows indicate that the focus of the classroom is the teacher, the board, or some other central point.

This chapter will help you make these and other decisions about room arrangement, equipment, and basic supplies. Each component is described, and guidelines and examples will help you plan.

# ■ Five Keys to Good Room Arrangement

Remember that the classroom is the learning environment for both you and your students. It is not a very large area for up to 30 people interacting for long periods of time—as much as 7 hours in a day. Furthermore, you and your students will be engaging in a variety of activities and using different areas of the room. You will facilitate these activities if you arrange your room to permit orderly movement, keep distractions to a minimum, and make efficient use of available space. Depending on your instructional approach, you may need different arrangements for different instructional formats (e.g., whole-class, small-group; see Chapter 6). Use the following five keys as guidelines for deciding about your room's arrangements:

1. **Use a room arrangement consistent with your instructional goals and activities.** You will need to think about the main types of instructional activities that will take place in your class and then organize the seating, materials, and equipment compatibly. If your main activities include whole-group lessons, teacher-led small-group lessons, and centers, the classroom should be arranged to accommodate multiple purposes. For example, the whole-group instructional area (e.g., grouped desks or a rug to accommodate all students) should allow all students to see the instructional displays as well as provide a storage/surface area for your teaching materials. The small-group area may need a specific table or grouping of desks from which you can see all students and can simultaneously provide instruction and access materials for the small group. The centers will require several locations around the room where students can explore content independently. Holding all of these spaces within a single classroom takes careful planning.

2. **Keep high-traffic areas free of congestion.** Areas where many students gather and areas that receive constant use can be sites for distraction and disruption. High-traffic areas include group work areas, pencil sharpener, trash can, water fountain, certain bookshelves and storage areas, computer stations, student desks, and the teacher's desk. These areas should be widely separated from each other, have plenty of space, and be easy to get to. If students will be working at computers or in various parts of the room during a single lesson, make sure they can move easily from place to place. Classrooms with multiple computers may require the use of extension cords and surge protectors. Be mindful of the traffic hazards these can pose as well as of the local fire marshal's regulations.

3. **Be sure students can be seen easily by the teacher.** Careful monitoring of students is a major management task. Your success in monitoring will depend on your ability to see all students at all times. Therefore, be sure there are clear lines of sight between instructional areas, your desk, student desks, and all student work areas. Be especially conscious of the placement of bookcases, file cabinets, and other pieces of furniture and equipment that can block your line of vision. Stand in different parts of the room, and check for blind spots.

4. **Keep frequently used teaching materials and student supplies readily accessible.** Keeping materials accessible not only minimizes time spent getting ready and cleaning up, but also helps to avoid distracting slowdowns and breaks in the lesson

flow. If you or your students must stop to locate needed materials and supplies, you run the risk of losing student attention and engagement as well as instructional time and lesson flow (see Chapter 6).

**5. Be certain that students can easily see whole-class presentations and displays.** When you plan where you and your students will be for whole-class presentations and discussion, be sure that the seating arrangement will allow students to see the overhead projector screen or board without moving their chairs, turning their desks around, or craning their necks. Also, don't plan to conduct whole-class activities in a far corner of the room away from a substantial number of students. Such conditions do not encourage students to pay attention and make it more difficult for you to keep all students involved. Check out how well your students can see by sitting for a moment at desks in different parts of the room.

Applying each of these five keys will help you design workable room arrangements. The specific components that will lead to this goal are described next. By attending to these areas, you will address the important aspects of room arrangement.

# ■ Suggestions for Arranging Your Classroom

## Wall and Ceiling Space

Wall space and bulletin boards provide areas to display student work, instructionally relevant material, decorative items, assignments, rules, schedules, a clock, and other items of interest. Ceiling space can also be used to hang mobiles, decorations, and student work. The following points should be considered when preparing these areas:

**1.** At the start of school, you should have at least the following displays for walls and boards:
- Class rules (see Chapter 3)
- A place for daily assignments or the daily schedule
- Some decorative display to catch your students' interest, such as a bulletin board with a "Welcome Back to School" motif, or a display that includes the name of each child in the room
- A calendar
- Posted emergency escape routes (usually near the door)

**2.** Other displays that teachers find useful include an example of the correct paper heading and a content-relevant display, such as one highlighting a soon-to-be-taught topic. Many teachers also provide posters of useful strategies for content areas, such as reading, and informational charts on the steps in writing.

**3.** Displays may be used to help keep track of your students' locations. You may wish to create a poster with a pocket for each child. These pockets can be made of library cardholders or laminated halves of envelopes. Label each pocket with a child's name. Whenever a child leaves the room, he or she inserts a Popsicle stick or construction paper strip labeled with the destination. The same idea can be used to create a record of jobs or privileges, such as being the line leader or materials manager.

**4.** You will probably want to cover large bulletin board areas with colored paper, burlap, or other fabric. This paper comes on large rolls and is often kept in the school office or a supply room. You can trim the bulletin boards with an edging or border. (If you can't find this item in your supply room and you have a school budget for supplies, you can find it at a school supply center or online.) Be sure the types and quantities of paper or material on walls or ceiling does not violate safety or fire codes.

**5.** Don't spend too much time decorating your room. You will have many other important things to do to get ready for the beginning of school. A few bare bulletin boards will allow you to add displays later. Children can decorate a blank space for an art project or as part of a science or social studies unit. Don't overdecorate. Wall space cluttered with detail can be distracting and make a room seem smaller. Hanging mobiles and decorations from the ceiling can also be overdone. Your room will seem small enough when your 25 to 30 students are in it.

**6.** If you need ideas for decorating your room or for setting up displays, ask other teachers, look in other classrooms, check online, and leaf through teaching magazines (e.g., *The Mailbox*).

**7.** As the following cartoon suggests, whatever decorating ideas or displays you use should be age appropriate for your students.

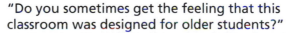

Cartoon reprinted courtesy of *Phi Delta Kappan* and James Estes.

## Floor Space

A good starting point for your floor plan is to determine where you will conduct whole-class instruction. Identify where you will stand or work when you address the entire class to give instructions. You can usually identify this area of the room by the location of a large board or projector screen. This area may need a place for items needed in presentations and an electrical outlet for the document camera (doc-cam). If you prefer to have your students gather on the floor for whole-class instruction, you may want to allow space for a large rug for this area.

Making a scale drawing of the classroom with templates for various furnishings (e.g., student desks, your desk, bookshelves, computer station) will decrease the number of times you have to move heavy furniture as well as save time. When you start arranging furniture, have extension cords in hand. They are easier to plug in before a heavy bookcase is standing in front of the outlet. Again, be aware of potential hazards with extension cords.

As you read the following sections, refer to Figures 2.1 and 2.2, examples of workable floor plans for an elementary school classroom. Note how each element has been addressed. These are just two of many possible alternative arrangements. Of course, you will have to adjust to whatever constraints exist in your assigned classroom (e.g., class size, shape, available furniture). If the classroom is small,

**figure 2.1** ■ An Example of a Workable Room Arrangement

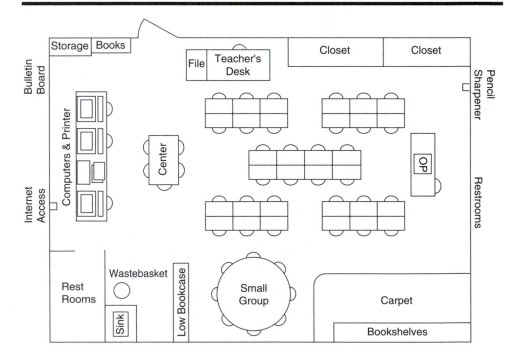

**figure 2.2** ■ An Example of a Double U-Shaped Arrangement with Easy Access to Special Topic Areas

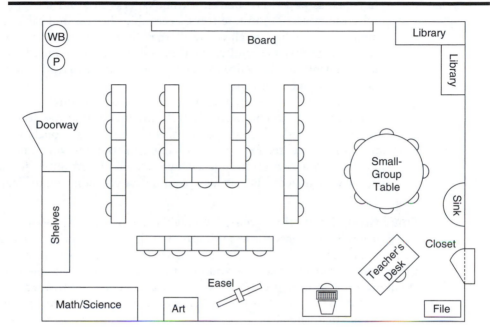

remove unnecessary student desks, other furniture, or equipment; if you have inadequate storage, perhaps you can locate an extra file or supply cabinet.

**Arrangement of Student Desks/Tables.**   Determine whether your seating arrangement will vary according to the type of classroom activity or will be permanent. After you have established the seating arrangement, decide whether you will assign students to seats or allow them to choose where they will sit. In Figure 2.1 student desks are arranged in clusters rather than in rows; however, no students are seated with their backs to the major instructional area. If the teacher displays material on the overhead projector screen, all of the students can see it by turning slightly in their seats.

- It is important to keep high-traffic areas clear, so don't put desks or other furniture in front of doors, water fountains, sinks, the pencil sharpener, or other traffic centers. Also, try to avoid having your whole-class arrangement face potential sources of distraction such as windows, computers, the small-group area, animals, or other eye-catching displays.
- Leave enough room around student desks so that you can move among and monitor the students easily or give them help during seatwork activities.
- Some classrooms are equipped with tables and chairs for students instead of desks. Table seating provides some unique grouping opportunities. To avoid

having students with their backs to instructional areas, seat students on only three sides of the tables. An additional problem is the storage of student supplies such as paper, notebooks, textbooks, crayons, and scissors. Milk crates under the tables, group tote trays, accessible shelves, and table-top boxes of community supplies are all viable alternatives for storage. Plan the location of such storage areas carefully, for they will be used frequently and often by many students at once. Give thorough consideration to traffic patterns around and near storage areas.

- Count the desks or chairs, and make sure you have enough.
- You may decide to change room arrangements during the year. If you begin the year with desks in rows, you may switch to a desks-touching arrangement later in the year (see Figure 2.2). Changes to routines can stimulate students' interest, and a new arrangement may increase opportunities for social learning. New arrangements may also require new procedures (see Chapter 3).

**Small-Group Instruction Areas.**   You will need an area where you can meet with small groups of students for lessons, group projects, or tutoring. Arrange this area so that you can observe the rest of the class from your position within the small group. Place your chair so that you face the whole class. Note the position of the small-group area in Figure 2.2. If you are seated facing out toward the room, you can monitor the whole class even when working with the small group. If you are seated in the opposite chair with your back to the class, you cannot see the whole class unless you turn around.

A table allows a small-group area to be used for activities that include writing or working with materials. When a table or extra chairs are not available, students may be asked to carry their chairs and place them in a circle (or to sit on a rug) for group instruction. An alternative is to assign seats so that students can remain at their desks or tables for small-group instruction while the teacher moves from group to group.

If many small groups will be working in your classroom at once (e.g., research groups, literature discussion groups, or writing-process groups), you will have to provide areas where they can meet. For instance, groups can meet on the floor, at student desks, or at the small-group table. Chapter 7 has additional information on arranging your classroom for cooperative groups.

**Computer Workstations.**   Most classrooms are now equipped with computers. This technology can greatly expand the learning opportunities available to students, but it must be managed carefully. Your location choices may be limited because of the need for wall outlets and Internet access, so consider placing the computer workstations first and then arranging other centers and activity areas. Some schools have computers on rolling carts to be shared among classrooms. With this situation, you will have to consider the ease in getting them in and out of the room as well as charging them. Place the computers away from chalk dust, liquids, and magnets.

When arranging your room, make sure that computer monitors are positioned so that you can quickly scan them to be sure students are on task. This is especially important when students have Internet access. Check all equipment in advance of student use. Get and store any necessary extension cords, cables, paper, printer cartridges, headphones, and other peripherals with the equipment.

Large groups of students around a computer can lead to disturbances and off-task behavior. Limit the number of students working on a computer to no more than four, and establish a policy that students at the computer have a purpose and a time limit so that this resource can be shared fairly. Teach students to save their work so they don't lose it if they are unable to finish their projects in a given time frame. Flash drives serve as a convenient storage tool.

**The Teacher's Desk, Filing Cabinet, Projector, and Other Equipment.** If you intend to use a teacher's desk during the school day (e.g., student conference, modeling journal writing), use the same monitoring principle in positioning the desk that you use when arranging the small-group area: Sit facing the students, and be sure that you can see all of them from your seat. Consider traffic patterns near your desk. For example, student desks should not be so close that students would be distracted by individuals approaching your desk or working with you there. If you are not planning to use a teacher's desk during the school day, you may consider placing the desk at the back of the room. Some teachers prefer a locking rolling cart to a desk.

Consider what access students will have to materials on your desk. If they can use materials stored on your desk such as a stapler, pens, or extra crayons, what are the procedures for obtaining these supplies? For example, may students get these supplies as needed, or do they have to ask your permission?

Other furniture items, such as a filing cabinet and storage cabinets, must be where they are functional. Seldom-used supplies can be safely tucked away in a corner or hidden from view. Furniture that contains items to be used frequently must be close by.

The teacher's computer is often kept on or next to the teacher's desk. If attendance and tardy reports are done by computer each morning, the computer needs to be easily accessed. When you are at the computer, keep lines of sight open so you can monitor students easily. Remember that all student records are confidential and should not be accessible to others.

**Bookcases and Other Storage.** Bookcases should be placed where they will neither hinder your monitoring nor obstruct students' ability to see chalkboards or relevant displays. Tall bookcases perpendicular to a wall create hideaways that prevent you from seeing the students behind them. When bookcases contain items used frequently, such as dictionaries or the classroom library, they must be convenient and easily monitored. Seldom-used items should be on an out-of-the-way shelf or in a cabinet. If students will access materials within cabinets, label the doors (e.g., with words or photographs). Place items students access at a reasonable height for them. Consider using a rolling cart for materials that may have to be moved from group to group, such as resources for a particular research topic.

"Miss Marpole, I need to talk to you about your seating arrangement."

Reprinted by permission of George Abbott/*Phi Delta Kappan.*

**Centers.**   A center is an area where students may work on a special activity or study a topic. Centers may be built around a thematic study topic in science or social studies, for instance, or around skill areas in a particular subject such as arithmetic or reading. Examples of types of centers in elementary classrooms include classroom libraries, listening centers, writing centers, science discovery centers, computer workstations, math centers, art centers, and dramatic play areas. The number and type of centers will vary according to grade levels and curriculum.

If you use centers in your classroom, consider carefully the location for each. For instance, if the center is to be a separate area of your room, such as the classroom library, consider dividing it from the rest of the class with a low bookshelf or table so you can still monitor students. Also, if you anticipate increased noise or activity at a center, locate it so as not to disturb other students. If any of your centers require electrical outlets, arrange them first. Be certain that all necessary materials and equipment at each center are available and functioning properly. Post instructions for equipment use and cleaning up the center.

Some teachers like to have a more informal area in the classroom, including, for example, an area rug, bookcases, a small table, or comfortable seating. Such an area can add an inviting, personal touch to the setting. Students might be allowed to use it for special projects, group work, or during free-reading activities (see procedures in Chapter 3). If you use such an area, design its location so that it won't interfere with or distract from other activities. Also, because this type of center requires extensive floor space, weigh its advantages against the loss of space for other activities and the crowding that may result.

**Pets, Plants, Aquariums, and Special Items.**  These attractions can add a personal touch to a room and provide learning experiences for children. However, the first week of school is already quite exciting for students, so it is not necessary to introduce such special features immediately. If you do bring in such items, place them where they won't distract students, especially during whole-class activities. They should be placed where they will neither impede movement about the room nor interfere with activities of individual students. Check to see whether any students are allergic to pets. Choose plants that are nontoxic. You may also want to consider assigning students responsibilities for the care of classroom pets or plants (e.g., feeding fish, watering plants).

## Material and Supply Storage

When you have decided on your wall and bulletin board displays and have organized your classroom space, you can concentrate on obtaining supplies and providing for their storage. Some supplies will be used frequently and should be readily accessible; other items will be seasonal or used infrequently, and they can go into deeper storage.

**Textbooks and Other Instructional Materials.**  Identify the textbooks and other instructional materials (e.g., dictionaries, encyclopedias, magazines, newspapers, maps, globes, and math manipulatives) to be used in your class. Make sure you have sufficient quantities for everyone. Determine which books the students are allowed to keep at their desks or take home and which must remain in the room for all students to use. Then find easily accessible shelves in a bookcase for everyday books and materials that will not be kept in student desks. If you don't know what supplemental materials are available or what the school policies are regarding these items, check with the school principal, media specialist, or another teacher.

**Student Work.**  If students do not have space to store their folders and journals, or if you prefer to keep them in a central location, make sure this area is easily accessible. For example, a milk crate can contain a hanging file for each student's work, journal, and folder. Some teachers utilize file baskets for students' work in each subject area. Students' computer-based work may also be saved on CDs or flash drives for future use (see also Chapter 6).

   If your students keep portfolios of their work, it may be easier for the students and you to keep up with them if there is a specific storage space for them. Locate this in an area that makes it easy for students to find their portfolios, place their work in them, and return them to a central spot. Also, consider if digital storage (e.g., photographs, scanned documents, videos) would be a viable tool for portfolios.

**Frequently Used Classroom Materials.**  A basic set of supplies for the children includes paper in varying sizes and colors, water-soluble markers, rulers, assorted pens and chalk for art projects, transparent tape and masking tape, a stapler, and glue. These and any other supplies that are used daily—science materials, math manipulatives, calculators—should be kept in a handy place such as on a worktable or shelves. Students are usually expected to supply such materials as pencils, erasers, pens, crayons, scissors, and notebook paper or tablets. Because you cannot count on all students to bring these materials at the beginning of the year, make sure you have a supply of these items. Also, give parents a list of supplies each child in your class will need. Some teachers include a request for class supplies such as hand sanitizer, tissues, and zipper storage bags.

**Teacher's Supplies.**    You will receive some materials from the school office for your own use. These items may include pencils and pens; paper; a large, lined display tablet; dry erase markers; scissors; transparent tape; ruler; stapler; paper clips; and thumbtacks. In addition, you should have a grade book, a lesson plan book, and teacher's editions for all textbooks. Ask about other supplementary books such as thematic resources or math or science standards. These items can usually be stored in your desk. Because some schools restrict paper use (particularly with photocopying) for budget purposes, be sure to note any limitations for the year and abide by them.

**Other Necessities.**    If your room does not have a clock and a calendar, obtain them. Both should be large enough to be seen from all areas of the room. You may wish to buy a desk bell or a timer if you will need it as a signal for starting or stopping activities. The following items may also come in handy: paper towels, soap, bandages, plastic gloves, and extra lunch money for emergencies. Some teachers keep a few basic tools such as a hammer, pliers, and screwdriver for minor repairs.

**Student Belongings.**    In addition to supplies that students store in their desks or in tote trays, you will need storage for items such as lunch boxes, book bags, outdoor clothing, lost-and-found items, and show-and-tell materials. Leave spaces for these items as you prepare your classroom. (You might prepare signs identifying each space.) If students bring items that are too large to be stored at their desks (e.g., musical instrument), or if their presence is likely to be distracting or to interfere with movement about the room, designate a storage location elsewhere in the room. Planning for storage will help keep your classroom from becoming cluttered and will help avoid the problem of misplaced belongings. Some classrooms have cubbies for student items. Consider labeling these with students' names.

**Seasonal or Infrequently Used Items.**    Holiday and seasonal decorations, bulletin board displays, and special project materials are used only on some occasions, as are calculators, protractors, templates, special art project materials, and science equipment. Because you do not need continual access to these materials, you can store them at the back of closets, in boxes on top of cabinets, or even out of the room if you have access to outside storage space.

To organize and keep track of your activities as you arrange your room and get your equipment and supplies ready, you will find it helpful to use the checklist at the end of this chapter. Each aspect of room arrangement has been listed, and space has been provided for noting what has to be done and for checking off each area.

# ■ Chapter Summary

Organizing the furniture, equipment, materials, and supplies in the classroom is a necessary beginning task for teaching. Five keys guide the placement of these items: (1) Use a room arrangement consistent with your instructional goals and activities, (2) keep high-traffic areas free of congestion, (3) be sure students can be seen easily by the teacher, (4) keep frequently used teaching materials and student supplies readily accessible, and (5) be certain students can easily see whole-class presentations and displays. Classroom arrangements differ according to multiple constraints (e.g., number of students, grade level, available furniture) and can change to meet varying purposes (e.g., instructional formats; see Chapter 6). Establishing a physical space for learning that is safe, practical, and instructional is a critical aspect of your management plan.

# ■ Further Reading

Bitter, G. G., & Legacy, J. (2008). *Using technology in the classroom* (7th ed.). New York: Pearson Education.

*This text is an introductory explanation of technology and its use for teachers and students. The initial chapters are designed for those new to technology. Later chapters are accessible to those new to technology as well as helpful to those familiar with the technology described.*

Butin, D. (2000). *Classrooms.* Washington, DC: National Center for Educational Facilities (ERIC Report No. ED446421). Available at www.edfacilities.org/ir/irpubs.html

*The author discusses classroom design. Trends in classroom design principles and major issues in the use of classroom space are summarized. The Web site has articles dealing with classroom design in content areas, as well as links to many related Web sites.*

Diller, D. (2008). *Designing classrooms for literacy: Spaces and places.* Portland, ME: Stenhouse.

*This book offers suggestions for the elementary teacher to promote and support the development of literacy with particular attention to the design and arrangement of the learning environment.*

Evertson, C. M., & Poole, I. R. (2004). *Effective room arrangement*. Nashville, TN: Vanderbilt University, Peabody College, IRIS Center (iris.peabody.vanderbilt.edu). Click on "Resources," then on "Accommodations" (left column), and then on "Case Studies" (middle column) to link to this case study set.

> *This Web site contains many activities and case studies for accommodating special needs students in the regular education classroom.*

Fraser, B. J., & Walberg, H. J. (Eds.). (1991). *Educational environments: Evaluation, antecedents and consequences*. Oxford, England: Pergamon.

> *Classroom environments are much more than physical arrangements; they include organizational, instructional, and interpersonal dimensions. Their effects, moreover, depend substantially on how students perceive or experience the environments. This book thoroughly explores many aspects of learning environments, connecting them to a variety of social, institutional, and personal factors.*

Huffman, H., Jernstedt, G., Reed, V., Reber, E., Burns, M., Oostenink, R., et al. (2003). Optimizing the design of computer classrooms: The physical environment. *Educational Technology, 43*(4), 913.

> *This article suggests two guiding principles as a framework for effective classroom design that includes technology: promoting student attention and allowing for periodic shifts in learner activities.*

Jones, R. A. (1995). *The child–school interface: Environment and behavior*. London: Cassell.

> *Jones presents an analysis of how children's behaviors are influenced by the various environments they encounter at school. The author's point of view is ecological, incorporating the physical setting of the classroom as one of the contributors to children's behavior, along with social and organizational factors.*

Meager, J. (1996). Classroom design that works every time. *Instructor, 106*, 70–73.

> *The author, a veteran classroom teacher, describes a number of charts, bulletin board ideas, and graphs that can be used to feature content and prompt desirable student behavior. Issues of the magazine* Instructor *are often a good source of ideas and activities for classroom use.*

Weinstein, C. S., & David, T. G. (Eds.). (1987). *Spaces for children: The built environment and child development*. New York: Plenum Press.

> *Chapters address how characteristics of the physical setting influence the behaviors and development of children. Guidelines for constructing and arranging environments are provided, based on educational and developmental research. Ideas for including children in planning their spaces are included.*

teacher.scholastic.com/tools/

> *This site includes a classroom set-up tool. Under "Teacher Resources" choose "Tools," and then select "Class Set-Up Tool."*

# ■ Suggested Activities

The following activities will help you plan and organize your classroom space.

1. Figure 2.3 shows how one teacher arranged a classroom. There are several potential problems with this room arrangement. How many can you find? Suggest one or more ways to correct each problem. (See the key for this activity in the Appendix.)

2. a. Examine Figure 2.4. Based on the room arrangement, what activities would you expect to be common in this classroom? What kinds of participation will be expected from students?

   b. Picture yourself as a student in the classrooms depicted in Figures 2.3 and Figure 2.4. Place yourself in various areas of the rooms. Can you see what you need to see? Now place yourself as a teacher in the rooms. Can you see all students? Can you circulate freely among desks and work areas?

   c. The teacher whose classroom is depicted in Figure 2.4 anticipated having 28 students in her class. She has just learned that she will have at least 33 at the beginning of the year. How can she rearrange her room to accommodate the five additional students without losing the advantages of the arrangement she has designed?

3. Visit other teachers' classrooms, and examine their room arrangements. Use the items in the checklist at the end of the chapter and the five keys to room arrangement listed

**figure 2.3**  ■  A Room Arrangement with Potential Problems

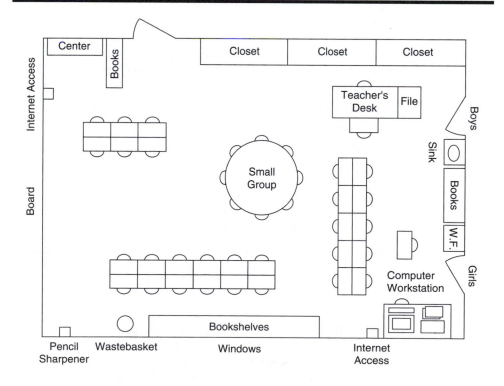

**figure 2.4**   ■   One Teacher's Planned Room Arrangement

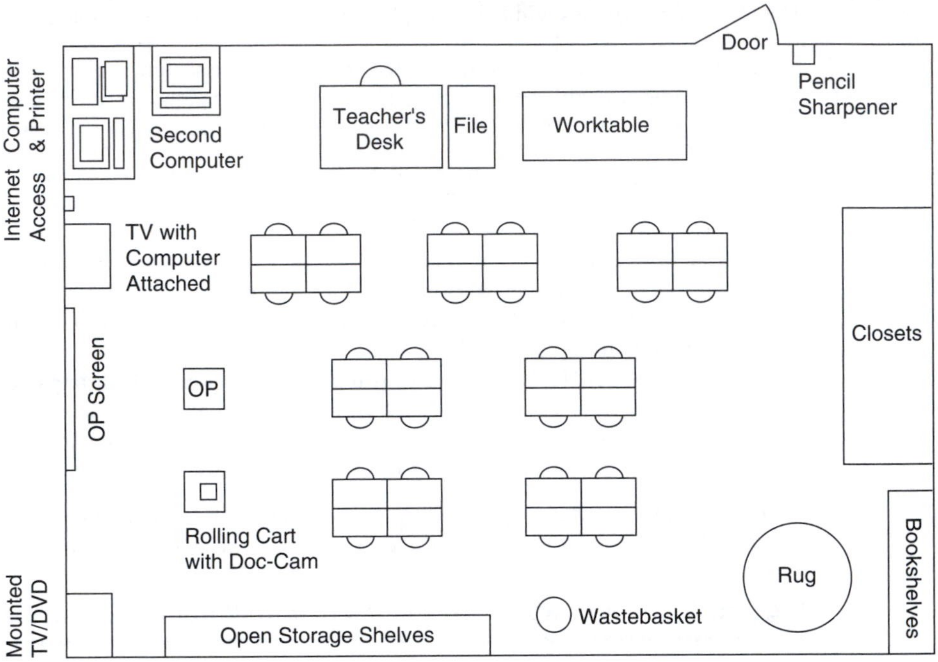

there (discussed on pp. 13–14) to guide your observation and analysis. If you have a specific problem, ask several teachers for suggestions, and see how they may have coped with a similar problem.

4. Cheri is a repeating first grader who missed most of her first-grade year for medical reasons. She has a syndrome that is characterized by fragile bones, so for Cheri, simple jostling or bumps can result in broken bones. She walks with leg braces and often uses a walker. Cheri is protectively seated beside the teacher's desk, separate from the other students. Here Cheri has easy access to her walker. Her academic work shows that she is progressing with her peers, but her social skills are below grade level. From this information, where could you seat Cheri to help her increase positive interaction with peers and maintain safe movement to and from groups and in and out of the classroom? Select A, B, or C in Figure 2.5, and explain your choice.

5. Several short articles and examples of room arrangement and classroom design for K–12 can be found at www.learnnc.org, a Web site maintained by the University of North Carolina. Enter the phrase "room arrangement" or "classroom design" into the site's search tool. From this site identify three tips for arranging your classroom that you plan to implement.

6. To the checklist at the end of the chapter, add five or more other room arrangement needs you will want to address as you set up your classroom. Make notes about where you will obtain these items.

**figure 2.5** ▪ A Room Arrangement to Facilitate Access and Interaction for a Student with Special Needs

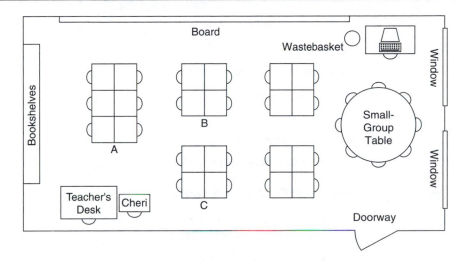

7. The decisions you make as a teacher (e.g., how you want students to interact with you, with each other, and with the content) reflect what you believe about teaching and learning—that is, your philosophy of education. Your decisions will have important consequences for the success of your instructional activities. Thinking about your beliefs in advance will allow you to respond thoughtfully rather than reactively when problem situations arise. How does the classroom arrangement influence the teaching and learning of a classroom? Sketch two or more classroom arrangements that are resonant with your beliefs about teaching and learning.

# Checklist for Organizing the Classroom

| Check When Complete | Subject | Notes |
|---|---|---|
| | **Bulletins Boards, Walls, and Ceilings** **Floor Space** | |
| ☐ | A.  Student desks/tables | _____ |
| ☐ | B.  Small-group area | _____ |
| ☐ | C.  Computer workstations | _____ |
| ☐ | D.  Teacher's desk and equipment | _____ |
| ☐ | E.  Bookcases and other storage | _____ |
| ☐ | F.  Centers | _____ |

☐      G.   Pets, plants, and special items     _____

**Materials and Supplies Storage**

☐      A.   Textbooks and trade books     _____

☐      B.   Student work     _____

☐      C.   Frequently used classroom materials     _____

☐      D.   Teacher's supplies     _____

☐      E.   Other necessities     _____

☐      F.   Student belongings     _____

☐      G.   Seasonal or infrequently used items     _____

**Five Keys to Good Room Arrangement**

☐      1   Arrangement consistent with instructional goals and activities     _____

☐      2.   Traffic areas free of congestion     _____

☐      3.   Students easily seen by the teacher     _____

☐      4.   Frequently needed materials accessible     _____

☐      5.   Students able to see all teaching displays     _____

---

**MyEducationLab**

Now go to www.myeducationlab.com to:

- Take a Quiz to test your mastery of chapter objectives.
- Study chapter content with an individualized Study Plan.
- Deepen your understanding of particular concepts and principles with Classroom Management Simulations.
- Apply what you have learned in the chapter to your work with children in Building Teaching Skills exercises.

**CHAPTER 3**

# Establishing Classroom Rules and Procedures

Now that your room arrangement has prepared the physical space of the class, you must consider how you will frame students' social space. An effective classroom has patterns and routines in place that make interaction and movement easy to organize and accomplish. For students to have a successful year in your classroom, they must understand and practice the behaviors you expect of them. Because you will want appropriate and cooperative behavior to become the norm in your classroom, think about how your students will know of these expectations and begin to adopt them consistently. A carefully planned system of rules and procedures makes it easier for you to communicate your expectations to your students, and it helps ensure that the procedures you set up will be workable and appropriate.

Some of the first questions to ask yourself are What are rules and procedures? How do you develop, teach, and reinforce them? The goal of this chapter is to help you answer these questions and develop a sound system of rules and procedures for your class.

## ■ What Is an Effectively Managed Classroom?

An effectively managed classroom is one that runs smoothly, with minimal confusion and downtime, and maximizes opportunities for student learning. It is not possible for a teacher to conduct instruction, or for students to work productively, if they have no guidelines for how to behave, when and how to move about the room, where to sit, when they may or may not interrupt the teacher, and the amount of noise that is acceptable. Consider this example:

*At 8 A.M. when the beginning-of-school bell rings, 21 of Ms. Smith's 26 fourth-grade students are in the classroom. Most are not at their desks but are milling about the room and talking noisily. Ms. Smith calls out above the din, "Everyone, sit down!" With much effort, she succeeds in getting most of the children in their seats; however, three students are still standing and talking. The teacher goes to the front of the room and tries to begin a discussion of the previous day's field trip, but few children are listening. A few students straggle in at 8:06. Two others leave their seats. The teacher asks the children what they liked about their field trip. Only a few students respond. There is already some evidence of inattention: Several students are not facing the teacher, and others are quietly conversing among themselves. The teacher abandons the discussion and asks a girl to pass out papers. At 8:09 students are sitting with nothing to do while the teacher talks with children who have walked up to her desk. At 8:10 the teacher goes to the front of the class and announces that today she will show them something new. Two students are talking loudly, but the teacher ignores them. Three other students leave their seats: One goes to the drinking fountain, one to the pencil sharpener, and one to visit with another student. The teacher tells students to prepare for journal writing. Immediately two students leave their seats to borrow paper, and the noise level in the room increases. About half the students get out notebooks. The students by the far wall are quiet, but they seem to be ignoring the teacher. One student goes to the closet, another to the pencil sharpener. Ms. Smith calls out, "Everyone, be quiet and get out your journals!" Several students call out, "What for?"*

### Vignette Reflection

Respond to the following prompts with a peer (or in writing).

1. How would you describe the social space (teacher–student, student–student interactions) of this classroom?
2. What are some things you feel could be adjusted to improve this social space?
3. Imagine you are a student in this class (select one of the following: student on time, student on task, student late to school, student needing journal paper). Describe your surroundings and the impact this has on you and your learning.

Observers of this classroom might criticize Ms. Smith for allowing students to get away with so much misbehavior. "Be stricter," they might say. "Punish the misbehaving students" or "Develop more interesting lessons to capture student interest." Some might even suggest that Ms. Smith set up a reward system to encourage good behavior. Although these suggestions could be helpful under some circumstances, they do not address the fundamental problem in this classroom: The students have not learned the behaviors that are expected of them, nor has the teacher established procedures to guide student behavior. Problems are evident in several areas: the beginning-of-day routine, bringing materials for class, talking when the teacher is leading the class, out-of-seat behavior, attending to the teacher, and responding to questions.

Of course, even if the students know what is appropriate, they will not necessarily behave as they should. (For that reason, this book will not end with the present chapter!) However, giving the students a clear set of expectations for what is appropriate is a major step toward establishing a positive classroom environment.

Keep in mind that the unique setting created by elementary school organization makes it essential to have a good set of classroom procedures. You will work with 25 to 30 students every day. Although your students will leave the room for lunch, recess, and perhaps some instruction, you will generally be limited to a single room with limited space and materials. You will be responsible for teaching many cognitive skills to a diverse population of students, and at the same time you will have to handle administrative tasks, arrange for appropriate materials and supplies, and evaluate students. To do these things well, you and your students need an orderly environment with minimal disruption and wasted time, leaving everyone free to concentrate on the critical tasks of learning. The rules and procedures you establish with students will reflect the goals you have for yourself and your students.

# ■ Preliminary Considerations

## Definition of Terms

*Goals* are target aspirations not necessarily attained every day. However, long-term goals determine our daily actions. You should carefully consider your personal goals and the goals you want your students to achieve during the year. Discussing goal setting with your students is an important way to establish common values regarding class activities. Keep in mind that your beliefs and the goals you set will influence the expectations you communicate to your students.

*Expectations* are desired behaviors or outcomes. Within a classroom, a teacher can make his or her expectations known to students, or the teacher can cause students to guess at the expectations. It is much easier for students to meet a teacher's expectations when they know what these expectations are. Teachers can make their expectations known to students by directly teaching the classroom rules and procedures, providing opportunities for students to practice them, and consistently responding to students' behavior. A teacher's consistent responses can include both positive consequences to reinforce appropriate behavior and negative consequences to deter inappropriate behavior.

*Rules* and *procedures* refer to stated expectations regarding behavior. A rule identifies general expectations or standards for behavior. For example, the rule "Respect other persons and their property" covers a large set of behaviors that should always be practiced. Rules may indicate unacceptable behavior as well as expected, appropriate behavior, although teachers sometimes manage to write rules that are only positively stated (e.g., "We ask permission before talking in class"). In addition to general rules, many teachers have a rule or two governing a specific behavior that could become an issue or that they want to prevent (e.g., "Gum chewing is not allowed").

Procedures also communicate expectations for behavior. Procedures help students meet the expectations of the stated rules in specific situations. Procedures are directed at accomplishing something rather than prohibiting some behavior or defining a general standard. For example, you will set up procedures with your students for collecting assignments, turning in late work, participating in class discussions, using the bathroom, and so on. Some procedures (such as use of equipment at a center) are sufficiently complex or critical that you may want to post guidelines in addition to practicing them with the students. However, many procedures are not written because they are very simple or because their specificity and frequency of use allow students to learn them rapidly.

The rules and procedures you design will depend on the kind of classroom community you want to develop. For example, different rules and, especially, procedures will be necessary in a classroom where most instruction is teacher led than in one where students work largely independently or in small groups.

## Identifying School Rules and Procedures

In most schools teachers are expected to enforce a set of school rules. School rules are usually expressed in a code of conduct that specifies desired and prohibited student behaviors (e.g., school handbook). Often such codes of conduct identify possible consequences for prohibited behaviors. It is to your advantage to apply school rules consistently in all classes and areas of the building, making it easy for students to learn them. These rules also acquire more legitimacy in the eyes of some students because they are everyone's rules. In addition to rules and procedures that regulate student behavior, all schools have certain administrative procedures that must be followed by every teacher (e.g., keeping attendance records). You should know your school's rules and procedures before the year begins so you can incorporate them into your own classroom system. You can find out about school rules for students and administrative procedures for teachers at a school orientation meeting or from a teacher's handbook, a building administrator, or another teacher. Pay careful attention to the following:

1. Behaviors that are specifically forbidden (e.g., running in the halls, bringing certain items to school) or required (e.g., being in possession of a hall permit when out of the classroom during class time, bringing a note for absence/tardiness).

2. Consequences for rule violations. In particular, note the responsibility you have for carrying out the consequence, such as reporting the student to the school office. If the school does not have a policy for dealing with certain rule violations, you must decide how to handle them yourself.

3. Administrative procedures that must be handled during class time. Some administrative tasks occur infrequently (e.g., assigning textbooks at the beginning of the year). Some administrative tasks are daily occurrences, including taking and recording class attendance, talking with previously absent students, and filing an attendance report with the office. Other tasks (e.g., handling school lunch cards or hall passes) occur frequently, so you will need a record-keeping system and a safe place to keep any money you may be handling. You will also need a procedure for allowing students to leave the room to go to other parts of the building. Some teachers have an attendance chart for students to indicate their presence each day. At one glance, you can tell who is absent without interrupting ongoing activities.

Procedures in these areas will often already be established and followed throughout the school. If standardized procedures have not been implemented in the school in some area, you may find it helpful to talk with experienced teachers about how they handle it.

When you have information about school rules and procedures, you will be ready to begin planning for your own classroom. We will present guideline rules first, then those for procedures.

## ■ Planning Classroom Rules

Many different rules are possible, but a set of four to eight rules should be sufficient to cover the most important areas of behavior. Here are four general rules that encompass many classroom behaviors.

**RULE 1. Respect and be polite to all people.** This rule is general; be sure to give sufficient examples and explanation so that both you and your students clearly understand its meaning. You will have to define *polite*, and you may want to extend this definition to include not hitting, fighting, or name-calling. You may also want to emphasize that "all people" includes you, the teacher.

**RULE 2. Be prompt and be prepared.** This rule includes guidelines that underscore the importance of schoolwork. *Prompt* may refer to the beginning of the school day, transition to group work, and moving to individual tasks. *Being prepared* acknowledges the importance of having the right materials, as well as the mental attitude, to be successful in schoolwork.

"That's Ms. Clamhouse. She runs a tight ship."

Courtesy of Tony Saltzman.

**RULE 3. Listen quietly while others are speaking.** This rule will prevent call-outs and other interruptions of lessons. You can use the discussion of this rule to teach the students the procedure for how to comment or ask a question (e.g., raise a hand and wait to be called on).

**RULE 4. Obey all school rules.** Including this rule gives you an opportunity to discuss whatever school rules are pertinent to your supervision of students outside your classroom (such as on the playground or in the cafeteria). It reminds students that school rules apply in your classroom as well as out of it. It also suggests that you will monitor their behavior in the areas covered by the school rules.

These or similar rules are often found in well-managed classrooms. However, what makes the classroom well managed is not the posting alone, but rather that in these classrooms the rules are also taught and consistently reinforced. The provided rules should not be considered a definitive list. You may decide to use other rules (e.g., a rule prohibiting a specific behavior) or different wording. Some teachers may find these rules too general and might prefer to have more rules with greater specificity.

When presenting general rules, discuss your specific expectations with students. Emphasize the positive parts of the rules rather than just their negative counterparts to help students learn how to behave appropriately. You must be explicit about behaviors that are not acceptable when such behaviors might occur frequently (e.g., being out of seat, call-outs). These specific behaviors may be incorporated in your set of rules or be discussed when presenting procedures associated with specific activities. Be sure your presentation includes concrete examples, and be sure you explain any terms the children at your grade level might not understand. Role-playing situations that model the rules in practice can be helpful.

The rules you choose will be implemented on a continuing basis. You will discuss them with your students on the first day or two of class, strongly emphasize this focus for the first couple of weeks, and consistently reinforce the rules thereafter. Posting the rules allows you to create a strong expectation about behaviors that are important to you, as does sending a copy of the rules home for parents' review and signature. You will refer to specific rules as needed to remind students of appropriate behavior. Your posted rules need not (and cannot) cover all aspects of behavior in detail.

The rules you develop, teach, and reinforce are demonstrated by students when they follow the procedures you establish for your classroom. As you teach students the rules, identify the specific procedures associated with them. For example, the rule "Respect and be polite to all people" has a number of possible procedures associated with it that help students meet this expectation. Students can demonstrate respect and politeness by taking turns at the water fountain, using courtesies ("please" and "thank you"), following teacher-provided directions, listening to the intercom when announcements are made, and walking quietly through the hall to avoid disturbing other classes. Each of these actions can serve as a distinct procedure within your class to support students in following the rule. (Procedures are discussed in the next section.) The connection of rules and procedures is equally important when you develop the rules yourself or when you have students participate in the development of rules.

## Student Participation in Rule Setting

Student involvement in rule setting can take many forms. In any classroom, students should discuss the reasons for having rules and clarify the need for and the meaning of particular rules. It is useful for students to generate concrete examples of the kinds of behaviors a particular rule covers. However, teachers must be prepared to supply positive examples (e.g., "Respecting property means putting extra supplies away so that others may use them") to supplement the mostly negative examples students tend to give (e.g., "Respecting property means not writing on the desk").

You can involve students in a discussion of the class rules by asking for their suggestions and asking them to name specific behaviors that everyone should practice to create a good climate for learning, one in which students feel comfortable participating. Many teachers utilize corresponding children's literature as a springboard for these discussions.

Students might volunteer suggestions such as "listen carefully," "don't interrupt," "don't call names," and "encourage others." After receiving a number of suggestions, organize the list into one or more general categories such as "respect for others." If the goal is a rule that encourages effort and persistence, then ask students for examples of behaviors that foster success and learning. If students give examples such as "turn in work on time," "pay attention," "ask for help when necessary," and "do your own work," summarize them in a general guideline, such as "Always do your personal best." Student participation in such a discussion is advantageous because it demonstrates the reasonableness of the guidelines and their acceptance. In early elementary classrooms (K–3), this process may take several days. In many classrooms, role-playing is crucial for students' understanding of rules.

Many effective managers do not allow choice in rule setting. Instead, they clearly present their rules and procedures to students and provide explanations of the need for them. A teacher who establishes reasonable rules and procedures, who provides an understandable rationale for them, and who enforces them consistently will find that the majority of students are willing to abide by them.

# ■ Planning Classroom Procedures

If you have never analyzed the specific behaviors required of students in a typical elementary school classroom, you will be surprised by the complexity and detail in this section. Don't hurry through it, even though some items may appear trivial; the bits and pieces will combine to form the mosaic of your management system. We describe five categories: procedures for room use, procedures for individual work and teacher-led activities, transitions into and out of the room, procedures for small-group instruction, and general procedures. A sixth area, keeping students accountable for work, is presented in Chapter 4. Specific procedures for cooperative groups are found in Chapter 7.

Remember that procedures may need to be changed—or new ones added—as the year progresses. Procedures always need to be taught and practiced, which is stressed later in the chapter. As you read the discussion in the following sections, note ideas for procedures on the Checklist: "Classroom Rules and Procedures," at the end of the chapter.

## Procedures for Room Use

Certain areas of the room, and furniture and equipment within the room, need procedures to regulate their use.

**Teacher's Desk and Storage Areas.**   The best procedure is that students may not remove anything from your desk or storage areas without your permission.

**Student Desks and other Storage Areas.**   Just as students may not tamper with your desk, they may not bother the desks or storage spaces of other students. You can also help students learn good work habits by setting aside a few minutes each week for them to clean out and organize their desks and materials. (This is a good end-of-day activity for Friday.)

**Storage for Common Materials.**   Develop procedures for students obtaining commonly used supplies (e.g., scissors, markers, scrap paper, rulers) and resources (e.g., supplementary books, texts, encyclopedias, dictionaries). Some teachers utilize a rotating student helper position to access needed materials; others mark walkways past cabinets/shelves as one-way when multiple students are accessing the storage simultaneously. Still others find it helpful to label cabinet doors with a list or photographs of contents. Teach students when these materials may be used, whether permission is needed to use them, and how they may be taken and returned.

**Drinking Fountain, Sink, Pencil Sharpener.**   A common procedure is to allow the use of these facilities by only one student at a time and only when the teacher is not conducting a lesson or talking to the whole class. Some teachers require that students request permission to use the fountain or sink except during specified break times. Others provide specific times for pencil sharpening and keep a supply of sharpened pencils handy for breakages outside of these times.

**Restrooms.**   When restrooms are immediately accessible from or adjacent to the classroom, many teachers allow students to use these facilities one at a time, without asking permission, whenever the teacher is not conducting instruction. Establish a system that lets a student know when the restroom is occupied (e.g., a reversible sign on the door with a green light and a red light; knocking and waiting). It is a good idea to go over restroom-use procedures such as flushing the toilet, washing hands, wiping off the sink area, and disposing of paper towels. When restrooms are separated from the classroom, both group times (before lunch, after recess) and individual procedures should be established.

**Centers and Equipment Areas.**   Establish procedures for when an area may be used (perhaps during particular blocks of time only), whether special permission is needed, and how many may use the area at a time. You will need procedures for assigning students to centers or, if centers are self-selected, for guiding student movement among centers. Teachers often allow quiet talking in such areas as long as it does not disturb others. If talking is allowed, the area should be away from areas where students are expected to work silently. Post rules with instructions for equipment use, the number of students allowed, and cleanup at each area. Specifically for computers, students will also need procedures for

- Going to a specific computer
- Retrieving/storing data (flash drive or individual desktop-folder use)
- Accessing software/Internet sites (during assigned times or after completing an assignment)
- Sharing a computer (who controls the keyboard and for how long)

## Procedures for Individual Work and Teacher-Led Activities

Major concerns include keeping student attention, allowing for participation, and providing assistance when needed. Good procedures prevent or reduce interruptions and distractions that can slow down content-development activities or interfere with student learning.

**Student Attention During Presentations.**   Consider how students should behave when you or another student is presenting information to the class or while you are conducting a discussion or recitation. Typically, students are expected to face the presenter and listen attentively. In fact, teachers often translate this expectation into a general classroom rule such as "Listen carefully when the teacher or another student is talking." Teachers also expect students to remain seated at all times during presentations, to remain quiet, and to have only the books or other materials needed for the lesson on their desks.

**Student Participation.**   You must identify ways to allow students to ask questions and contribute to a discussion. During presentations and discussions, the simplest procedure is to require that students raise their hands, wait to be called on, and remain in their seats. Requiring that students raise their hands gives all students a chance to participate and allows you to call on students who do not have their hands up. Some teachers teach students to call on the next speaker to avoid having all interactions channeled through the teacher. In most circumstances, allowing students to call out answers or comments without permission results in some undesirable consequences, such as domination of participation by a few students, frequent inappropriate comments, and interruptions of discussions and presentations. Two exceptions to the "no call-out" procedure occur

1. When teachers want multiple students to provide a chorus response to a question. You can preface such an activity by announcing that students do not need

to raise their hands to respond. Teach students a signal for a chorus response, such as cupping one hand behind an ear or giving a verbal signal or prefacing the question with "everyone."

2. During activities in which hand raising might slow down or interfere with a discussion. True discussions do not involve raised hands; rather, you will need to teach the conversational conventions of listening for a pause, taking turns, and anticipating conversation direction.

Variations from the standard procedure of requiring raised hands usually should not be used early in the school year. Instead, follow a simple routine for several weeks until you are certain that students understand it. Then, if you choose to depart from the procedure, clearly communicate the difference to the students at the beginning of the activity.

**Talk Among Students.**   In many activities, quiet talk is an important part of problem solving. However, students must know when and how loudly they may talk. You must decide what your policy will be and communicate it to the students. The "no talking" rule is an easy rule to break and does not necessarily reflect a learning-oriented environment.

In your decision to allow students to talk to one another and to work together during individual work activities, you will have to establish specific limitations. For example, you might tell students that during certain activities quiet talking is allowed, but if it gets too loud, the privilege will be lost. It is best to demonstrate what "quiet talking" means and have students practice it to show you they can meet your expectation.

If students work at centers and in groups, you must define with them how much noise is acceptable. Many teachers find it helpful to have a "zero noise" signal for when they need to get the whole group's attention. A zero-noise signal could be your raising your hand or turning off the lights momentarily.

**Obtaining Help.**   When students are working at their seats and need help, have them raise their hands. It is not a good idea to allow them to call out or to come up to you whenever they wish because this can distract other students, congest a given area, or prevent you from completing instructional tasks. When they raise their hands, you may then go to them or have them come to you one at a time. Another procedure is to allow students to come up only if you are seated at your desk (or some other designated place) and not already helping another student. These procedures eliminate long lines of chatty students around your desk. They also allow you to control where you give individual assistance. If you choose to help students at a location other than their desks, choose one that allows you good visibility of the rest of the class. Some teachers help students think about their questions by having students ask themselves, "Can another student answer this?" If the answer is yes, the student asks another for help.

If students are encouraged to help each other, you will have to establish procedures for how and when. Some teachers establish the "C3B4Me" procedure, which tells students to ask three other students for help before they ask the teacher. Students need guidance in asking appropriate questions and learning how to help peers without merely supplying answers. Chapter 7 has suggestions for teaching these important skills.

**When Individual Work Has Been Completed.**   When students are assigned work at their desks, some students may finish before the next scheduled activity. This situation is frequently handled either by having students complete an additional enrichment assignment or by allowing these students to use the remaining time for free reading or work at a center or helping with classroom maintenance chores. You may also wish to have students who finish early serve as peer tutors for others. If you have enrichment activities that involve additional materials not in the students' possession, you must specify when these materials may be used, where they will be kept, and what the procedures are for returning the materials to the proper place. If many students frequently complete their work early, maybe assignments are too easy, or too much time is being allocated for seatwork activities.

## Transitions into and Out of the Room

**Beginning the School Day.**   You should establish a routine to open each class day. At the beginning of the year, you should lead this routine so that it is done efficiently and helps students "settle in" to the classroom. During the course of the year, students may begin to take over this routine without your guidance. The routine need not be elaborate or time-consuming. Many teachers begin with social items, such as a riddle for the day, a discussion of the day's lunch menu, the pledge of allegiance, date and birthdays, discussion of school events, or other items of interest. Some begin each day with a class meeting or a planning session during which students set their goals for the day. Such activities can be important for community building.

At this time you may also wish to collect money, permission slips, or other items brought from home. If much time is required for morning management tasks, have students begin work on a content-related activity to establish an academic focus, ensuring that students do not have dead time.

**Leaving the Room.**   Your students will leave the room en masse at several times during the day: at recess and for lunch, the library, music, computer lab, or some other instruction. A common technique is to have the children line up after appropriate materials have been put away, with the quietest table or row lining up first. Decide what behaviors are appropriate in line. Some teachers, particularly of younger children, have to specify where hands and feet should be while students are lined up. Some teachers have students clasp their hands behind their backs; others have students keep their hands at their sides. Line leaders can be helpful, and students enjoy the privilege. Because noise disturbs other classes, talking is usually forbidden while the line is passing through the halls. You will also need procedures for helping individual students know when and how to leave the room if they are working with a speech teacher, a special education teacher, or a peer mentor in another classroom.

**Returning to the Room.**   It is important that procedures be established for this transition, particularly after lunchtime. When students know what to do on returning, they can get started instead of waiting for you to direct them. Common procedures are entering the room quietly, taking their seats, and using the restroom, sink, pencil sharpener, or drinking fountain one at a time in each area. Note that these procedures get students ready for afternoon activities.

When students return from an out-of-room activity that has left them noisy or unusually chatty, or if they are very excited when returning from recess or lunch, your transition activity should give them time to wind down before you start academic work. For example, you might read aloud as they settle in and get ready for the next activity. Some research has found that students' attention is better after such transitions than when the teacher tries to enforce total silence and an immediate return to academic tasks. However, do not prolong the chatter unnecessarily, and be sure to gain student attention when you begin the next activity. Monitor students so that "wind-down" time doesn't become "wind-up" time.

**Ending the Day.**   An end-of-day routine ensures that student desks and work areas are cleared off, materials to go home are ready, and students leave on time. Planning ahead for the end of the day guards against hurried closings, lost papers, and a feeling of confusion and chaos. Possible routines include feeding room pets, straightening bookshelves, tidying up desks, picking up paper, and stacking chairs on the desks. Other important end-of-day tasks include briefly reviewing important things learned that day, foreshadowing coming events, and checking materials that will be taken home. If you have children who leave early to ride a bus, you may wish to do only the essentials with them and complete the rest of the routine after they leave.

## Procedures for Small-Group Instruction

One complication with using small-group instruction is that the teacher is often working with one group while the rest of the class is engaged in individual work. The dual focus complicates monitoring, providing assistance, and dealing with problems that might occur. Well-planned procedures are a must if small-group instruction is to be carried out smoothly.

**Getting the Class Ready for the Activity.**   Students must know what they are going to do during the time they are not in the group. Therefore, post the assignments by group, and discuss work requirements beforehand with the whole class. Note any materials that will be needed when students come to the teacher-led group.

**Student Movement into and Out of the Group.**   These transitions must be brief, quiet, and free from disruptions. Describe expected behavior to students: walk, no talking, bring needed materials. Develop a signal to tell students when to come to the group area. They should not automatically come when they see other students leave you because you may want to check student progress before working with the next group. Some teachers use a bell or a kitchen timer; others use a verbal signal.

**Expected Behavior of Students in the Group.**   The rules for attention and hand raising used in the whole class can also be used in the small group. However, with smaller numbers of students, some procedures must change, and these must be taught. Some teachers have each student who responds select the next student to participate. Sometimes the exchange between students can be more loosely structured.

**Expected Behavior of Students Outside the Small Group.**   You will have given instructions to students not in the group and posted their seatwork assignments. However, students may need help as they work. It is not a good idea to allow students to come up to interrupt you while you are in the group; therefore, establish a procedure to enable students to get help. One such procedure is to allow students to help each other. Another is to assign certain students the job of monitor. Students can then raise their hands, and the monitor can assist them. Permission to interrupt the teacher is given only to the monitor and only when assistance is absolutely necessary. Often students are told that they should skip the part of the assignment they are unable to do and that the teacher will help them later. You should check on their progress even while you are working with the small group. Look up frequently to scan the class for signs of difficulty. When you change groups, circulate around the room to help students before you call the next group. Students can raise their hands between groups, or they may write their names on the board for assistance when you are available.

**Use of Materials and Supplies.**   Small-group activities frequently require the use of materials and equipment. To avoid traffic jams, plan ways to distribute these items, and perhaps use more than one distribution place if necessary. Sometimes you can save time by placing needed materials on students' desks or worktables before class starts. Check equipment to make sure it functions, and have replacements on hand just in case. Student helpers can be assigned to distribute supplies and materials, to monitor supply areas, and to clean up work areas. If students need to bring special materials for group or project work, let them know far enough in advance so they can get them; you may have to arrange for safe places for their materials to be stored while work is in progress. If any of the equipment you need poses a potential hazard to students or can be easily damaged by carelessness, identify safety routines and demonstrate proper use.

**Using Multiple Groups.**   Some teachers use multiple groups extensively for a variety of tasks such as short- or long-term projects, peer coaching and other assistance, and review of content learned in other formats. Other examples include laboratory assignments in science, the preparation of group reports or projects in social studies and reading, and study groups organized to accomplish specific learning objectives. However groups are used, it is important to develop efficient routines that support the learning objectives.

Routines are typically introduced to the students whenever groups are first used, and they are practiced thereafter until the groups are working well. Students need to learn appropriate group behavior, especially if you intend to use groups extensively. Although you can monitor group work, the fact that six or seven groups may be working simultaneously at varying paces, using a variety of resources, precludes your being able to direct all the groups' activities. The procedures implemented for group work must be carefully chosen to encourage students to work independently toward instructional goals, to promote desirable interaction among students in the group, and to support efficient use of time. If students will frequently be working in groups and presenting the results to the whole class, mention the importance of attentiveness during group presentations. Detailed procedures that help cooperative group activities proceed smoothly are discussed in Chapter 7.

## General Procedures

**Distributing Materials.**   At the beginning of the year, books and supplies must be distributed to students. Develop procedures for recording book numbers, noting damage, and handling other details. These are covered in Chapter 5, along with other procedures for beginning the school year. In addition to the beginning-of-year materials distribution, you will have supplies, papers, and books to pass out every day. Unless you establish efficient procedures, much time can be wasted. Many teachers have student helpers pass out materials such as manipulatives, calculators, or papers during opening activities. For the distribution of books or supplies, a student helper can be assigned to each group. If you collect papers from assignments by group or by row and preserve the order while you are checking them, you can then redistribute them to the class in the same way. This makes it easy to hand the materials to one student at each table or in each row.

**Interruptions or Delays.**   While some interruptions cannot be postponed, most can be rescheduled. First ask to have the contact delayed until your planning time if possible. If delays or interruptions must occur while students are working, they should be taught to continue their work. Emphasize that they should be courteous and patient if you are interrupted in the middle of a lesson by a visitor or a phone call and that you will return to them as quickly as possible. If you will be detained very long, give the students something to do in case they finish their work before you return. Avoid leaving your classroom unless it is absolutely necessary. You retain liability for your students in this instance. In the rare case that you must be away from the room, make sure that a nearby colleague is aware of your absence and can check on your class.

**Restrooms.**   If restrooms are located away from your classroom, a hall-pass system may be established to monitor the number of students out of the room and to let students know whether they may leave. You might hang a restroom hall pass next to the hall door to be placed by the student around his or her neck or carried en route to the restroom. See if there is a schoolwide procedure to follow. Teaching students the procedure of recording their departure and return times on a sign-out sheet can assist them in making their trip efficiently.

**Library, Resource Room, School Office.**　When one or a small group of students must go to another area in the school, you will generally remain in the classroom with the rest of the students. For example, small groups doing research may go to the library. Schoolwide procedures are usually established to handle these situations. Find out whether a hall-permit system or some other procedure is used to regulate the movement of students in the halls. Also, review any school rules that govern behavior in transit or at the location. Make sure your students understand these procedures. Be sure the teacher in the other location (e.g., librarian) is prepared for these additional students.

**Cafeteria.**　Review the school policies for the cafeteria, and be ready to explain them to your class before they go to lunch, and after they return if necessary. If you are planning to (or must) sit with the students, decide ahead of time who will get to sit by you (and whether this will be at random or a privilege) or whether you will use assigned seats. If your students make too much noise or misbehave, you may wish to establish an incentive for good behavior or include lunchroom behavior as part of your in-class reward system.

**Playground.**　Safety rules are a must, and you should prohibit overly aggressive behavior and dangerous play. If any equipment on the playground poses a potential hazard, you will have to talk about it with your students. Make clear to your students what part of the school grounds they may use for recess. You should also establish some signal for getting students' attention when it is time for them to line up and return to the classroom; this could be a whistle or a raised hand. If you plan to play a game on the playground, announce this before leaving the room, telling students where they should go when they reach the playground.

**Fire and Disaster Drills.**　You need to know what school policies and routines have been established to protect the children and you. Teach these procedures ahead of time so that the class can review them just before each first drill. Maintain a current roster with emergency contact numbers to carry with you.

**Classroom Helpers.**　Teachers often use students to help with such chores as erasing the board, passing out materials and supplies, carrying messages to the office, watering the plants, tidying up, and feeding the animals. Students are often chosen to be line leaders. Some teachers use these activities as privileges or rewards for especially good or improved behavior, or they may use them to encourage some students to accept more responsibility. Other teachers make sure that every student has a job each week so that all are contributing to the classroom community.

Some teachers have a chart or bulletin board with slots for the names of students currently serving as monitors or helpers. A card is then made for each child, and this card is placed in the appropriate slot when that child has a particular room helper responsibility. Some teachers ask for volunteers for each job; others appoint students on a rotating basis or use jobs as rewards. Appointment is usually done at the beginning of the week, and the appointments last one or two weeks.

# ■ Chapter Summary

Classroom rules and procedures structure the social space of a classroom. To make this space appropriate for learning, the established rules and procedures must be taught, practiced, and consistently reinforced. Elementary students can often participate in the development of classroom rules and can benefit from active involvement in the establishment of these rules (e.g., role play) and from getting constructive feedback as they learn. For students to meet the expectations of the posted rules, classroom procedures outline the specific behaviors that should become routine. Procedures are needed in many areas, including how to use the room and its components, how to participate in instructional activities, how to transition between these activities as well as in and out of the classroom, how to complete assigned work, and how to meet expectations for other school areas and events (e.g., library, fire drill). An effectively managed classroom has the social space structured through rules and procedures to run smoothly and maximize student learning.

# ■ Further Reading

Castle, K., & Rogers, K. (1994). Rule-creating in a constructivist classroom community. *Childhood Education, 70*(2), 77–80.

*Creating classroom rules together can be a meaningful experience for children and teachers and can help establish a positive sense of classroom community. Student participation in rule making encourages active involvement, reflection, meaningful connections, respect for rules, sense of community, problem solving through negotiation, cooperation, inductive thinking, and a sense of ownership.*

Evertson, C. M., & Poole, I. R. (2004). *Norms and expectations.* Nashville, TN: Vanderbilt University, Peabody College, IRIS Center (iris.peabody.vanderbilt.edu). Click on "Resources," then "Behavior and Classroom Management" (left column), and then "Case Studies" (middle column) to link to these case study sets.

*This Web site contains many activities and case studies for accommodating special needs students in the regular education classroom.*

Evertson, C. M., & Poole, I. R. (2008). Proactive classroom management. In T. L. Good (Ed.), *21st century education: A reference handbook* (Vol. 1, pp. 131–139). Los Angeles: Sage.

*This chapter describes preventive actions teachers can take to prepare and manage the classroom environment effectively, including discussion of classroom rules and procedures.*

Fenning, P. A., & Bohanon, H. (2006). Schoolwide discipline policies: An analysis of discipline codes of conduct. In C. Evertson & C. Weinstein (Eds.), *Handbook of research on classroom management: Research, practice, and contemporary issues* (pp. 1021–1039). Mahwah, NJ: Erlbaum.

*The authors describe the history, purpose, and uses of schoolwide codes of conduct and conclude that using a code of conduct to support positive student behaviors is more efficacious than setting up a system of punishments that increases expulsion or suspension rates.*

Good, T. L., & Brophy, J. E. (2008). *Looking in classrooms* (10th ed.). Boston: Allyn & Bacon.

*This book is an excellent source of ways and means for teachers to develop into successful professionals. It synthesizes the knowledge base about teaching and provides research-based and accessible summaries about effective classroom practices. Particularly helpful are observational tools and rich examples of classroom practices that support teachers' professional development.*

# ■ Suggested Activities

1. Seek a local example or search online for an elementary school's schoolwide rules. Discuss with a partner: How would these rules impact your teaching if you were a member of the faculty?

2. Goals represent desired directions of student growth and may be academic, behavioral, or emotional. Write one goal in each area that you would consider appropriate for your students. Write one in each area for yourself. Consider how the goals you wrote are reflective of your philosophy of education.

3. As you think about planning your routines and rules, consider what role students will play in choosing and implementing them. Some teachers prefer that students participate extensively by helping formulate rules, by discussing their rationales, and by role-playing nonexamples and examples of following the rules. Other teachers prefer a more traditional, teacher-led system of rules and procedures. Still others prefer a blending of teacher and students working together. Write a response to these questions: Which approach resonates more strongly with you? Why? How does your preference relate to your developing philosophy of education?

4. Reconsider the vignette of Ms. Smith at the beginning of the chapter. Work with a partner to describe five procedures this teacher could put in place to have a smoother, more learning-oriented opening for the school day. (See the key for this activity in the Appendix.)

5. Read Case Study 3.1. It illustrates classroom procedures and rules for most major areas and will help you envision your own system of management. Create a list of reasons Mr. Abrams's class will probably run smoothly. How does his classroom compare with the one you envision for yourself and your students?

6. Case Study 3.2 illustrates a more complex classroom organization that involves introducing multiple areas and centers for student activities. List some of the advance planning decisions Ms. Miller has made. What procedures has she developed? How are they taught and monitored? What do you expect her classroom rules are?

7. Develop a list of four to eight general classroom rules. Be sure they emphasize areas of classroom behavior important to you and to the functioning of your classroom. Review them with an administrator or another teacher.

8. Make a copy of the checklist at the end of the chapter. Observe an elementary classroom for 30 minutes (or find an online classroom-observation video of similar length). Fill in as many blanks as possible in section III to describe the procedures in this classroom. Which procedures were most helpful to the lesson's progression? Were there any procedures you would recommend to better support students' learning? Consider how the checklist could help you plan your classroom procedures and help students meet your expectations. Where you have questions, ask other teachers their opinions/experiences.

9. Revisit Activity 4 in Chapter 2. What procedures would need to be established to make the environment safe for student movement, including Cheri's?

# ■ Case Study 3.1

## CLASSROOM RULES AND PROCEDURES IN A SECOND-GRADE CLASS

Mr. Abrams's students follow four rules: We use quiet voices in the classroom. We do our best work. We are polite and helpful. We follow all school rules. At the beginning of the year, Mr. Abrams and his students decide what "quiet voices" means and practice using quiet voices in different instructional activities. The students also role-play situations in which students are and are not using quiet voices. In this way, Mr. Abrams helps students connect classroom conversation procedures with their corresponding rule. When Mr. Abrams needs to get the attention of the class, he routinely uses a bell as a signal. He practices this signal with the students. When the bell rings once, they stop talking and look at him. He explains to the class that using the bell is a shortcut to save time, that he will ring the bell only once and not several times, and he expects students to respond immediately. He uses the bell in a very consistent manner and provides feedback to encourage student compliance.

Students identify the rule "We do our best work" as including the procedures for listening carefully when the teacher gives instructions, participating in class discussions, completing all assignments, turning in neat work, and using time wisely. Mr. Abrams provides brief examples and nonexamples for students to role-play this rule and corresponding procedures in action.

Procedures relating to the rule "We are polite and helpful" include listening quietly when the teacher or another student is giving a presentation, cooperating with other students during small-group work, sharing materials and supplies, and respecting others' opinions. Mr. Abrams explains to his students that during some discussions they can raise their hands and wait to be called on to allow everyone a chance to talk and be heard. His signal for this procedure is raising his right hand, and he practices it with the students. At other times students contribute to a discussion without raising their hands. His signal for this procedure is placing his right hand by his ear. He also practices this signal with the students several times. Consideration and respect for fellow students, the teacher, and other adults in the school are included under this rule. In addition, the school rules referred to in the fourth classroom rule govern behavior in the halls, cafeteria, and other common areas of the school grounds. Mr. Abrams makes sure to teach and consistently reinforce all corresponding procedures as the class travels to these additional locations.

Several other important classroom procedures provide guidelines for behavior in Mr. Abrams's classroom. Students are expected to stay seated at their desks whenever he presents directions or instruction to the class. At other times, they can leave their desks to get supplies, hand in papers, sharpen their pencils, and use the restroom adjacent to the classroom without asking permission as long as they do not disturb other students. For example, students can sharpen a pencil without permission except when the teacher is talking or when another student is addressing the class. No more than two students can be at the pencil sharpener at one time, one sharpening and one waiting. When the teacher is working with a small group or helping an individual, students may not interrupt. They stay at their desks and raise their hands to request help. Students who finish their work early may read books from the classroom library, go to one of the classroom centers, or play an instructional game. They may talk, using their quiet voices, but they may not disturb anyone still working on the assignment. Mr. Abrams connects each of these procedures to their corresponding rule as he teaches them to the class. When students forget or fail to follow one of the procedures, Mr. Abrams reminds them.

# ■ Case Study 3.2

## USING CENTERS IN A MULTITASK CLASSROOM

Ms. Miller designed her classroom with centers for listening, reading, writing, and creating. Special-interest centers on topics the class is studying in science, social studies, or math change every month or so. Although each child has an assigned place at a table, students are seldom in their seats; instead, they work on a variety of projects individually, in pairs, and in groups. When they meet as a whole class, they gather on a carpet instead of in traditional rows of desks. On any given day in November, a visitor may see an active, busy, somewhat noisy place, but it is easy to discern that there is a sense of order and purpose to the tasks the students are doing.

This classroom didn't get this way all at once. Much of the first six weeks of school was spent preparing students to work independently and collaboratively. On the first day of school, Ms. Miller taught cues for when to gather on the rug and when to return to seats. She explained that there would be times when they could talk with each other, but that during "rug time" they were to raise their hands so only one person would be speaking at once. Ms. Miller prepared a poster with the day's schedule and "center time" clearly marked. She went over it with the students before posting it on a highly visible bulletin board. She referred to the poster during the first weeks of school when giving students instructions for activities, or she asked students to tell her when certain activities were to start or stop.

Centers were introduced one at a time, over several weeks. When each new center became available, Ms. Miller presented it to the whole class, demonstrating the material found there and pointing out times on the day's schedule when it would be available. She also pointed out two signs in each center. One lists the procedures for the center. For example, the sign in the reading center says, "Silent readers may leave the center to find a quiet place to read. Students reading aloud to each other should stay in the center." Every list of procedures ends with instructions for cleanup. The second sign lists the capacity of that center. For example, the listening center has only four sets of earphones, so its capacity is four. Ms. Miller explained to the students that they may sign up for centers each morning when they arrive at school. One period of the day is allotted to "free center time," when students may go to the centers they have chosen. During free center time, students cross their names off the sign-up sheets when they leave the center so other students may enter.

Another period is "assigned center time," when Ms. Miller decides who should be in each center. After each new center was introduced, Ms. Miller saw that every student visited it during assigned center time. She monitored the center's use carefully, making sure that all students understood the use of each new center before another center was introduced. Even after all centers have been introduced, Ms. Miller continues to monitor them and brings up problems she sees for discussion during rug time. She balances the available centers so that if activities at one center require her attention, the other centers have more familiar activities available on which students can work independently.

# Checklist: Classroom Rules and Procedures

| Check When Taught to Students | Area | Procedures |
|---|---|---|
| I. What are my short-and long-term goals for myself this year? _____ | | |
| II. What are my short-and long-term goals for my students this year? _____ | | |
| III. With these goals in mind, what will be my basic procedures for the following areas? _____ | | |
| | **Room Use** | |
| ☐ | A.  Teacher's desk and storage areas | _____ |
| ☐ | B.  Student desks and storage areas | _____ |
| ☐ | C.  Storage for common materials | _____ |
| ☐ | D.  Drinking fountains, sink, pencil sharpener | _____ |
| ☐ | E.  Restrooms | _____ |
| ☐ | F.  Centers or equipment areas | _____ |
| ☐ | G.  Computer stations | _____ |
| ☐ | H.  Board | _____ |

### Individual Work and Teacher-Led Activities

☐     A. Attention during presentations      _____

☐     B. Participation      _____

☐     C. Talk among students      _____

☐     D. Obtaining help      _____

☐     E. When individual work has
       been completed      _____

### Transitions into and out of the Room

☐     A. Beginning the school day      _____

☐     B. Leaving the room      _____

☐     C. Returning to the room      _____

☐     D. Ending the day      _____

### Procedures for Small-Group Instruction

☐     A. Getting the class ready      _____

☐     B. Student movement      _____

☐     C. Expected behavior in the group      _____

☐     D. Expected behavior of students
       outside the group      _____

☐     E. Materials and supplies      _____

☐     F. Using multiple groups      _____

### General Procedures

☐     A. Distributing materials      _____

☐     B. Classroom helpers      _____

☐     C. Interruptions or delays      _____

☐     D. Restrooms      _____

☐     E. Library, resource room, school office      _____

☐     F. Cafeteria      _____

☐     G. Playground      _____

☐     H. Fire and disaster drills      _____

☐     I. Classroom helpers      _____

---

**MyEducationLab** ─────────────────────────────────────────

Now go to www.myeducationlab.com to:

- Take a Quiz to test your mastery of chapter objectives.
- Study chapter content with an individualized Study Plan.
- Deepen your understanding of particular concepts and principles with Classroom Management Simulations.
- Apply what you have learned in the chapter to your work with children in Building Teaching Skills exercises.

## CHAPTER 4

# Procedures for Managing Student Work

In Chapter 3 we presented procedures for establishing an orderly classroom but indicated that additional procedures would be needed to keep students accountable for their work and learning. An accountability system is a set of additional procedures aimed at encouraging students to complete assignments and to engage in other learning activities. Ultimately, the goal of any accountability system is to help students develop into independent learners; thus, your procedures should give as much responsibility as possible to the students themselves, rather than having the students depend on either you or their parents to see that assignments are completed.

As we discuss student accountability, it is easy to focus on the products students create, such as completed assignments and test scores. After all, these are the tangible, measurable outcomes of the activities you engage in with students each day. However, it is important not to lose sight of your goal as a teacher: to facilitate learning and to foster an understanding of the value of that learning.

Your accountability system should lead you and your students to examine their learning and the learning process in which they are engaged. If you are checking written work daily but are not critically examining what students are learning by doing these assignments, the purposes for doing academic work may be lost. Students may come to see their written work as a task to be completed that doesn't relate to what they learn, in which case your system will not function to support learning as you intend.

Each day of the school year you will give your students assignments that they will be expected to complete in the classroom or at home. These range from discussion to research to simple recall. Depending on the assignment, it may provide opportunities for exploration, for original thinking, for practice and application, or for repeated exposure to content. Such experiences are crucial for student learning. Thus, your accountability system should encourage students to become motivated and independent learners. Your support of consistent and successful engagement in student assignments is critical scaffolding toward this end. If students do not care or are not held accountable for their work and learning, many problems can occur. Consider the following example:

> It is the second month of school, and Mr. Paul's third-grade class is finishing its fairy tale unit. As a culminating project, five groups of students have been creating their own fairy tales. For this assignment, the group members were to work together to write and illustrate a fairy tale and on the last day of this unit present their fairy tale to the rest of the class.
>
> Mr. Paul has been disturbed by the lack of cooperation in all of the groups. He has noticed that many groups have been off task. Members have also argued about story lines, characters, and settings, and these arguments have led some students to work alone. Many of the students have turned to Mr. Paul for answers, whereas he wanted them to turn to their peers for help. Mr. Paul has also noticed that some of the groups did not follow the procedures he established for this activity. For instance, he asked them to write and illustrate their books on only one side of their writing paper. Many used both sides of the paper, and their markers and pens bled through the paper, making the story and illustrations difficult to see.
>
> As the groups are presenting their fairy tales to the rest of the class on this final day, they are very disorganized. Some groups have not decided ahead of time who will read and show the illustrations. Other groups lack presentation skills, such as clearly displaying their pictures for everyone to see.
>
> After the last group has presented, Mr. Paul dismisses the students for recess and sits at his desk. He wonders what he can do to improve the groups' skills. It is clear from their careless manner that the students have not taken responsibility for this project and have not believed it is important.

### Vignette Reflection

Discuss with a partner your responses to the following questions:

1. What are some of the difficulties students are experiencing with this project?
2. How might a written description of the project look?
3. What are some of the issues preventing the project from matching Mr. Paul's expectations?

From the vignette, it seems that many of Mr. Paul's students did not feel very accountable for their work. It is possible, of course, that the assignment was too difficult or was not explained adequately, but it is also likely that Mr. Paul's procedures have not helped the students develop good work habits or understand the importance of cooperating and presenting information effectively to others.

This chapter focuses on classroom procedures that communicate the importance of assignments, that enable students to understand what is expected of them, and that help students take responsibility for their learning. The critical areas include communicating assignments and requirements, monitoring progress (including self-monitoring), and providing feedback (including self-evaluation and reflection). The Checklist "Managing Student Work" will help you organize your planning in these areas, and four case studies of accountability systems for elementary teachers are provided at the end of the chapter.

# ■ Clear Communication of Assignments and Work Requirements

Students need a clear idea of what their assignments are and what is expected of them. This means that you must be able to explain all requirements and features of the assignments. You should also provide a reason for doing the assignment or explain what students may gain from the effort: reinforcement, discovery, understanding, challenge, or usable skills. Oral explanation alone is not sufficient because not all students listen carefully, some students may be absent when the assignments and requirements are discussed, and the assignment itself may be complex. In addition, there is often more to completing assignments than doing the work accurately. Accuracy alone may not reflect learning. You must also consider standards for neatness, legibility, and form. Although you do not want to encourage an overemphasis on form to the detriment of learning, students need to understand what will be expected of them. Consider the following three areas when developing your standards.

## Instructions for Assignments

In addition to telling students what the assignment is, post the assignment and important instructions in an easily viewable location. Also, teach students to copy the assignment into their notebooks or on the first line of their papers so they will have a record of it if they need to complete work at home. Go over instructions orally with the class, indicating where the instructions are displayed in the room. Whenever appropriate, use an example to show students how their papers should look. After giving instructions, check for understanding by asking students to restate them in their own words so you know that they understand what to do.

When you are giving directions for independent work to several groups in preparation for reading group time, be sure the assignment for each group is clearly labeled. For primary grades especially, you might assign a color to each reading group. Use a marker of that color to write the assignments on the board, or use paper of that color when duplicating worksheets. Use the same location for each group's assignment every day so groups will know where to look without your help.

When you are giving directions for group work, move students into their groups first. Make sure you have everyone's attention again before thoroughly explaining your expectations. Check the understanding of at least one member of each group by asking such questions as, "What will your group need to do first?" For older students, provide a set of written instructions to each group, especially when the group task is a complex one. As students become more skilled at group work, they may be able to generate work plans on their own.

## Standards for Form, Neatness, and Due Dates

When you have developed a standard set of requirements for written work, students will then learn what is generally expected, and you will have to explain only exceptions or changes as they occur. Students need to know what paper to write on, what

*"Oh no, not homework again."*

heading to use, whether to write on the back of the paper, whether to color any part of it, how to number, whether to use pen or pencil, and whether to erase errors or to draw lines through them.

Decide on a standard but simple heading for papers, and post a sample heading to review with students the first time they are to use it. Remind them of it during the early weeks of school until they use it properly.

Finally, due dates should be reasonable and clear; exceptions should not be made without good cause. Tell students your policy for turning in work on time, and follow it consistently. If you regularly extend the due dates for assignments, students may learn that they can negotiate for extra time and may not use their time well. In general, insist that work not done on time be completed at home or after school. This assumes, of course, that students possess the necessary knowledge or skills to do the work on their own.

## Procedures for Absent Students

When students are absent, they miss instruction, directions for assignments, and assistance they may need in getting tasks under way. Establishing routines for handling makeup work is helpful and will avoid the interruption of instruction. You may not require that students complete each assignment they missed while they were absent, but students who miss critical assignments may need to make them up. Consider the following ways to help students catch up:

1. Arrange to meet briefly with students who have been absent to discuss makeup assignments. If you post weekly assignment lists for each subject on a bulletin board, in a folder, or on your class Web site, you can point out which assignments are to be completed. For young children, you may need a packet of makeup work in a special "makeup folder." Let students know how much time they have to complete it.
2. Establish a regular time, such as 15 minutes before or after school, when you will be available to assist students with instruction they have missed. In addition, you can designate class helpers to help at particular times of the day (usually during independent activities).
3. Designate a place where students can turn in makeup work and where they can pick it up after it has been checked (e.g., baskets or trays labeled "Makeup Work").
4. Determine how students who have missed group work will make it up. Assist groups in planning for the inclusion of absent members and in helping them catch up.
5. For students whose absence you can prepare for in advance (e.g., religious holidays), discuss with the students and parents a plan for completing the work.

# ■ Monitoring Progress on and Completion of Assignments

## Monitoring Work in Progress

Monitoring student progress helps you identify students who are having difficulty and enables you to encourage other students to keep working. After you have made an assignment, monitor students carefully. Don't immediately begin working at your desk or become involved with an individual student without first checking to see whether all students are starting and can do the assignment. If you don't check, some students may not start, and others may begin it incorrectly. Two simple strategies can help to avoid this situation. First, if everyone in the class is doing the same assignment, you can assure a smooth transition into independent work by beginning it as a whole-class activity; that is, have everyone get out paper or other materials, and then answer the first question or two, or work the first few problems, together as a group, just as you would conduct a recitation. For example, ask the first question, solicit an answer, discuss it, and have students record it on their papers. Not only will this procedure help ensure that all students begin, but any immediate problems with the assignment can be resolved.

A second way to monitor student involvement in the assignment is to circulate around the room and check each student's progress periodically. This way corrective feedback can be given, and students can make progress. Note the progress of all students, not just those who raise their hands for help. Check frequently with students who become easily confused or distracted. Also, check in with small groups as they begin working to assure each group is on the right track.

If you are working with reading groups while some students are doing independent work, don't wait until the end of reading time to check on students outside the reading group. Check in with them between meetings with groups to be sure they are doing the work correctly.

Shoe-New Business © 1990 Macnelly. Distributed by King Features Syndicate.

Some longer individual assignments may not be due for several days or even a week or longer. Examples include notebooks, reports, and science or social studies projects. In this case, be especially careful to monitor progress. Define stages in the project or assignment; then set deadlines and goals for each of the parts, or have students develop work plans on which they report daily. Collect and check assignments at each stage, and provide feedback. This helps students learn to organize their time and makes it easier for you to monitor and evaluate their progress. If students engage in long-term projects often, support them in developing their own subgoals and deadlines, first as a whole group and later individually.

Discuss the criteria for evaluation, and solicit input to encourage students' awareness and commitment to high standards. Teachers often use such discussions to develop a rubric, that is, a set of outcomes and, perhaps, rating scales for evaluating important outcomes. Students can be encouraged to use the rubric for monitoring their own or their group's progress. Group projects require special attention to feedback and monitoring. Identifying a timeline for progress checkpoints (e.g., proposal, midproject progress report, group presentation) will help you and the students stay on course. We present more material on managing student work in groups in Chapter 7.

## Monitoring the Completion of Assignments

Monitoring the completion of assignments has several components. First, establish regular procedures for turning in completed work. Second, note whose papers have been turned in. Many different systems are possible. For example, you might have students put completed work in individual "mailboxes"; you can then determine at a glance whose boxes are filled and whose are not. Or you might have students put completed papers on a certain corner of their desks so you can spot them as you move around the room. This procedure is useful when you do not intend to collect the papers. Another procedure is to have students put their work in different baskets for each subject for you to grade, record, and return with feedback. As an additional help, you may give students individual checklists to help them keep track of their own assignments.

Some teachers teach students to keep an assignment notebook for homework. Each day students copy homework assignments into the notebook, and each evening parents initial the notebook after the assignment is completed. Teachers can also use the notebooks to communicate with parents about upcoming events or projects, and parents can write comments or questions to teachers in the notebooks.

Consider also how you will collect work. When all students are turning in materials at the same time, one efficient procedure is to have papers passed in a given direction until you have all papers in your hands. Materials such as notebooks or journals that are bulky might be collected by designated helpers and stacked in a particular spot. Papers or assignments turned in by students at varying times can be placed in labeled baskets, trays, or plastic containers. Having students identify their papers by an assigned number corresponding to alphabetical order makes sequencing these papers a fast task for easy recording. Locate drop-off spots away from congested areas or areas that might be distracting to students. Let students know the procedure you expect them to use. Following it consistently saves time and prevents confusion.

## Maintaining Records of Student Work

An important part of your monitoring system is your record of work completed or skills mastered. You may be provided a printed grade book, access to digital grade book software, or both. In a printed grade book, you should have a place for recording the names of students who are absent each day—for example, by putting an *a* in the corner of the appropriate space. When setting up your grade book, you can devote several lines per student and record grades and scores for each subject on a separate line, or you can use a different page for each major subject. Color coding entries can help identify weighted scores (e.g., tests, long-term projects).

If you have students from another teacher's class for instruction in a subject, leave space for those additional students on the page for that subject in your grade book. You will need to supply the other teacher with report card evaluations, and it will be helpful to have all of the information in one place.

Digital grade books function much the same way but can add the benefit of parental access to scores, missing work, and attendance. These programs have the additional advantage of creating progress reports quickly for every student. If you plan to keep student grade records on the computer in an electronic file, determine whether your school's computer system automatically backs up information in each teacher's classroom computer. If not, be certain to do so yourself, and/or maintain a paper copy of academic progress information.

Record grades or other evaluations (e.g., E, S+, S, U) for major assignments and test results in your grade book. You may also want to evaluate other classwork such as worksheets or workbook pages. This practice is not as common in the primary grades as in the intermediate grades, where more emphasis is placed on grading, and a more complete record of daily work in major subjects is useful. However, some primary grades maintain a checklist of mastered skills that are part of the school district's grade-level or subject-area standards. If students will be accountable for mastery of these standards, create a space for this in your grade book. Note that students' grades and other personal information are confidential. Protect your grade book, printed summaries, and/or passwords to maintain data security.

Consider your grading system carefully. Avoid systems that give very large weights to single tests or assignments. Also, realize that using a zero for missing assignments results in "catastrophe" grading (Carifio & Carey, 2009), in which one or a few such scores make a failing grade inevitable. Your grading system should permit students to stumble occasionally but still be able to recover sufficiently to succeed overall.

## Managing Student Portfolios

Teaching students to keep portfolios of their work has become a standard practice in many elementary classrooms. For example, students may keep a writing portfolio that shows the progress of their writing from first to final drafts. Helping students create portfolios can be an effective way of showing a student's progress and teaching students to self-assess by selecting and reflecting on their work.

Portfolios also provide teachers with a useful tool for parent conferences and holistic grading. Depending on the purpose of a portfolio, students may have more or less input into the selection of portfolio entries and the eventual evaluation of the complete portfolio. However, over time children should be supported to make more choices about what to include and why. Digital documentation for e-portfolios (via scanners, digital cameras, and electronic files) can save storage space and can easily be stored on a flash drive or CD.

## Managing the Paperwork

Keeping up with all of the papers can be overwhelming. One way to avoid mountains of "back papers" is to look over, grade, record, and return assignments quickly. Not only is this timely feedback for your students, but it also helps you to spot students who are "fading" and to diagnose areas needing whole-class remediation. Be realistic about your grading capabilities. If you are behind in grading six sets of papers and are planning to assign essays due in two days, rethink your plans. Allow yourself enough grading time to do the job well—on the last paper as well as the first. Try making a grading schedule to distribute a huge task into manageable segments rather than plowing through until you are exhausted. Instead of collecting, checking, grading, and returning each assignment, try another routine: Go around the room to check each student's work. Record a grade or note completion as you move to each student's desk. This type of checking is fast, personal, and efficient and is especially effective for written assignments that require holistic assessment.

If you plan to have students pass papers up, you can prevent "straggler" papers by describing, modeling, and practicing the procedure for how it is to be done. Returning papers is simplified when they are already filed together, labeled by subject, and even organized by rows or groups. Papers may be distributed by students; consider using weekly "assistant teachers."

# ■ Feedback to Students

Good monitoring procedures are essential for providing quality feedback to students, and frequent and regular feedback is more desirable than sporadic appraisal because it reduces the amount of time students spend making errors. Appropriate times for feedback will occur as you monitor work in progress and after it is completed. Try to give students immediate and specific feedback: Tell them how they are meeting your expectations, what they need to do to correct errors, and then check their corrections.

Although feedback about completed work cannot occur until after an assignment has been checked, checking should be done within a day of work completion so that students can benefit from the feedback. Consider also having your students

Hi & Lois © King Features Syndicate.

help you. At most grade levels, students can check their own work occasionally. Use this strategy only for assignments they are capable of checking accurately, such as arithmetic worksheets or spelling quizzes that have specified right answers. Teach students a consistent system for marking right or wrong answers. Displaying correct answers can make checking work in class proceed smoothly and accurately.

Remember that student checking is not done for a grade. It provides students with only some quick feedback so they can know what they did correctly and you can know what help they may need. Papers that require a recorded grade should be checked and graded by you.

Pay attention at the beginning of the year to the completion of assignments. The first time a student fails to turn in an assignment with no apparent reason, talk with the student about it. If the student needs help, provide it, but require that the student do the work. If the student neglects two assignments consecutively or begins a pattern of skipping occasional assignments, call, send a note home, or email the parents. Be friendly and encouraging, but insist that the work be done. Don't wait until the grading period is over to note problems with assignment completion or assume that the report card grade will communicate this information effectively. The parent(s) can be the teacher's strongest ally in ensuring that a child takes schoolwork seriously, so do not hesitate to contact parents. Most parents will appreciate your concern and provide you with support from home. Your school may have a policy regarding contacting parents by email.

You may also want to communicate with parents by having students take checked assignments home regularly. Be sure that this includes good work, not just poor work. You can occasionally have parents sign and return the papers as a way of rewarding and motivating students to keep up their good work. Use a large envelope or a two-pocket folder to convey the materials home rather than sending them loose. This envelope or folder is also a convenient holder for other important documents that go home for signing or for the parents' information. Be sure that the child's name is on the folder or envelope. Taping a signature sheet on the front with a place for the date and the number of papers included can ensure that parents see all of the student's work. Consider a specific day weekly to exchange these papers with parents. Keep the returned, signed papers until the end of the marking period in case questions arise. Students can then select portfolio entries from this completed work.

Another means of giving the children feedback is to display good work. Do not make standards for "good" so stringent that some children can never meet them. Effort and progress may be more appropriate criteria. Be sure to keep the students' grades private.

Finally, teach students how to reflect on and record their own progress. Older children can keep a sheet with test scores or assignment grades. Steps on a ladder, circles on a caterpillar to color in for each completed assignment, or some similar visual device can be a good motivator for younger students. Students who select their own portfolio entries can write about the learning each piece represents or about why they included particular materials. Remember your ultimate goal is to help students develop into lifelong, independent learners.

# ■ Chapter Summary

Student work provides teachers with an opportunity to see what the students are learning and where they may need additional instruction. Managing the ebb and flow of student work requires teachers to communicate clearly what is being assigned, how to do it, when to do it, where to turn it in, as well as how to make up the assignment if a student is absent. In addition, students need teachers to monitor the students' progress on assignments in order to check instructional clarity and to assist students with learning in the process. Managing the student work after it is completed means maintaining accurate, up-to-date records; providing timely feedback to students; and teaching students how to reflect on their own work. When teachers effectively manage student work, they provide solid instructional communication to students on a regular and consistent basis.

# ■ Further Reading

Brophy, J. E. (2004). *Motivating students to learn* (2nd ed.). Mahwah, NJ: Erlbaum.

> *A practical guide for helping teachers develop classroom practices for motivating students within the realities of the classroom. The book's focus on motivational principles rather than motivational theorists or theories leads naturally into discussions of specific classroom strategies and synthesizes that portion of the motivational literature most relevant to teachers.*

Burns, M. (1995). The 8 most important lessons I've learned about organizing my teaching year. *Instructor, 105*(2), 86–88.

> *Many of the ideas in this article focus on planning for instruction. Their implementation would be a big step toward managing student academic work, and they are well worth considering by new or experienced teachers.*

Evertson, C. M., & Poole, I. R. (2004*). Fostering student accountability for classroom work*. Nashville, TN: Vanderbilt University, Peabody College, IRIS Center (iris.peabody.

vanderbilt.edu). Click on "Resources," then "Behavior and Classroom Management" (left column), and then "Case Studies" (middle column) to link to this case study set.

*This Web site contains many activities and case studies for accommodating special needs students in the regular education classroom.*

Kuhn, D. (2007, June). How to produce a high-achieving child. *Phi Delta Kappan, 88*(10), 757–763.

*In this short article, the author considers what schools are and should be doing to provide meaningful learning experiences for students. She describes key research, including the work of Carol Dweck (Stanford), and makes clear recommendations for focusing instruction in ways that motivate students to know the hows and whys as well as the whats of subject matter.*

Leahy, S., Lyon, C., Thompson, M., & Wiliam, D. (2005, November). Classroom assessment: Minute by minute, day by day. *Educational Leadership, 63*(3), 19–24.

*This article outlines how to consider assessment for rather than of student learning. Emphasizing the importance of formative evaluation, the authors share five strategies for maximizing the use of assessment to promote student learning.*

Mergendoller, J. R., Markham, T., Revitz, J., & Larmer, J. (2006). Pervasive management of project-based learning. In C. Evertson & C. Weinstein (Eds.), *Handbook of research on classroom management: Research, practice, and contemporary issues* (pp. 583–615). Mahwah, NJ: Erlbaum.

*This chapter describes research on the management of project-based learning, including ways of helping students manage themselves and work with peers on long-term projects. The authors emphasize that although students play an important role in many project-management activities, the teacher remains the senior partner ensuring that students understand and fulfill their responsibilities.*

Shores, E., & Grace, K. (2005). *The portfolio book: A step-by-step guide for teachers.* Upper Saddle River, NJ: Pearson Prentice Hall.

*This work provides portfolio assessment techniques in easy-to-manage steps covering several major features in one book: portfolio assessment, practical applications, usable forms, emphasis on family involvement, and teacher reflection.*

rubistar.4teachers.org/index.php

*This site includes several ready-made rubric templates for multiple subjects, types of assignments, and grade levels. Use of the site is free and does not require you to sign in unless you plan to save your designed rubric to the server.*

www.apa.org/education/k12/classroom-data.aspx

*This site shares the teaching module Using Classroom Data to Give Systematic Feedback to Students to Improve Learning, providing some dos and don'ts of managing student work for the purpose of improving learning.*

www.lburkhart.com

*This site includes tips for technology integration in elementary, middle school, and special needs classrooms.*

# ■ Suggested Activities

1. Having procedures for managing students' work can help you create a fair, documented basis for student assessment and allow timely feedback to students. These procedures also enable students to practice personal organizational skills and responsibility. How does what you believe about teaching and learning (your philosophy of education) influence the way you design your accountability system?

2. Return to the opening case study of Mr. Paul. Discuss with a partner what suggestions you could offer at this point for introducing the project in a way that might prevent some of the difficulties students experienced?

3. Case Studies 4.1 to 4.3 illustrate accountability procedures that encourage student responsibility. Create a list of those procedures that you can incorporate into your classroom.

4. Case Study 4.4 illustrates problems that can occur if certain accountability procedures are not in place. Use the information in this and in previous chapters to diagnose Mr. Ambrose's problems. What steps could Mr. Ambrose take to improve the situation in his class? Compare your ideas with the key in the Appendix.

5. Use the checklist at the end of the chapter to organize your planning as you develop an accountability system. Can you think of additional accountability procedures you will need?

6. Go to the Internet site www.atozteacherstuff.com/Tips, then click on "managing papers." What tips can you find that would prevent the student protest "I know I turned it in"?

7. Interview a practicing elementary teacher to ask questions regarding his/her management of student work. Write a list of five procedures this teacher uses that you would like to incorporate in your classroom, and describe why you feel these procedures would be helpful.

# ■ Case Study 4.1

## MANAGING STUDENT WORK

To help students check their homework and to encourage them to help each other, Ms. Alvarez's fourth-grade students work in teams of four and go over homework problems together. Ms. Alvarez has taught her students how to take turns reading the problems, answering the questions, and encouraging and helping one another. Each team member takes a turn reading the problem aloud and then gives his or her answer to the problem. Team members rotate leading the discussion of the questions until all questions have been answered. From time to time, Ms. Alvarez plans activities and conversations that reinforce the collaborative environment she strives for in her classroom, as well as reviewing procedures for her "group check."

The students use the "group check" process when checking their homework. When a team member reads the answer, the other members give a "thumbs up" if they had the same answer. If someone's answer differs, the student quietly says, "I disagree." Each team member talks through the problem and reworks it to see where the error might be. This process continues until each team comes to consensus about the homework problem.

On one question involving the area of a circle, Jake did not draw his circle the same size as his team members did. When Anita gave her solution, Jake said, "I disagree. I think!" Jake and his team members discussed the sizes of the circles and what they would need to do to draw to scale. They used their compasses and redrew the circle, being careful to note the radius given in the problem. As it turned out, Jake's answer was correct; he had drawn his circle to the correct scale. Jake and his team members marked the problems that were difficult for them on their papers. When Ms. Alvarez brought the class back together, she discussed problems that were difficult for the team to agree on and what questions they still had.

Ms. Alvarez uses this information as a cue to the problems that were difficult for the majority of the class. She plans additional class instruction to clarify this learning. Having the team members first check their work together frees Ms. Alvarez to move around the room and help teams that need assistance. Her "group check" system helps her avoid standing at the front of the room and calling out answers.

At the end of the morning activity, one person from each team collects the team's homework folders and files them in the team members' portfolios, stored on a nearby shelf. When Ms. Alvarez has a conference once a week with her students, their portfolios are within reach. If she notes that students need additional support, she works with them individually or in small groups.

## ■ Case Study 4.2

### KEEPING STUDENTS INVOLVED DURING CENTER ACTIVITIES

Ms. Avery designates a section of the board for listing the daily schedule for centers. Today's schedule consists of the following activities and times:

|  | **Reading Group** | **Research** | **Math** | **Science** |
|---|---|---|---|---|
| 9:00–9:20 | Spotted Owl | Gorilla | Panda | Panther |
| 9:25–9:45 | Panther | Spotted Owl | Gorilla | Panda |
| 9:50–10:10 | Panda | Panther | Spotted Owl | Gorilla |
| 10:15–10:35 | Gorilla | Panda | Panther | Spotted Owl |

Center time typically consists of four stations, one of which is teacher directed. At the beginning of center time, Ms. Avery presents directions and shows the students the necessary materials for each station.

The reading groups in Ms. Avery's class are flexible. Sometimes they are created around the students' interests; sometimes they are formed to practice certain skills, such as learning about main ideas, cause and effect, and inferring. At present the students have selected four endangered animals (spotted owl, panther, panda, gorilla) for in-depth study, and the reading groups were formed to study each animal. In addition to their reading groups, small groups of students are developing research projects on their chosen animals.

During today's center activities, the students will meet with Ms. Avery for their reading groups. They will also continue with their research projects, using Internet and print resources the teacher and students have found. At the math center, they will complete a practice sheet on long division; manipulatives and other aids are provided for the students at this station. For science, the students will observe the animals in the class terrarium and record their observations in their science logs, making comparisons with their selected research animals.

When Ms. Avery meets with each reading group, she sits where she can see the entire class. She scans the class frequently and signals children when necessary to keep them engaged. She does so by making eye contact or sometimes calling individuals' names softly to prevent or stop inappropriate behavior. Because Ms. Avery does not want interruptions while she is in the reading circle, she has assigned one helper for each group. To prevent overreliance on the helpers, Ms. Avery has taught the children to request assistance only for situations that prevent them from doing any work at all. If they can skip the problem or question and move on, they are to do so and wait for help from her.

When the timer rings, she dismisses the reading group, and the other groups clean up their stations; place their writing, practice sheets, and journals in appropriate baskets; and move to their next stations. Ms. Avery circulates around the room checking on student progress, answering questions, and helping students. Between groups, her checks usually take no longer than 5 minutes, after which she is ready to call the next group. Ms. Avery has made sure that this monitoring time is built into her schedule.

# ■ Case Study 4.3

## USING TECHNOLOGY IN AN UPPER ELEMENTARY GRADE

Ms. Curry's fifth-grade science class has been learning to do research on the computer using Web-based resources. Later students will present their projects using software designed for school-age students that accommodates short videos and other graphics. Students are to complete two multimedia research projects during the year, but Ms. Curry decides to limit the choices for the first project to make it easier for students to begin quickly and to focus on learning the content. This also allows her to adjust the assignment for student ability levels. When she introduces the first research project on cells, Ms. Curry provides two handouts describing requirements: (1) a description of the topic and a list of slide categories the computer presentation should include, and (2) a general outline of requirements for the project, a calendar of checkpoints, a due date for the assignment, and information about how the project will be graded.

Ms. Curry does an initial multimedia presentation for the class as an example and goes over all directions step-by-step. She emphasizes two main requirements: appearance and sources to be included. To illustrate guidelines for appearance, she provides examples of color selections for backgrounds and text to show which color combinations can be easily read and which cannot. She also includes appearance standards such as size and clarity of fonts defined in detail. The second main requirement concerns appropriate sources (using reliable Web sites) and citations (Web sites, graphics, or video). At least one of the cards or slides has to include a graphics or video file rather than written text. Ms. Curry provides a printout of her sample presentation to each student, posts one on the bulletin board, and posts a link to the file on her class Web site. She also indicates the days the class will be scheduled to work in the computer lab and provides a sign-up sheet for using the classroom computers during class-work time or study hall.

Before the first multimedia project is due, students receive a check-off sheet that they use to determine whether they have met all the requirements before submitting their disks. She uses this to evaluate their work and to record grades for each presentation, which she discusses with each student.

# ■ Case Study 4.4

## POOR WORK AND STUDY HABITS IN A THIRD-GRADE CLASS

Mr. Ambrose's third-grade class has been fairly well behaved, with little disruptive behavior. Most students follow his procedures, such as those for staying in their seats during whole-class presentations; raising hands during discussions; and using the pencil sharpener, restroom, and other areas of the room appropriately. Some social talk occurs during independent work activities, but it does not escalate into chaos, and students usually settle down when requested. However, students have been less task engaged lately, and many students have been tardy turning in assignments. They complain that they don't know when assignments are due, and some don't turn in their work at all. To make assignments explicit, Mr. Ambrose has begun to record the daily assignments on the board. Because some assignments are not due until the following day, he leaves the previous day's assignments on that board also, so students will know when each subject's assignment is due for both days.

Today, during a 1-hour period of individual and group work, several students asked what they were supposed to do—despite the fact that Mr. Ambrose had listed the morning assignments on the board and repeatedly pointed out where they could be found. After several students turned in papers before they were called for, Mr. Ambrose explained, "Remember that class assignments not finished during class time are supposed to be kept until the next day, even if you get them done later in the day, unless I call for them. If you finish the homework during independent work time, it can be placed in the turn-in box then." Students continued to act confused, not only about when assignments were due but also about how to do the work.

Mr. Ambrose frequently works at his desk during independent work time, but he allows students to come up one at a time if they need assistance. They follow this procedure well, although some of the lowest-achieving students seldom come up. Quiet socializing and other off-task activity go on among students whose seats are located away from the teacher.

Mr. Ambrose has ample activities for students. For example, during a recent 1-hour segment he gave students an assignment and then a quiz (students were told to hold their papers until after the quiz was completed). An extra-credit assignment was listed on the board for students who finished the regular work early. As he handed out the quiz and gave instructions, some students continued to work on the assignment. Later they had to go to Mr. Ambrose to find out the instructions for the quiz, and several did not have enough time to complete it. Mr. Ambrose has told students that they must work harder and do their best or their grades will suffer, but this seems to have had an impact on only the most motivated students in the class.

What steps could Mr. Ambrose take to improve the situation in his class?

# ■ Checklist: Managing Student Work

| Check When Taught to Students | Area | Notes |
|---|---|---|

**Communicating Assignments and Work Requirements**

| | | |
|---|---|---|
| ☐ | A. Where and how will you post assignments? | _____ |
| ☐ | B. What will be your standards for form and neatness? | _____ |
| ☐ | C. How will absent students make up assignments? | _____ |
| ☐ | D. What will be the consequences of late or incomplete work? | _____ |

**Monitoring Progress on and Completion of Assignments**

| | | |
|---|---|---|
| ☐ | A. What procedures will you use to monitor work in progress for individuals? | _____ |
| ☐ | B. What procedures will you use to monitor work in progress for groups? | _____ |
| ☐ | C. How will you determine whether students are completing assignments? | _____ |
| ☐ | D. How will you manage completed assignments? | _____ |
| ☐ | E. Will students keep portfolios? If so, how will entries be selected, and how will students reflect on them? | _____ |
| ☐ | F. What records of student work will you retain? | _____ |
| ☐ | G. How will you encourage students to monitor themselves? | _____ |

**Feedback**

| | | |
|---|---|---|
| ☐ | A. What are your school's grading policies and procedures? | _____ |

☐     B. What kinds of feedback will you
provide, and when? _____

☐     C. How will you encourage students
to reflect on their own progress? _____

☐     D. What will you do when a student
stops doing assignments? _____

☐     E. What procedure will you follow to
share student work with parents? _____

☐     F. How will you handle grading
disputes? _____

---

### MyEducationLab

Now go to www.myeducationlab.com to:

- Take a Quiz to test your mastery of chapter objectives.
- Study chapter content with an individualized Study Plan.
- Deepen your understanding of particular concepts and principles with Classroom Management Simulations.
- Apply what you have learned in the chapter to your work with children in Building Teaching Skills exercises.

**CHAPTER 5**

# Getting Off to a Good Start

The beginning of school is an important time for classroom management because your students will learn attitudes, behavior, and work habits that will affect the rest of the year. It is in the first few weeks of school that students learn the behaviors expected of them and how to accomplish school tasks successfully. They also learn in what ways these tasks are meaningful to them and why success is worth pursuing. Much of this is communicated simply by how you treat your students and what you expect of them from the very first day. Careful planning for the beginning of school sets the stage for the rest of the year.

Your major goal for the beginning of the year, then, is to strengthen each student's belief that school tasks are worth doing and that he or she can be successful. To accomplish this, you must obtain student cooperation in two key areas: following your rules and procedures and engaging successfully in all learning experiences. Attaining this goal will make it possible for you to create a positive climate for learning throughout the year.

A concern for establishing appropriate behavior does not imply a lack of concern for student feelings and attitudes. Instead, the intent is to create a classroom climate that helps children feel secure and confident and keeps preventable problems from occurring. Therefore, some of the suggestions in this chapter focus directly on cognitive goals, whereas others incorporate student concerns and other affective considerations.

The major topics in this chapter are creating a positive climate, teaching rules and procedures to the students, and deciding on the classroom activities you will use during the first week of school. Communicating with parents, special problems, and preparing for a substitute are also discussed. A checklist is offered to help organize your planning, and two case studies of the beginning of the year will give you many ideas about how to begin.

# ■ Creating a Positive Climate in Your Classroom

Having a good management plan before the school year begins is essential, but its effectiveness in building community will depend on the presence of a positive classroom environment. Your goal is not to be the ruler of a classroom kingdom but to be the designer and facilitator of an interactive classroom community. The foundation of a positive climate is positive interactions between teacher and students and among students. A positive environment encourages students to be excited about their school experience and about learning.

Students are with their teachers almost 50 percent of their waking hours during the school year, so it is easy to see how teachers are major influences in young people's lives. This large investment of time, plus teachers' influence on students, requires the creation of a positive and safe environment in which students can be challenged, feel free to explore, support one another, and engage in constructing their own knowledge (see Chapter 8).

Like all human beings, children have a strong need to belong to a group. You can promote that sense of belonging in a number of ways (Erwin, 2003; Pianta, 2006):

1. **Speak courteously and calmly.** Students need to hear teachers saying "please," "thank you," and "excuse me." These courtesies become expected and are modeled by the students. A calm voice indicates acceptance and self-control. If children feel threatened or frustrated, knowing that the teacher is not upset is reassuring.
2. **Share information.** Learn each student's name as soon as possible and engage in activities that help students learn more about each other. Introduce yourself and share something about your outside interests. Speak personally with your students to get to know them individually.
3. **Use positive statements as often as possible.** Often negative behavior is more noticeable than positive; therefore, we tend to comment on it more often. Perhaps we also feel compelled to mention negative behavior because we believe it will improve students' behavior. The opposite is usually true. Not only do negative statements cause a student to feel negative, but they also tend to create a negative environment that affects everyone.
4. **Establish a feeling of community.** Conduct class meetings on a regular basis for class building, problem solving, and content-related discussions. One of your first meetings can be on establishing class rules and procedures (see Chapter 3).

While building a positive relationship with individual students is seen as one of the most critical predictors of student success, understanding the concept of authority is also important to the health of the community. To feel safe, children need to know that there is a source of authority within the classroom (Brophy, 2004; Hoy & Weinstein, 2006). The power of authority naturally lies with the teacher, but how that power is used has a critical influence on the learning community.

# ■ Teaching Rules and Procedures

One of the surest ways to communicate your expectations for student behavior is through a planned system of classroom rules and procedures. How best to teach this system to your students is an important consideration. The term *teach* is used purposely; you will not communicate your expectations adequately if you only state the rules and procedures. Here are three important aspects of the teaching process:

1. **Describing and demonstrating the desired behavior.** Use words and actions to convey what behavior is acceptable or desirable. Be as specific as possible. For example, do not simply tell students you expect good behavior while you are out of the room; tell them what "good behavior" means—staying in seats, no talking, keep working. Demonstrate desired behavior whenever possible. For example, if you allow "quiet talking" or "classroom voices" during center time, show what this means. If the procedure is complex, present it step-by-step. For example, lining up requires that students know when to line up (the teacher gives permission by tables or rows), where and how to go (push chairs under tables and then walk without talking), expected behavior in line (hands off others, no talking in halls, walk—don't run). You do not have to do all of the demonstrating; students enjoy showing the class the correct procedure.
2. **Rehearsal—practicing the behavior.** Rehearsal serves two purposes: It helps children learn the appropriate behavior, and it provides you with an opportunity to determine whether they understand and can follow a procedure correctly. Complex procedures may have to be rehearsed several times. Practice is especially helpful for primary-grade children; however, older elementary school children can also benefit from rehearsal when procedures are complex or unfamiliar.
3. **Feedback.** After you have asked students to follow a procedure for the first time, tell them whether they did it properly. If they need to improve, tell them that, too. Be specific in your feedback—for example, "Thank you for putting your materials away quickly. Please stop the talking at Table 2." If many students do not follow a procedure correctly, repeat one or more of the steps listed here. If only a few students are off track, ask them to describe what they are supposed to do so that you can see whether they have understood your directions. Finally, the fact that students follow the procedure correctly once does not mean they will do so consistently. Watch carefully, and be prepared to give reminders and feedback as appropriate.

The following example illustrates how to teach procedures; it shows how a complex transition procedure was taught to a second-grade class.

*Ms. Stevens explains to her students that she expects them to move quickly and quietly from one activity to another so they will have time to do all the things planned. She shows them the kitchen timer and makes it ring. When they hear this bell, they should put away the materials they are using and move to the next activity as quickly as possible. She says, "After reading, I will ring the bell, and you are to put your reading materials in your desk as quickly as possible. You should then get up from your desk and walk quietly to the rug so we can begin our Spanish lesson. Are there any questions?" A student asks if she will always ring the bell for Spanish, and Ms. Stevens says she will.*

*Ms. Stevens then tells the class that she would like them to practice. "You have paper and pencil on your desk for story writing. I will give you time to finish the story later in the day. Right now, when I ring the bell, put your materials in your desk, and come quickly and quietly to the rug." At this point, Ms. Stevens rings the bell. Students immediately begin putting away their materials and moving toward the rug. However, several students line up to get drinks of water, and one goes to the restroom. When everyone is on the rug in a circle around Ms. Stevens, she refers to the clock on the wall and says, "It took us 3 minutes to put the materials away and get to the rug. You are second graders now, and I think you can move faster than that. I think you should be seated on the rug in a circle in 1 minute. Also, it was not time to get a drink of water or to use the restroom unless it was an emergency. Do you all understand?" The students all nod solemnly.*

*Ms. Stevens tells students to return to their desks, get out their paper and pencils, and get set to practice again. The students go quickly back to their desks and take out their materials. Ms. Stevens rings the bell again, and students go through the routine, this time more quickly. After everyone is settled, Ms. Stevens smiles and thanks the students. "You've done a super job. It took you only 1 minute to get to the rug. I'm really proud of you."*

### Vignette Reflection

Discuss with a partner your responses to the following questions:

1. What are the steps to this procedure?
2. How did Ms. Stevens teach it?
3. What feedback was offered as students practiced?
4. What will Ms. Stevens likely have to do for the next several transitions?

## Teacher Authority

*Teacher authority* refers to your right to set standards for student behavior and performance and to the likelihood that students will follow your lead in their decisions and behaviors. When students do as you expect, they are vesting you with the authority to lead them. When they intentionally engage in behaviors contrary to your wishes, they are disputing your teacher authority.

Teacher authority can be derived from multiple sources (Pace, 2003; Spady & Mitchell, 1979). Under *traditional* authority, students are expected to behave because the teacher is the adult in charge, much as children are expected to obey their parents. Teachers who rely exclusively on this form of authority will find dealing with upper elementary students problematic when that authority is challenged. *Bureaucratic* authority derives its legitimacy from the teacher's ability to use grades to reward effort and performance, and to use prescribed consequences for desirable and inappropriate behaviors. *Expert* or *professional* authority is based on teacher knowledge and skills: Students may accept the teacher's decisions about curriculum and academic tasks because of the teacher's expertise in the subject matter. Finally, some teachers utilize *charismatic* authority; they are expressive and outgoing, or they engage students with their interactive style and good communication skills. Students follow these teachers' lead because they like and are attracted to them. Pace (2003) found that teachers derived their authority from several sources rather than relying on just one. For example, a *charismatic* teacher might use *bureaucratic* and *traditional* authority with students who don't respond positively to his or her interpersonal style.

Mention of teacher authority can make some persons uncomfortable because the term suggests "authoritarian" and thus evokes an image of repression and arbitrary governance. However, there are several forms of authority (see sidebar). Furthermore, society depends on authority as a key aspect in organizing its social and work groups. In the same way, schools depend on student acceptance of legitimate authority in order to create a safe setting in which teaching and learning can occur.

Another perspective on authority makes a distinction between *authoritarian* and *authoritative* leadership. Authoritarian teachers mandate rules without rationales, try to control students through threats and punishment, and assign

Shoe-New Business © 1982 Macnelly. Distributed by King Features Syndicate.

consequences arbitrarily. In contrast, authoritative teachers explain the basis for actions and decisions, give students more independence as they demonstrate maturity and a willingness to behave responsibly, and administer consequences fairly and proportionately. Regardless of the style of teacher authority, or combination of styles, authoritarian behavior invites challenges and resistance, whereas authoritative leadership invites cooperation.

It's a useful exercise to pay attention to how students react to your use of authority and then consider ways to adjust your approach when appropriate. No single approach is best in all circumstances, so try to be flexible and open to feedback.

# ■ Planning for a Good Beginning

Planning for a warm and friendly learning environment for your students is a positive first step in starting the year. In the beginning, you must consider the management strategies of choosing teaching rules and procedures and a system for ensuring student accountability (discussed in Chapters 3 and 4). You now need to plan activities for the first several days of school.

## Planning for the First Days of School

Planning activities that will allow all your students to be successful will make students feel more secure and confident and will encourage good effort. Initial assignments should be easy and should require only simple directions. In this way, the children can learn lesson routines quickly and encounter little difficulty in completing assignments.

For the first few days, limit the lessons to those that can be presented and explained to all students at the same time. Do not try to group students for instruction for at least several days, and if you can, avoid individual testing or activities or assignments that require lengthy work with individual students and keep you from monitoring the whole class. If you are involved with a small group or with an individual, you may not see important behaviors and events that may grow into problems. Don't overload yourself or your students with unnecessarily complicated activities. Your students will already be learning many new procedures during the first few days of school.

Plan your activities to take into account the students' perspectives, concerns, and need for information about their new and unfamiliar classroom. A variety of activities—including some with physical movement, music, and provision for occasional short breaks—provides the changes of pace that help maintain interest and alertness throughout the day. In addition, you can stimulate excitement in the curriculum and its activities if you foreshadow interesting things the students will be learning this year.

Keep in mind that not all of your students may be present the first day of school. Many times, students will enter or leave the school during the first couple of weeks. For record-keeping purposes, create a temporary grade book and attendance sheet that you can transfer to your official records once your class roster is settled.

## Some Typical Activities

Activities for the first school day and for several days thereafter are not necessarily presented here in the sequence you will follow, nor will you use each activity every day. Examine the two case studies at the end of the chapter to see how different teachers put the pieces together.

**Greeting the Students.**   Prepare student name tags ahead of time, but have extra materials on hand for students who are not on your roll. Decide how name tags will be fastened on. If you intend to use safety pins, be sure your students can fasten them, or plan to do it for them. Other options are tape, commercial stick-on tags, or a length of yarn so the name tags are worn like necklaces. In addition to name tags, you might tape a name card to the top of each student's desk.

When students enter the room, greet them warmly, help them get their name tags, and get them seated. If you have taped their names to their desks, the matter of seating is settled. In some cases the roster of students is not definite, so you may have them find a desk that "fits" them so that they will be comfortable throughout the year. Explain that seating may change later.

Make a seating chart or label the desks as soon as practicable, making any necessary adjustments later. Some teachers use a grid, putting student names into the boxes in pencil until classes have stabilized and seating is set. Another strategy involves using sticky notes on a heavy sheet of 8 1/2 × 11-inch paper and keeping it in a plastic sleeve. This allows you to move, add, or subtract students as necessary. An added advantage is the flexibility if you decide to rearrange desks. Sticky notes can be arranged in any configuration. In addition, you can color code individual notes to inform a substitute of information about students' needs, allergies, and/or roles.

Don't allow the students to wander around the room or become noisy. As students enter, provide a simple puzzle, a bulletin board–themed coloring sheet, or a piece of paper with open-ended questions such as "I am thinking about . . .," "I have a question about . . .," or "I wonder what _____ is like in school" to give students something to do at their desks. As soon as most students are present, begin with the introduction. Remember later in the day to let students talk about how they solved the puzzles or what they wrote on their papers.

**Introductions.**   You will want to tell the students something about yourself; however, an extended autobiography is not necessary. A few personal notes and something about your interests are appropriate. Have students introduce themselves—nothing more than a name is necessary, but some teachers have the children tell something about themselves (e.g., favorite color, naming family members). The introductory activity should not take too long, however; there will be plenty of opportunity later to get acquainted, and you do not want students to become restless.

**Room Description.**   Introduce students to their classroom by pointing out and describing areas of the room, especially areas that they will be using on the first day (e.g., where they may put their coats, lunches, or other items from home). Particularly for kindergarten, plan also to do a school tour (e.g., library, cafeteria).

**Get-Acquainted Activities.**   Teachers frequently include a get-acquainted activity as part of their first-day plan. Such activities can help students feel that the teacher and others know them better and care about them as individuals. Teachers often describe the goal of such an activity as helping students feel more secure and comfortable with their classmates. The activities are also used to foster a greater sense of class cohesiveness. One of the following get-acquainted activities can be used early in the first day for a change of pace after the room description or after the initial discussion of rules and major procedures:

- Have pairs of students learn each other's names and something about the other person (e.g., hobbies, interests). Then have students introduce their partners.
- Use a name game to help students remember names and to add interest to introductions. For example, have students make up an adjective to go with their own names (e.g., Happy Holly, Curious Carl), or have students use the name of a game they like (e.g., Nintendo Nick). As students introduce themselves, have them name the other students who came before them (or perhaps the previous five students) along with their descriptors.
- Make copies of a line drawing of the school's mascot. Let students sign their own copies and write personal facts (e.g., names of brothers or sisters, pets, likes and dislikes, favorite activities or foods) on the drawings. Post these on a bulletin board so students can read about each other.
- Ask students to complete a brief questionnaire identifying their interests, favorite subjects, hobbies, and so on. Upper elementary students can complete a series of open-ended statements that reflect their interests or preferences (e.g., "Today I feel . . ." or "The thing I do best is . . .").

The activities described next can be used the first day or later in the week, after students are more acquainted with one another or after you have had time to prepare for the activity.

- Make a puzzle with student names. For example, leave out a few letters in each name for students to fill in, or list first and last names in separate columns in scrambled order, and let students match names. Students can also identify names arranged in a seek-and-find puzzle.
- Set aside a few minutes before the children leave to review the day's activities and to discuss with the students what they learned, found difficult, liked best, and so forth. Say a few words about upcoming events and activities. Comment on good work and behavior to reinforce your expectations and to keep the tone positive.
- Have students from last year's class—you'll need to plan this well ahead—write letters to students in this year's class, telling them what to expect, what was fun about the year, suggestions for study, and what they learned during the year. Share these letters with your students.

- Have students bring a paper bag containing three to five objects—such as books, pictures, or toys—that tell something about themselves. Let students use these props to introduce themselves on the second or third day of school. Split the activity into two segments, if necessary, to maintain attention and interest.
- Make up a questionnaire in the form of a scavenger hunt; for example, "Name a student who has three brothers and who plays soccer." Let students work in groups to see how many of their classmates they can identify.
- Have students bring in one item or a picture of an item that represents them. Students will explain the meaning of their items to the class and then put them on a bulletin board, forming a collage of student interests and experiences.

**Presentation and Discussion of Rules, Procedures, and Consequences.**   Soon after the introductions, usually after the initial room description, present the major rules and procedures. School rules should be covered along with your classroom rules. Major consequences associated with the rules should be described at the same time. Plan to review the rules later, perhaps on the second and third days, to underscore their importance and help students remember them. Some teachers then test students on the rules, documenting each student's knowledge and understanding of them. Posting the rules is a common way to remind students. You may also have copies made of the rules and procedures and send them home for parent signatures. See Chapter 3 for a discussion of writing rules with your students.

Teach important procedures as they are needed, rather than all at once. For example, during this initial discussion you will probably want to teach procedures for using restrooms and the pencil sharpener, moving about the room, obtaining help, asking questions, and talking. Later in the day, as they are needed, teach other procedures such as those for major transitions (e.g., ending the day, leaving and entering the room at lunch time or before and after recess) as well as procedures associated with the cafeteria or other out-of-room areas. Your opening routine (see Chapter 3) will probably be used on the second day of school, so you may wish to wait until then to describe it.

"The hardest part about goin' back to school is learning how to whisper again."
Family Circus © Bill Keane, Inc. King Features Syndicate.

Procedures for special equipment such as computers can wait until you're ready to use that equipment, and small-group procedures should not be introduced until those activities begin. The idea is to provide students with the information they need to successfully complete the activities required of them in the first days of school and to help them feel confident in their new classroom environment. It may take several minilessons and practice with feedback across the first few days to help students learn these routines.

On the second day of school, review the rules and major procedures students need to know. This reinforces your expectations for appropriate behavior and reminds students of rules and procedures they may have forgotten. When correcting student behavior at the beginning of school, remind students of what rule was broken. In the primary grades particularly, you will have to observe students carefully for several weeks to be sure they are following procedures correctly and to give cues, prompts, and feedback to help them learn class routines.

When you present your class rules and procedures, set a positive tone by emphasizing the benefits to everyone: "These rules are intended to help us have an enjoyable class in which everyone can learn. We all know that our classroom will work better when everyone respects everyone else's rights" or "When we allow someone to speak without interrupting, we are showing that we are good listeners." If some procedure or rule is difficult to follow, you might acknowledge this as you discuss it: "I know it isn't easy to remember to raise your hand before speaking when we are having an interesting discussion, but doing so will give everyone a chance to participate" or "It will be hard not to start using the equipment right away, but we need to wait for directions so no one is injured." Explanations such as these help students understand and accept what might otherwise be seen as arbitrary rules.

**Content Activities.**   Be sure to select activities that are uncomplicated. Assignments should allow for differences in speed of completion; be sure to have backup activities for students who complete work early. Consult your teacher's manuals and curriculum guides and talk with experienced teachers to get ideas about appropriate beginning content activities for the subjects at your grade level.

**Productive Time Fillers.**   Periodically, you will have to fill in time between activities or before and after major transitions. For example, students may complete an assignment earlier than you anticipated, but there may not be enough time to finish another activity before starting the next event on the day's schedule. There may also be times when students need a short break after an intensive lesson. Filling these times with constructive activity is better than trying to stretch out an already-completed task or just letting students amuse themselves. Ideas include having a good book to read to the children or some simple games that can be played in the classroom (e.g., Seven Up, Name Bingo, Baseball Math, Spelling Bee). Use handouts with puzzles, riddles, or story starters for creative writing. You can also lead the children in group exercises, sing songs, listen to a good children's story, or have a bulletin board of creative writing ideas. You might have a "share and tell" time in which students focus on telling what they know about a particular topic (e.g., pets, hobbies). Ask other teachers for ideas, and accumulate a file so you will be ready with a filler when one is needed.

**Administrative Activities.**   If you use textbooks, you will have to distribute them. You may wish to issue only one or two textbooks on the first day; some teachers wait a day or two before distributing any textbooks and use handouts for assignments, especially if class enrollment is likely to change. When you do give out books, you may have to record book numbers for each student, perhaps using a standard form. You should also determine school policies in this area. For example, some schools require that books issued to students be kept covered at all times. If so, you will need a supply of covers on hand, and you must teach the children how to cover the books. In lower grades, it might be better to do the job yourself or enlist the help of parents or an aide. Even in higher grades, some students will have forgotten how to cover books. Plan to show the whole class, and schedule plenty of time for this event.

Determine whether there are any materials that students must take home with them on the first day or later in the week (this might include information about the breakfast and lunch program, school policy on attendance, time of arrival and departure for children, etc.). Keep a file of extra copies of these materials for students who enter school later in the year.

## Communicating with Parents and Guardians

Up to now we have focused on preparing for the beginning of school and establishing early positive relationships with your students. However, a vital part of relationship building will be to connect with parents and families in ways that involve them in their children's schooling.

Parent involvement is a positive factor in children's academic and social growth (cf. Jeynes, 2005; Walker & Hoover-Dempsey, 2008). Current research suggests that parent involvement may make its most important contribution through its influence on the student beliefs and behaviors that lead to achievement (Hattie, 2009; Walker & Hoover-Dempsey, 2006). As parents find significant ways to participate in their children's schooling, they model for their children the importance of education and help bring together the cultures of home and school.

**Establishing Formal and Informal Communication.**   One of your first steps at the beginning of school will be to establish some means of formal communication with homes, such as sending a letter containing essential information about your class that has not already been covered in school handouts. This beginning link with families opens the door to further contact. Sometimes teachers at one grade level collaborate on one letter. Otherwise write one of your own, and have it ready to be sent home with students at the end of the first day. Include the following points in your letter:

- A brief introduction of yourself
- Materials or supplies the child will need

- Statements about school policy, achievement, and progress
- Your conference times and how parents may contact you
- Curriculum units you will teach and special events coming up during the year
- Events especially for families (e.g., back-to-school or school preview night, open house, special events, parent–teacher conferences)
- Information about homework, including calendars and assignment sheets, requests to sign homework, and other daily or weekly information available on your voice mail and email
- Invitation to be classroom volunteers
- School, classroom, or student newsletters
- Breakfast and lunch programs (if this information has not already been provided by the school)

Depending on your school's population and demographics, you may want to consider bridging possible language barriers and include a translation of your letter in the predominant language. You may also wish to attach a handout describing class rules and major procedures (especially those relating to assignments) along with a survey or questionnaire asking parents about their child and their hopes and expectations for the coming year. In this way parents can also alert you to special problems that you may need to know about.

Your letter should be cheerful and friendly but, above all, neat, legible, grammatically correct, and free of misspellings or typos. It is easy to be overwhelmed at the beginning of the year with the abundance of tasks and to let this letter be rushed. But you want to create a good impression and a professional image, and you have only one chance to make a good first impression! Ask a friend to proofread the letter to be sure it is clear, correct, and easy to read. You may also want to consider sending two copies of important letters and enclosures, one for parents to keep and one to be returned with their signatures so you know they received it (see an example letter at the end of the chapter).

While the early letter home is an important initial contact with parents and families, it is only a first step, a one-way formal communication wherein you provide them with information. Your ultimate goal is to establish a dialogue between home and school and to invite more interactive communication as the year proceeds. Begin implementing some of the following measures in your subsequent contacts with parents:

- Encourage classroom visits
- Engage in brief conversations and exchanges during school programs and events
- Make and encourage phone calls
- Exchange notes via paper or email
- Plan informal home visits

Technology adds additional considerations for communicating with parents. The privacy of students and the confidentiality of their records require that teachers be cognizant of how they and their students use technology. For example, parental permission must be sought in writing to post any student work, name, likeness, or photograph online. It is also helpful to know your district's email policy for communications with parents. Written communication online can have different interpretations. Know how to phrase and format text so that it is courteous and professional. Keep in mind that all communications written from a district-owned computer (even a teaching journal you type for yourself there) are accessible by subpoena.

Additionally, teachers need to remember the potential lack of equitable access at home. Not all families may be able to access email messages or receive text updates; therefore, it is important to retain communication through other avenues (e.g., paper notes home, phone calls) rather than alienate students by forcing their families to disclose they are a noncomputer family (Seiter, 2005). For other suggestions about how to reach out to parents, visit the Web site content.scholastic.com/browse/article.jsp?id=4143.

**Barriers to Effective Communication.**    In spite of your best efforts to establish positive relationships with parents, you may encounter obstacles stemming from *practical, psychological*, and *cultural* sources. In terms of *practical* difficulties, hardships imposed by low income, poverty, work schedules, child care, transportation, language barriers, or limited educational background can make families feel either inadequate to interact with the schools or unable to do so (Finders & Lewis, 1994).

*Psychological* barriers can derive from a parent's unhappy school history, memories of poor achievement or mistreatment at school, or personal struggles with poor mental or physical health. If these factors come into play, parents may feel intimidated by perceived school authority and may be poorly equipped to participate (cf. Gavin & Greenfield, 1998; Hoover-Dempsey et al., 2005). Schools' and families' mutual misunderstandings of school values and practices as well as perceived differences in home and school expectations can raise *cultural* barriers to parent involvement (cf. Delgado-Gaitan, 2004; Drummond & Stipek, 2004). All these factors require that teachers take into account the multiple influences on student learning and behavior and shape classroom policies to serve both student outcomes and family involvement.

Walker and Hoover-Dempsey (2008) offer research-based suggestions for improving family–school partnerships. Some of these ideas require the commitment of the entire school both administratively and at the classroom level; others offer teachers suggestions for bridging home and school.

- Improve school climate by developing welcoming strategies that respect and capitalize on family strengths.
- Work with the existing parent–teacher structures to include a variety of ways parents can be involved.
- Collaborate with after-school programs as points of contact.
- Capitalize on student-centered events (e.g., concerts, athletic events, student programs) that draw parents in, and ask for volunteers.

These and many other suggestions are available in the literature; see Further Reading for references.

## Special Problems

It is not possible to predict every problem that could occur in the first few days of school, but it is possible to identify several that occur commonly, occasionally, or rarely. If you are prepared for the commonly occurring problems and at least not surprised by the occasional or rare event, you will be able to respond appropriately.

**Interruptions by Office Staff, Parents, Custodians, and Others (Common).**  If you can reschedule the issue for a noninstructional time, do so. If it cannot be delayed, manage the interruption without leaving the room. Invite the person into your room, and face your students as you talk with the person. If the interruption is likely to last more than a few seconds, or if you must leave the room, give students something to do before continuing the conference (e.g., continue working, read silently, rest heads on desks). Let the person wait, not your class. Have materials for one or two planned activities ready for an unforeseen or lengthy interruption. Remember that your liability for your class continues even when you must leave the room and have provided suitable supervision.

"I know I can train them to be thoughtful, productive citizens if I can ever get past 'sit.'"

© Martha F. Campbell. Used by permission.

**Late Arrivals on the First Day (Common).**   Greet late arrivals as warmly as you did the other students. Tell them you will talk to them about what they missed as soon as you can but that for now they must wait in their seats. Show them where to sit, and incorporate them into the present activity. When you have the total class involved in independent work, meet with these children to explain anything they may have missed.

**One or More Children Are Assigned to Your Class after the First Day (Common).** Try to meet with these students before school so that you can explain rules and procedures to them and handle necessary paperwork. If you have already distributed books to the class, make sure these students also get texts. If you can't meet these students ahead of time, use the first available opportunity while the rest of your class is occupied. Be warm and welcoming with these students; you want to communicate that you are pleased that they have joined the class, not that they are inconvenient! Appoint one or more responsible students to be "buddies" with the new students to help familiarize them with the classroom and school procedures and rules. The amount of assistance you can expect from these buddies depends on their grade level. Be sure to monitor new students carefully to help them adjust to your class and to learn appropriate behavior.

**A Child Forgets Lunch Money or Supplies (Common).**   Be familiar with your school's policies. The principal or school nurse may have an emergency fund for students without lunch money. Some schools allow students to charge a lunch in an emergency. It's a good idea to keep a couple of lunches' worth of small change on hand. Also, have one day's worth of supplies available for students who forget theirs. If a student continues to forget supplies, you may have to check with parents to see that they are aware that the materials are needed. If you suspect that the family cannot afford the supplies, see whether your school or parent–teacher organization has funds for helping such students.

**Large Amounts of Paperwork during the First Week of School (Common).** This may be difficult, but try to do as little paperwork as possible during class time. Plan to spend extra time before and after school, and arrange your personal schedule to accommodate it. This will pay off in reduced tension over the long run. If you must do clerical work during class time, do it quickly while the children are engaged in activities. Monitor the class while you work, and avoid losing eye contact with your students for long periods. Create a checklist (a spreadsheet program works well) for all paperwork and money the children will be turning in during the first few days of school. A glance at your master checklist will show you which children need reminders.

**A Child Forgets Bus Number or Misses Bus (Occasional).**   Know your school's dismissal routines and times. Help to avoid this type of problem by rehearsing bus procedures with students. Consider putting a sticker or other label on younger students, identifying how they are to get home (e.g., car, bus number, walker). This way you or another adult in the building can assist any confused students quickly. Make certain that students are not left alone while waiting for a ride, and reassure them that the parent or other person picking them up will arrive soon. Have bus numbers and parents' and emergency phone numbers on hand for when problems do arise.

**Shortage of Textbooks, Vital Equipment, or Materials (Occasional).**   Before school begins, check on the availability of textbooks and your equipment, and find out your school's procedures for getting the needed materials into your room. When you discover shortages, report them to the school office. If you must begin the year without enough texts, you may be able to have students share books, or you might arrange to share a class set with another teacher. If you have no texts at all in some subject, you might find earlier editions of the text in storage to tide you over. Depending on the subject, teacher-prepared materials may be sufficient.

**A Special Needs Student Has Difficulty Understanding or Following Directions (Occasional).**   Seat the student close to you, and engage the student in simple activities. Work individually with this student only after the rest of the class is busy. As soon as possible, talk to the resource teacher to determine what the student is capable of doing; then plan the student's educational program. If possible, talk to the teacher from the preceding year for suggestions. You will also find it helpful to set up a conference with the parents soon after the year has begun. For further suggestions, see Chapter 11.

**Crying (Occasional).**   Younger children especially may cry for no apparent reason early in the school year. Sometimes the crying stops fairly quickly if you can distract the child and engage him or her in some activity. Sometimes it helps to assign a friend to accompany the child to get a drink of water, wash his or her face, and then come back to join the class. Be understanding and try to find out the possible cause for the tears, but do not reinforce the crying by giving the child excessive attention or sympathy. If the crying is not disruptive, the child can remain in his or her seat until the episode is over. If the crying is disruptive, take the child out of the room, or have someone from the office come to get him or her.

**Wetting (Occasional).**   Although accidental wetting is more common with younger children, it sometimes occurs even in the upper grades, especially during the first few days of school. This kind of accident is extremely embarrassing to the child, and the teacher should make every effort not to add to the child's discomfort. Have paper towels on hand to facilitate the cleanup, and handle the matter as privately as possible. Arrange to call home, or have an office worker call to request a change of clothes. Later, talk privately with the child to determine why he or she did not go to the restroom in time. With some younger children, you may have to contact the parents and keep a change of clothes at school as a precaution. In general with younger children, the teacher must schedule regular restroom breaks and even remind some children to use the restroom regularly.

**A Child Becomes Very Sick or Is Injured (Rare).** Prior to the first day, identify the ways you can contact the school office for emergency help. If the child has a known medical condition (such as asthma) and you have been previously informed of what to do, follow directions and stay calm. In other cases, phone the office, or send a messenger requesting someone to come to get the child. Do not leave the child unattended. Activate the 9-1-1 emergency system if a student's health appears in jeopardy.

**A Schoolwide Emergency Arises (Rare).** Know the policies for handling school emergencies (e.g., fire, tornado, lockdown). Keep calm, follow the procedures given (e.g., lining up, class gathering location), and make sure to take a class roster with emergency contact information with you.

## Preparing for a Substitute

During the first weeks of school, create a handbook for the substitutes who may teach in your absence. Always assume that these people have never been to your school before. This handbook should include the following:

- Class roll
- Seating chart
- Copy of your classroom rules and consequences
- Daily schedule
- List of medical alerts and medication times for various students
- Emergency lesson plans (in case you are unable to leave current ones)
- Names of teachers and students who can provide assistance
- Emergency procedures
- Map of the school

Leave this handbook in a prominent place in your classroom or in the school office so that it is immediately available when a substitute arrives. Tape a note permanently to your desk ("Substitute's notebook in bottom drawer").

# ■ Chapter Summary

Beginning the school year organized and prepared is vital to setting a successful direction for students. One key to beginning the year is establishing a positive climate in the classroom through modeling courtesy and kindness, communicating effectively, including all students, and building a sense of "we." Planning for the first days of school also includes providing activities that acquaint students with one another and with you; teaching the classroom rules, procedures, and consequences; and focusing content activities to review previous learning. Elementary teachers also plan the first days of school to build relationships with students' families. Letters of introduction in print typically include information that parents need (e.g., class supply list, classroom rules, teacher contact information, highlights of key content/activities/dates for the year, weekly routines). Finally, teachers prepare at the beginning of the year for the unexpected (e.g., interruptions, sick child, extra paperwork) by anticipating these potential problems and having a plan in mind if they arise. Effective classroom management begins before the first day of school with thorough planning and preparation and is renewed each day that follows.

# ■ Further Reading

Brophy, J. E. (2000). Teaching. In H. J. Walberg (Series Ed.), *Educational practices*. Brussels, Belgium: International Academy of Education. Available at www.ibe.unesco.org/en/services/online-materials/publications/educational-practices.html

*This booklet, prepared for the International Bureau of Education, synthesizes much of what is known through contemporary research about teaching. As an easy-to-read description of good teaching, this booklet presents overarching themes, research, and classroom descriptions for classroom climate, learning, curriculum, discourse, activities, engagement, and assessment. Reading this publication could easily prompt thoughtful preparation for the start of a school year.*

Erwin, J. C. (2003). Giving students what they need. *Educational Leadership*, 61(1), 19–23.

*This article emphasizes the importance of teacher–student relationships as an integral tool of classroom management and the need to create those conditions that encourage internal motivation and student responsibility, as opposed to external motivation, which gives teachers full responsibility for motivating students.*

Pianta, R. C. (2006). Classroom management and relationships between children and teachers: Implications for research and practice. In C. M. Evertson & C. S. Weinstein (Eds.), *Handbook of research on classroom management: Research, practice, and contemporary issues* (pp. 685–709). Mahwah, NH: Erlbaum.

*The author condenses the research literature on teacherstudent relationships to show the importance of these interactions for the individual student as well as the classroom community.*

Randolph, C. H., & Evertson, C. M. (1995). Managing for learning: Rules, roles, and meanings in a writing class. *Journal of Classroom Interaction, 30*(2), 17–25.

*The authors argue that management and content are interwoven. As teachers and students negotiate ways of interacting with academic content and with each other, and as they define the roles that each plays, they establish meanings that influence what academic content can be learned and how it is learned.*

Walker, J. M. T., & Hoover-Dempsey, K. V. (2008). Parent involvement. In T. L. Good (Ed.), *21st century education: A reference handbook* (Vol. 2, pp. 382–391). Los Angeles: Sage.

*This entry explains the importance of involving parents in the classroom, as well as provides recommendations for doing so.*

Wiske, M. S. (1994). How teaching for understanding changes the rules in the classroom. *Educational Leadership, 51*(5), 19–21.

> *This article discusses how attempting to share authority and responsibility with students violates traditional classroom and school norms. The author implies that teachers must remain open to and accepting of the uneasiness this change causes both in themselves and in their students.*

ci.kern.org/tesa/

> *This Web site for the Teacher Expectations and Student Achievement (TESA) intervention program (Kern County, Los Angeles) is designed to increase academic performance as well as diversity and gender awareness, to promote a positive classroom climate, and to reduce discipline problems.*

www.proteacher.com

> *This Web site for teachers includes tips for planning and message boards on a range of topics in elementary schools.*

teachersnetwork.org/NTNY/nychelp/need_to_know/parcontact.htm

> *This Web site, sponsored by the New York Teachers' Network, lists many helpful letters and announcements you can use as ideas for beginning home–school communication with your students' parents or guardians.*

# ■ Suggested Activities

1. Return to the vignette of Ms. Stevens earlier in the chapter. Write a response to the following questions: What style of authority does Ms. Stevens demonstrate? How will her teaching of this initial procedure affect her future teaching? (See the key for this activity in the Appendix.)

2. Respond to the following questions with a partner: Can you remember what it was like to start school when you were attending elementary school? When adults are asked to recall school beginnings, they can rarely remember much detail about what teachers did, but they often remember their own personal experiences, problems, or concerns. Do you remember a year when you felt especially welcomed? Was there a year when you felt left out or unexcited about your new class? How should you attempt to take your students' concerns into account at the beginning of the year? Because your personal concerns and anxieties may be heightened during those critical days, how can you deal with your own feelings and accommodate student concerns at the same time? How will your beginning-of-the-year choices reflect your philosophy of education?

3. Read Case Studies 5.1 and 5.2, which describe teachers beginning the year in diverse settings. As you read them, consider the following questions:
   a. To what extent are the principles described in this and previous chapters in evidence in each case?

    **b.** In spite of subject-matter and grade-level differences, there are similarities between the teachers. Identify as many of them as you can.

    **c.** What differences are apparent between the teachers in their beginning-of-year activities? Which activities would you use? Why?

    **d.** In Case 5.1 the teacher uses a literature-based approach to frame activities for students. In Case 5.2 the teacher makes extensive use of groups for cooperative learning. How do these approaches affect the way each teacher begins the year?

**4.** What do you think your students' goals and concerns will be at the beginning of the year? How can your classroom management plan accommodate them?

**5.** Read the suggestions for home–school letters on the Web site teachersnetwork.org/ NTNY/nychelp/need_to_know/parcontact.htm. How could you adapt one or two of them for your classroom?

**6.** Talk with teachers who have had several years' experience at a grade level you would like to teach. Ask them what activities they use during the first few days and how they sequence them. Teachers are often willing to share handouts and ideas. You might also ask someone to look over your lesson plan for the first day and give you suggestions.

**7.** What are some ways you can initiate and sustain a positive climate in your classroom? Make a list, and interview other teachers for their ideas.

# ■ Case Study 5.1

## BEGINNING THE YEAR IN A LITERATURE-BASED PRIMARY CLASSROOM

### First-Day Activities

| Time/Activity | Description |
|---|---|
| 8:00–8:35 Greeting students | Ms. Gonzalez greets the children as they enter, helps them put on their name tags, and checks the pronunciation of their names. She gives the students laminated name strips and tells each one to choose a desk and place the strip on it. She also tells students to put their lunch boxes in the basket, hang their book bags on their labeled coat hooks, and place their supplies on the round table at the side of the room. |
| | As the first students settle at their desks, Ms. Gonzalez lets each one select a piece of construction paper, write his or her name on it, and decorate it. When students have finished, they get to choose a cubby that will hold their personal belongings and tape the construction paper to the back wall of the cubby. She has placed a tape dispenser at each end of the cubbies for the students to use. Ms. Gonzalez also asks the early-arriving students to help their later-arriving classmates. As the rest of the students arrive, Ms. Gonzalez helps them settle into the classroom, checks supplies, talks with parents, and monitors students' progress. She uses a prepared set of extra materials to welcome a student not yet on her roster. |

**First-Day Activities**

| Time/Activity | Description |
|---|---|
| 8:35–8:40<br>Introducing teacher | After all buses have arrived and she feels that her students are settled, Ms. Gonzalez moves to the next activity. She does not call roll because she can tell who is absent by the remaining laminated strips. She records attendance in the school software system.<br><br>Ms. Gonzalez, who has taught at this school for many years and already knows several of her students, briefly introduces herself and tells the children that she is looking forward to an exciting year with them. She notices that many of the children are curiously looking around the room, so she starts by describing the classroom and a few class procedures. |
| 8:40–9:00<br>Describing room | Ms. Gonzalez begins by pointing out the classroom library, and she tells students that they may get books from the library after they have finished their assignments. The students may use the beanbags and comfortable pillows while they are in the library, or they may take the books to their desks. She also shows the listening center next to the library and points out that this center can accommodate only two children at a time. Next she shows how to operate the CD player and headphones. She notes the four computers next to the listening center. Ms. Gonzalez says they won't be using the computers until next week, but she tells the students what kinds of activities they will learn to do with the computers. She also highlights materials in the science discovery center, gives procedures for this area, and tells the students that four children may work at this center at one time. |
| 9:00–9:25<br>Drawing self-portraits | Ms. Gonzalez holds up her self-portrait, which she drew the previous day, and they discuss what self-portraits are. Ms. Gonzalez then distributes construction paper to the students and asks them to draw their own self-portraits. She also asks them to write two things about themselves on the back of the pictures.<br><br>As the children begin, Ms. Gonzalez circulates, offers assistance, and monitors their progress. When some children become concerned about their spelling, she tells them to try their best, listen to the sounds in the words, and write what they hear. As children finish, Ms. Gonzalez tells them to select a book from the class library or go to the listening center. |
| 9:25–9:30<br>Procedures | At 9:25 the timer rings. Ms. Gonzalez tells the children that she uses the timer to signal the end of an activity. When they hear the timer ring, they should look at her for further directions. Ms. Gonzalez sets the timer again, and the students practice this procedure as the final students complete their self- portraits. She tells the children that it is time to go to the playground, so they need to practice lining up to leave the classroom. She says she will dismiss them by tables, and they should push their chairs under their desks. She demonstrates pushing in chairs and asks a student to show how it can be done quietly. She then asks students to line up quietly without crowding the person in front of them. As she dismisses each table, she compliments students for following directions. |
| 9:30–10:00<br>Playground | While students are on the playground with another teacher, Ms. Gonzalez prepares for the next activity. |

*(continued)*

**First-Day Activities**

| Time/Activity | Description |
| --- | --- |
| 10:00–10:10<br>Restrooms | Ms. Gonzalez meets her class in line at the playground and explains how they will return to the classroom. Once all of the students are at their desks and are looking at her, Ms. Gonzalez explains the restroom procedures. She lets one or two students practice with hanging a restroom pass on the doorknob and knocking to be sure no one is in the restroom before they open the door. She then demonstrates the use of the sink, soap, and paper towel dispenser. Students who wish then leave their seats to use the restrooms according to the procedures while Ms. Gonzalez reviews the morning with the class. When the timer rings, all students who wished to do so have taken a turn at the restrooms. |
| 10:10–10:30<br>Circle time | When all the students are at their desks and looking at her, Ms. Gonzalez asks them to bring their self-portraits and quietly form a circle on the floor. Everyone, including Ms. Gonzalez, shares a self-portrait and two interesting things about him- or herself. |
| 10:30–11:00<br>Story and song | Ms. Gonzalez follows this activity by reading a story about self-esteem. She then teaches the students a song called "I Like Me." She has written the words and has drawn several picture cues on a large sheet of chart paper. They practice reading the words several times; then Ms. Gonzalez sings the song. She then repeats the song, and the students join in the singing.<br><br>As she dismisses the students from the circle, she collects their self-portraits. Ms. Gonzalez chooses this time to review lunch procedures. Students practice getting their lunch boxes and quietly lining up for lunch. Before they leave, Ms. Gonzalez reviews the lunchroom rules and walks the class to the cafeteria to introduce them to the lunch monitor. |
| 11:00–11:30 | Lunch. |
| 11:30–11:50 | Recess. Ms. Gonzalez takes a turn on recess duty, supervising children's play and interactions. |
| 11:50–12:10<br>Reading aloud | As the students reenter the room, Ms. Gonzalez reviews the restroom procedures with a sign she displays on the restroom doors. She allows students to follow the restroom procedures while she sits in a rocking chair with the class seated around her on the rug and reads aloud. |
| 12:10–12:30<br>Discussing school rules | The class remains seated around the rocking chair, and Ms. Gonzalez explains the school rules. There are two: (1) Remain quiet in the hallways, and (2) individual students must have a hall pass. After they discuss the rules, Ms. Gonzalez asks two children to repeat them to the rest of the class and explain what they mean. |
| 12:30–1:00<br>Developing<br>classroom rules | The discussion of school rules leads directly into the development of classroom rules. The students remain seated on the rug but shift their attention to the board. Ms. Gonzalez uses a doc-cam to project on the board. She asks a student to turn off half of the classroom lights so the class can see the screen.<br><br>She tells the students they will have to raise their hands and wait to be called on during the discussion because everyone will need to hear all of the suggestions. She asks the students to suggest rules they feel are |

**First-Day Activities**

| Time/Activity | Description |
|---|---|
| | necessary for their classroom. The students raise their hands. Ms. Gonzalez calls on them and writes their responses. At this point, she is careful not to make evaluative comments on the students' ideas. She wants them to brainstorm suggestions. The students then discuss their ideas and often expand, connect, or modify them. |
| | Ms. Gonzalez ends this activity when she notices the students' attention beginning to fade. She tells them that this is a good start to their classroom rules and that they will continue with them tomorrow. At the end of this activity, the students return to their desks. |
| 1:00–1:35<br>Graphing activity | Ms. Gonzalez focuses the students' attention on an easel where she has hung a large graph. The graph is drawn on brightly colored paper and is titled "How I got to school today." The graph is divided into four columns. A picture of a car, a bus, a bicycle, or a pair of shoes is at the bottom of each column. She asks the students how they got to school this morning. Did they come in a car? Did they ride the bus? Did they ride their bikes? Did they walk? As the students raise their hands, Ms. Gonzalez gives them a picture of a car, bus, bike, or shoes. The students write their names on their pictures and tape them in the appropriate columns on the graph. |
| | After all of the pictures are placed on the graph, Ms. Gonzalez asks the students to count the number of pictures in each row and determine which row has the most and the least. She draws a bar graph that corresponds with the number of pictures in each row. She explains that the class will be learning a lot of new things this year. They will be doing science projects, math, writing, and so on. She asks them to think about things they would like to know. |
| 1:35–2:15<br>"What do I want to study this year?" | Ms. Gonzalez hangs another large piece of paper on the easel. In the middle of the paper is the question, "What do I want to study this year?" Again, she asks students to raise their hands and wait to be called on because everyone should listen to the topics. Ms. Gonzalez creates a semantic map with all of the suggestions. She knows that many of the topics will be covered because they correspond with her curriculum guide. Other topics will be pursued through individual and small-group projects. |
| 2:15–2:30<br>Getting ready to go home | Ms. Gonzalez reviews the day's activities by asking, "If your mom or dad asks you what you did today, what will you say?" She also asks questions about the procedures and school rules. She reminds the students to check their personal belongings and distributes notes to be taken home, including one to remind students (and inform parents) to bring an item about themselves tomorrow (e.g., picture, stuffed friend, favorite book). She asks them to leave their name tags on their desks so they can use them the next day, and she shows them how to stack their chairs. She checks to see that everyone has the things to take home and rehearses with the students the proper procedure for being dismissed. They are to leave their desks table-by-table and line up by the door. She asks two students to demonstrate lining up. When the bell rings, she leads the students out the classroom door and down the hall to the proper outside door for dismissal. |

**Second-Day Activities**

| Time/Activity | Description |
| --- | --- |
| 8:00–8:20 Greeting students | The teacher greets the students at the door and asks them to put on their name tags, get their journal notebooks from their cubbies, and put their items from home in their cubbies. On the board, she has written the journal topic: "What I liked best about my first day of school." She tells the students they may either write or draw a picture. She takes attendance, fills in the lunch count, and assists the students as they write. |
| | The timer rings to signal the end of this activity, and the teacher asks everyone to close the journals. She lets them go by tables to put their journals in their cubbies and gather on the floor. She reminds them of the procedures for leaving their desks and gathering on the floor (quickly and quietly). |
| 8:20–8:50 Introducing morning activities | Ms. Gonzalez shows the students the helper chart. Every student has a job, and the jobs rotate daily. She asks the pledge leader to come to the front of the room and lead the class. She helps the pledge leader point to the words as the students repeat the pledge. She then asks the calendar person to add today's date to the calendar and name the month, day, and year. The weather person tells today's forecast and uses the weather section from the newspaper to record today's expected high and low temperatures. Ms. Gonzalez guides the weather person through the forecast. The song leader leads the students through the "I Like Me" song they learned the previous day. Again, Ms. Gonzalez helps the student point to the words while the class sings. |
| | Three students volunteer to share what they wrote in their journals. While those students get their journals, Ms. Gonzalez tells the class that journal writing will usually be the first activity every morning. After the students share, Ms. Gonzalez tells each student one thing she liked about his or her writing. |
| 8:50–9:25 Developing classroom rules | Ms. Gonzalez then asks the class to look at the dry-erase board. She turns on the doc-cam and reviews the ideas they brainstormed yesterday for classroom rules. She asks the students whether any of the rules are alike. As the students begin to group the similar ideas, Ms. Gonzalez reminds them to raise their hands. She writes their ideas on another sheet. After they develop six broad categories, she asks the students to think about a title for each category. When titles have been proposed for each category, she asks the students whether these would be appropriate classroom rules. After some minor rewordings, the students and Ms. Gonzalez are satisfied with the rules. |
| 9:25–9:30 Procedures | The teacher asks the students to line up at the door. Several students use this time to get a drink of water or go to their cubbies. Ms. Gonzalez asks everyone to come back to the rug, and she asks a student to repeat the procedure for lining up. Ms. Gonzalez dismisses the students again and compliments them for following the procedure. |
| 9:30–10:00 P.E. | While the students are in physical education, Ms. Gonzalez writes the classroom rules on a piece of chart paper. |
| 10:00–10:30 Role-playing classroom rules | When the students reenter the room from P.E., they go to their seats, and the teacher points out the rules and asks each student to sign the chart. She lets each table go to the chart paper in turn. She asks the students where the rules should be posted, and they decide to hang the poster listing the rules on the wall by the board. |

**Second-Day Activities**

| Time/Activity | Description |
|---|---|
| | Small groups of students volunteer to role-play an example of each rule. The small groups practice and present their demonstration. The other members of the class guess which rule the group is presenting. |
| 10:30–11:00<br>Math activity | The teacher asks the students to return to their seats, and when they are seated, she asks for their attention. She is standing at the front of the room and holding geometric figures (circles, triangles, squares) made from colored construction paper. Magnets are attached to the figures so they will stick on the board.<br><br>Ms. Gonzalez tells the students they are going to play a guessing game. She is going to make a pattern on the board with these figures, and the students will have to decide which figure goes next in the pattern. After they complete several of these examples, she asks each of them to continue this game with a partner.<br><br>Because this is the first time the students will be working cooperatively, Ms. Gonzalez lets them begin with partners rather than in groups of three or four. As she passes out the materials, she asks them which classroom rules should apply to this activity. Several respond that they should listen to their partners and not interrupt them. Others say they should help each other. The teacher tells the students they can remain at their seats or move to a spot on the floor. She allows them 1 minute to move. As the students make patterns for their partners, she circulates throughout the room and offers assistance. She sets the timer to signal the end of the activity.<br><br>When the timer rings, the majority of the partners stop their patterning activity and turn to the teacher. A few continue to work, so she asks a student to tell what the procedure is. Then she sets the timer again. When it rings, everyone turns to her. She asks the partners to put the geometric figures in the storage bags. When she dismisses the students, they give her their bags of figures and quietly line up for lunch. |
| 11:00–11:30 | Lunch. |
| 11:30–11:50 | Recess. |
| 11:50–12:10<br>Reading aloud | Restroom break. Ms. Gonzalez sits in the rocking chair, and the students gather around her as she reads a story they have selected from the class library. |
| 12:10–1:00<br>Writing sample | Ms. Gonzalez likes to collect a writing sample from each of her students early in the year. This sample goes in the student's portfolio and serves as a baseline for the student's writing progress. Because the class has been sharing about themselves, this writing sample will be part of a book called *All about Me*. Ms. Gonzalez has prepared a small book with lines at the bottom of the pages for writing and spaces for illustrations. She brainstorms ideas for the book with the students and reminds them to use invented spellings if they need to.<br><br>The students return to their seats, and Ms. Gonzalez monitors their progress, paying close attention to students who are frustrated. Several children are concerned about their writing, so she tells them to draw the pictures first and then write about the pictures. As some students finish before the timer rings, they go to various centers in the room. |

*(continued)*

**Second-Day Activities**

| Time/Activity | Description |
| --- | --- |
| 1:00–1:15<br>Sharing | When the timer rings again, Ms. Gonzalez asks whether anyone wants to share his or her book. She collects the books from the students who do not want to share, and everyone gathers on the rug. Four students share, and everyone listens attentively. Students comment on the books and applaud the volunteers. Ms. Gonzalez takes up these remaining books and then dismisses students in groups of four to get their items from home out of their cubbies. |
| 1:15–1:55<br>"Getting to<br>know you" | When all students are seated, Ms. Gonzalez models how she would like the students to share their items from home. She tells about her photograph, the people in it, and why they are important to her. Then she stands, walks the photo around the circle, and is reseated. All the students share their items following this pattern. |
| 1:55–2:15<br>Sustained silent<br>reading | While they are still in the circle, Ms. Gonzalez explains the procedures for sustained silent reading. She says this will be the last activity every day. The students will select one or two books or magazines and find a quiet place to read. After they choose a place, they will remain there until the timer rings. Ms. Gonzalez says she will also be reading during this time.<br><br>She dismisses the students two at a time from the circle. They put away their sharing-time objects, select books, and quietly choose a place to read. After they are all reading, Ms. Gonzalez reminds a few students to be quiet. She also reads, but she keeps a close eye on the students.<br><br>Even though 20 minutes has been set for today's silent reading, Ms. Gonzalez knows that after the procedures are taught, the students will read for only 7 or 8 minutes. This amount of reading time will steadily increase throughout the school year. |
| 2:15–2:30<br>Getting ready<br>to go home | When the timer rings again, Ms. Gonzalez dismisses the students two at a time to return their books and collect their belongings to go home. When the students are ready to go, Ms. Gonzalez leads a brief review of today's activities and the classroom rules. |
| 2:30<br>Dismissal | Ms. Gonzalez reminds the students how to line up and calls the bus riders to line up first. She compliments the students on another good day and leads them out of the room. |

# ■ Case Study 5.2

## BEGINNING THE YEAR IN A FIFTH-GRADE MATH CLASS USING COOPERATIVE LEARNING

Ms. James teaches math in a departmentalized fifth grade. She repeats the same lesson with four groups of fifth graders each day. The following narrative describes the first day of class for the initial group of students.

**First-Day Activities**

| Activity | Description |
|---|---|
| Before the bell | Students attend a schoolwide assembly to welcome them and introduce new faculty members. Classes are dismissed by grade level to walk with their first-period teachers to their rooms. Desks are arranged in seven groups of four or five students each. Ms. James has placed a yellow folder marked with the period and group number on each group of desks. As students enter, Ms. James tells them that they may sit wherever they choose today but that seats will be assigned later in the week. |
| Initial greeting (4 minutes) | The teacher smiles and introduces herself, telling students about her family and some out-of-school interests. She tells students she is a hard worker, and she also expects them to work hard. She says she will be in her room starting an hour before school, and she will stay in her room until 4:30 each day, so students can come in if they need more explanation or assistance. "The most important thing in this class is trying. We will all make mistakes and get stuck, but by working together we will be able to solve the problems and learn a lot of new things." |
| Introduction (10 minutes) | Ms. James says that even though students have all studied math for the past 5 years, she is curious about whether they know how important and useful it is. She elicits ideas about how math might be useful, and she asks students to raise their hands and wait to be called on before speaking during this activity. During the discussion, she calls attention to a bulletin board that has several colorful posters highlighting math applications. Ms. James thanks students on several occasions for raising their hands and for listening well. When a couple of students call out, she reminds them to raise their hands before she calls on them. |
| | Ms. James comments on the grouping of desks. She explains that in her classes students work in groups much of the time and that this can be very helpful in learning. She says they won't always work in groups; they will also keep an individual notebook and take tests by themselves. For many assignments, however, they will be expected to work together and assist each other in understanding the content and solving problems. She comments that students often find this to be not only a good way to learn but an enjoyable one as well. A student asks whether she can choose her group. Ms. James responds that she must reserve the right to arrange the groups. Because group membership will change at times, however, students will have an opportunity to work with a variety of other students. Ms. James also emphasizes that working in groups with others is a good way to get to know them. "It's important that you be able to work with anyone in school, just as you'll have to outside of school," she comments. |
| Initial presentation of procedures (6 minutes) | Ms. James thanks the students for raising their hands before speaking. She says she has a few other procedures that will be needed for the class to run smoothly and she will go over some of them now and save the others for later, when they start group work. She says that during class, when she is talking or when a student is presenting something to the whole class, they are to remain in their seats. If they wish to comment or ask a question, they should raise their hands and wait for their turn. At other times, when they are working in groups or on individual assignments, they may talk if it is to someone in their group and it is |

*(continued)*

**First-Day Activities**

| Activity | Description |
|---|---|
| | about the assignment. She demonstrates the appropriate volume for small-group conversation. If they need to sharpen a pencil or get materials during work times, they may do so without permission as long as they do not disturb others. |
| Initial group task (8 minutes) | The teacher designates students in each group as Chair #1, Chair #2, Chair #3, and so on. She tells them that when they work in groups, different Chairs will have different roles and that these rotate so that each student gets a chance to do different things. "Chair #1, please open the group folder on the desk and look in the right-hand pocket. Take out a yellow card and a class card for each student." She asks Chair #1 in each group to distribute these items. Ms. James then has students make yellow name cards for their desks and fill out class cards for her. While students work on this task, she returns to her desk for a couple of minutes to attend to administrative matters, repeatedly checking students' behavior. She then asks Chair #1 to collect the class cards. |
| Description of procedures (10 minutes) | Ms. James asks Chair #2 to look in the left-hand pocket and get out the blue sheet listing classroom policies and procedures and to give one to each group member. She tells students that everyone will need a three-ring binder for this class and that this page should be the first one in it. She then reviews the classroom and school policies regarding absence and tardiness, leaving the room, makeup work, tests, and detention for violating rules. She explains that if she gives a warning to a student and it's ignored, she will assign a lunch detention, and the student will have to bring lunch to her room at noon and eat it there. She says, "If I have to come find you, it will be doubled." She has students write their names on the blue sheets and return them to the folders, to be put in the three-ring binders when they bring them. |
| End of period | Ms. James notes that time is almost up. She says that she'll explain her grading policies and class activities tomorrow. "Chair #3, if there is a new student in class assigned to your group tomorrow, would you please be responsible for helping him or her get a copy of the class policies, name card, and class card." She asks the students to return their name cards to the folders and remain in their seats until she dismisses them. When materials have been returned to the folders and each group is seated and quiet, she dismisses the class by group. She picks up the yellow folders and replaces them with blue ones for the next class. |

**Second-Day Activities**

| Activity | Description |
|---|---|
| Before the bell | Ms. James distributes folders for each group. She greets students as they enter, asking them to take their seats with the same groups as yesterday. She directs a few new students to join groups. |
| Opening the period (3 minutes) | Ms. James greets the students warmly as soon as the bell rings. She reminds them that they are in groups and have a designated number that will be the same as yesterday's. She reminds Chairs #3 of their responsibility to help new members of the group. |

**Second-Day Activities**

| Activity | Description |
| --- | --- |
| Diagnostic test (15 minutes) | "Before we get started on today's lesson, I'd like you to answer some questions. This will not be for a grade, but I would like you to do your best. Your answers will help me understand what topics we need to review and also help me make group assignments. Turn your paper over when you finish." Ms. James distributes the diagnostic test and tells students to show their work. She monitors as students complete the test and collects the papers as they are turned over. |
| Description of procedures and grading policies (8 minutes) | The teacher reviews talk and movement procedures in groups. "Use group voices, please. Talk loudly enough to be heard by others but not so loudly that groups near you will hear. Like this." She demonstrates. She gives students a one-page handout describing her grading policies and explains them in detail; she then asks students to write their names on and place this handout in their notebooks with the rules sheet. If students have not yet brought a binder, she has them store this sheet in the folder with their blue sheets from yesterday. |
| Preparation for group activity (4 minutes) | Ms. James announces an activity for learning about working in groups as well as learning math concepts. She asks students to volunteer ideas about what it takes to be a good group member. Stressing positive examples, she supports especially the ideas of sharing, helping, listening, encouraging, and working hard. |
| Math lesson (20 minutes) | Ms. James begins by reading an article from *USA Today*, which states that the average fifth grader in the United States watches 1,000 minutes of television a week. She asks the students whether they are surprised by this fact and then asks them to estimate how many hours of television that would be each day. She stresses that they are *estimating* and that *exact* computations are inappropriate. Next, she asks students to share what they think the article means by "the average fifth grader." She then explains that the students will be calculating how many days of television the average fifth grader watches in 1 year. She asks Chair #4 at each table to open the folders and distribute the materials. She says she will ask someone in each group to report on the group's solution. After the groups have worked for about 5 or 6 minutes, Ms. James calls on one person from each group to report on the group's results; she prompts students as needed as they describe the solution process their group used. She asks students to assess the possible effects of this amount of TV watching. |
| Wrap-up (5 minutes) | Ms. James asks students to comment on their roles in their groups. She also asks for suggestions about what works best for various roles. She praises the students for their creativity in developing solutions and for their effort. She announces that table assignments will change tomorrow and then dismisses the class as the next period's students begin to gather at her door. |

**Third-Day Activities**

| Activity | Description |
| --- | --- |
| Before the bell | Ms. James places a stack of book covers and the yellow group folders on each group of desks. On top of this stack, she lays a sheet identifying |

*(continued)*

**Third-Day Activities**

| Activity | Description |
| --- | --- |
| | the group members' names. As students enter, Ms. James tells them to check the name list at each group of desks to find their groups. |
| Textbook checkout (15 minutes) | Ms. James tells students they will stay in their groups for several weeks. She assigns Chair numbers to the group members and asks Chair #4 from each group to get texts from several stacks at the back of the room. While students cover their books, the teacher circulates from group to group and records book numbers. |
| Content activity and a new teaching strategy (17 minutes) | The teacher reviews concepts from yesterday's lesson. She asks Chair #2 to distribute materials from a box in each group. Students use the materials to work along with the teacher as she demonstrates various ways problems can be solved. She tells students they will now work in pairs, and she writes "Pair Share" on the chalkboard. Students will choose a partner from their group, work with him or her to solve a problem, and then take turns explaining the solution or demonstrating the steps to each other. "It is not enough just to work out a solution. Each of you must be able to explain to your partner how you arrived at it." Afterward, Ms. James asks volunteers to demonstrate and explain their solutions. |
| Group work (18 minutes) | Students are now given problems to solve as a group. These are somewhat more difficult and require several steps. Ms. James asks each group to work together to develop a way to solve each problem. She asks Chair #3 to record the solutions and Chair #5 to be moderator to make certain that everyone contributes (or if the group has only four members, Chair #4 moderates). The teacher reviews briefly, based on yesterday's discussion, what these roles entail. As the groups work on the problem, the teacher checks on progress. She then has several groups report to the class. Afterward, students are given an assignment, due the next day, which they work on for the remainder of the class. Students may work together on problems, but they are expected to show their own work on the assignment. |
| Wrap-up (5 minutes) | With about 5 minutes remaining in the period, the teacher asks students to put away their work. She says that unfinished problems should be completed as homework. Then she begins a short discussion about appropriate helping by asking students what it feels like not to understand something. She also asks about ways they might react if they were in that situation. "Everyone will experience those feelings and do some of those things, especially if they're made to feel unintelligent. In this class, though, we will learn from our mistakes, and no one should be embarrassed by not understanding something. Also, helping other students is a great way to gain in understanding. I certainly understand math much better now that I have taught it than I did when I was a student." Ms. James explains that everyone will have opportunities to explain problems and answer questions in this class, but if there is something they don't understand, they should ask for another explanation. She and the class then discuss how to explain in ways that are most helpful. The class is dismissed. |

**Sample Letter to Parent**

Dear Third-Grade Parent/Guardian,

My name is Ms./Mr. [Name]. I am your child's teacher, and I am looking forward to working with you this year to help your child succeed in third grade. I hope we can meet in person at our school's open house on [date] from [time] to [time]. To make sure you have access to me when you need it, the telephone number to our classroom is [telephone #]. If you call during instructional times, it will automatically go to voice mail. If you leave a message with a phone number, I will return your call as soon as possible. I am also available by email at [email address], which you can find on our class section of the school Web page [URL]. Please help me to have access to you when needed by completing the attached information sheet with your emergency and preferred contact information.

The school supply list for our class is attached and can also be viewed at our school Web site. Please help your child bring these items to class by Monday. Also, please notice that the list includes a field-trip fee for the year. This fee covers the cost of all field trips we will be taking. You may pay this fee at any point prior to the first field trip on [date].

Our class will study several themes across the year, beginning with "Families." Your child will be completing some class assignments during the next 2 weeks that will include talking with you about your family. If you have a unique tradition or special family story that you would be willing to share with our class as a part of this theme, please contact me by phone or email, or send a note with your child.

Finally, in order for our class to function efficiently, effectively, and as a community, we have a set of class rules. Please read the attached sheet listing the rules, sign that you have read them with your child, and return the signed sheet to me by Monday.

Again, I look forward to working with you this year.

Sincerely,

[signature]

Attached: Contact Information Sheet (*Please complete and return by Monday.*)

School Supply List (*Please send items by Monday, field-trip fee by [date].*)

Our Class Rules (*Please read with your child, sign, and return by Monday.*)

## ■ Checklist: Preparing for the Beginning of School

| Check When Complete | Item | Notes |
|---|---|---|
| ☐ | A. Are your room and materials ready? (See Chapter 2.) | |

☐    B.   Have you decided on your class procedures, rules, and associated consequences? (See Chapters 3, 4, and 8.)

                                             _____

☐    C.   Are you familiar with the parts of the school that you and your students may use (e.g., cafeteria, office and office phone, halls, restroom facilities, computer lab, resource room) and any procedures for their use?

                                             _____

☐    D.   Do you have a complete class roster?

                                             _____

☐    E.   Do you have file information on your students, including information on reading and math achievement levels from previous teachers, test results, emergency contact numbers, and any other information?

                                             _____

☐    F.   Do you know whether you have any students with disabilities who should be accommodated in your room arrangement or in your instruction? (See Chapter 11.)

                                             _____

☐    G.   Do you have adequate numbers of textbooks, desks, and class materials?

                                             _____

☐    H.   Do you have the teacher's editions of your textbooks?

                                             _____

☐    I.   Do you know the procedure for the arrival and departure of students on the first day? for every day after that?

                                             _____

☐    J.   Are students' name tags ready? Do you have blank ones for unexpected students?

                                             _____

☐    K.   Do you have your first day's plan of activities ready?

                                             _____

☐    L.   Does your daily schedule accommodate special classes (e.g., physical education, music) or "pull-out" programs (e.g.,

Title I reading, resource room
students, programs for the gifted)?    _____

☐    M. Do you have time-filler activities
prepared?    _____

☐    N. Do you have a letter ready to send
home to parents with information
about needed school materials?    _____

☐    O. Do you know when and how you
can obtain assistance from school
staff (e.g., the resource teacher,
school nurse, librarian, office
personnel, counselor)?    _____

☐    P. Do you have a plan to handle a
child's or school emergency?    _____

---

**MyEducationLab**

Now go to www.myeducationlab.com to:

- Take a Quiz to test your mastery of chapter objectives.
- Study chapter content with an individualized Study Plan.
- Deepen your understanding of particular concepts and principles with Classroom Management Simulations.
- Apply what you have learned in the chapter to your work with children in Building Teaching Skills exercises.

## CHAPTER 6

# Planning and Conducting Instruction

Let's assume that the steps you have taken so far to ensure that your classroom will run smoothly have worked. Your classroom is organized, you have thought about the climate to be established and the expectations you want to communicate, you've developed and taught your rules and procedures, and you have accountability systems in place to manage student learning. You have been utilizing lessons that have reviewed previously learned content while setting these routines and procedures in place. Now that your students are attentive and ready to participate, what do you do? Remember, your purpose is not just to have a smoothly running classroom; your purpose is to help students learn and to help them ultimately take responsibility for their learning.

It is at this point that management and instruction meet. Well-planned lessons with a variety of developmentally appropriate activities support the positive learning environment that careful management decisions create. Dry lessons with limited opportunities for students to participate are boring and erode students' motivation; this is when management problems begin. Interesting, relevant, well-planned lessons are the key to holding student attention.

As you may have noticed, not all people learn in the same way. These different modes have been called learning styles or learning preferences. Because children learn in different ways, varying the activities and the formats for learning gives you a better chance of meeting the different learning preferences in your class. You should not think, however, that you have to determine each child's preferred learning style and accommodate that style in every subject. It is just as important for students to understand that they can be successful in instructional formats that may not seem easiest to them (Brophy, 2004).

This chapter describes how to plan and conduct instruction in ways that support the kinds of learning you want for your students regardless of content area. Combining this information with knowledge from the content areas will help you teach each subject more effectively. The chapter is divided into three sections. The first one discusses the planning decisions you must make. The second section discusses Kounin's concepts for managing instruction. The final section discusses transition problems that can arise between activities.

# ■ Planning Instructional Activities

When you choose instructional activities for your classes, consider primarily whether an activity will lead to learning and what kind of learning you want to encourage. Activities that lead to better memorization are different from those that enhance reflective thinking or problem solving. Next, consider whether the activity will maintain student involvement. Also consider the sequence of activities for and the amounts of time spent on the various subjects in the curriculum. Such considerations lead many elementary teachers to plan reading and at least some language arts activities for the first 2 hours or so of each morning. These activities usually require sustained effort and often involve a combination of small-group, whole-group, and individual work formats. Involvement in these activities is more difficult to maintain later in the day, when students are less alert and more fatigued.

Establishing a daily schedule with specific times for various subjects will help you remain conscious of time so that you do not shortchange subjects taught later in the day. Furthermore, students will be better able to pace their own work if they know the schedule. When you plan your schedule, try to arrange change-of-pace activities to follow periods of sustained effort or intense concentration. For example, you might arrange reading or language arts activities so that they come before recess or physical education. If you cannot schedule such activities conveniently, at least give students a brief break, and lead them in exercises or a song or two, or give them time to stand and stretch if they have not had the opportunity to move around.

When you plan your daily schedule, you may find that your school district has established guidelines for the amount of time to be allotted to each subject. Also, special teachers may be assigned to teach a particular subject at certain times of the week. Thus, you may find that your class will be taught physical education on Tuesdays and Thursdays from 1:30 to 2:00 and will have music on Mondays and Wednesdays from 10:30 to 11:00. Obviously, your schedule will have to be set accordingly. In addition, some students may be pulled out for other classes (e.g., Title I, speech). If several students are out of the room at the same time, you will need to plan your content instruction for when they return.

At the beginning of the school year, good planning requires extra effort. Over-planning (preparing more activities than can be accomplished in a particular time) and underplanning (preparing too little for the amount of time available) can occur, particularly with inexperienced teachers. It is better to overplan and then be flexible in implementing the plan. Activities not completed one day can serve as starters for second and third days.

## Types of Planning

You will engage in several levels of planning, both long range (by the year and by the term) and short range (by the unit, the week, or the day). These levels of planning should be coordinated. Accomplishing the longer plan requires dividing the work into terms, the terms into units, and the units into weeks and days.

The lesson outcomes you envision will determine your planning goals and objectives, and your plans should reflect these intended outcomes. Many of these outcomes are determined by state or local curriculum guidelines or by mandated testing, but you should keep in mind that you are also teaching for understanding, appreciation, and application. Thus, your plans provide road maps that help transform the available curriculum into activities, assignments, and learning experiences that are meaningful. In developing your plans, keep two important considerations in mind: first, which skills and concepts students must learn, and second, through which activities they can become interested partners in the learning enterprise.

## Types of Instructional Activities

For each subject you teach, you will design activities to help students construct new knowledge, acquire and practice skills, consolidate and extend knowledge, and receive feedback about their learning. The basic components in teaching are (1) content development, (2) discussion, (3) recitation or reinforcement, and (4) feedback. These components may be accomplished in a variety of instructional formats (see Table 6.1). In the following sections, two common types of instructional activities are described: whole-group instruction and teacher-led small-group instruction. Chapter 7 explores the format of cooperative learning group instruction in detail.

**Whole-Group Instruction.**   Whole-class presentation is often the major vehicle for introducing and teaching content activities. During content development, you may present new information, elaborate on or extend a concept or principle, conduct a demonstration, show how to perform a skill, or describe how to solve a problem. Whole-group content development activities are appropriate for learning goals such as exposure and familiarity and for the efficient presentation of new material.

During content development, the teacher takes an active role focused on helping students think about the new content, relate it to what they know, and apply it. One chief management concern is making sure that students are active, not passive. Therefore, you will have to find ways to involve students in the development of the

**table 6.1** ■ Formats for Instruction

| Format | How Formed | Purpose | Advantages | Disadvantages |
|---|---|---|---|---|
| Whole Group | Whole group | To deliver information on new content or skill(s) to all at one time | ■ Covers much information in little time ■ Everyone hears the same information | ■ Does not meet needs of many students when used as the only method of instruction |
| Small Teacher-Led Group | Teacher-formed homogeneous groups using set criteria | To provide activities to meet specific needs, either remedial or enrichment | ■ Able to check more accurately for student understanding | ■ Some students may be engaged in long periods of seatwork without being actively monitored |
| Small Collaborative Group | Teacher-formed equivalent heterogeneous groups (formal cooperative learning) or | To reinforce previously taught content and foster social skills (Note: Individual grades are a *must* to achieve these purposes.) or | ■ More opportunity for students to "interact" with material being presented or | ■ Sometimes only two or three of the four to five students benefit from doing the work or |
| | Random selection with teacher guidance as needed to form heterogeneous groups | To experience a process or produce a product with no individual or group academic grading involved | ■ Social skills fostered | ■ Difficult to check for individual student's understanding during activity |
| Student Pairs | Teacher or student selected based on reciprocal learning needs | To enhance collaborative learning through collaborative/reciprocal processes | ■ Can involve both students ■ Fosters social skills ■ Facilitates reciprocal learning | ■ One student may do all the work/thinking |
| Individualized Instruction | One student | To meet individual student needs (IEPs, absentee makeup work, enrichment, remediation of content or skills) | ■ Teacher–student ratio a plus ■ Remedial/enrichment help easily given | ■ May be time-consuming ■ Some students may not be actively monitored |
| Centers and Stations | Teacher created with equitable student access designated in a variety of ways | To enrich, extend, practice, apply new learning, and/or remediate content and/or skills | ■ Enriches student understanding ■ Students can practice skills ■ Students can apply new learning | ■ Difficult to manage time at center and problematic for nonreaders ■ Requires preparation time ■ Difficult to monitor |

Adapted from *Creating Conditions for Learning: A Comprehensive Program for Creating an Effective Learning Environment* (8th ed.) by C. M. Everston, 2010, Nashville, TN: Vanderbilt University, Peabody College. © Vanderbilt University. Reprinted with permission.

lesson. Teacher questions are used for this purpose, allowing the teacher to check student understanding and to encourage students to contribute to steps in problem solving, to apply concepts or principles, and to analyze ideas.

In addition to presentations and questions, content development should include sample problems or other demonstrations of understanding of the new content. These not only help students learn the new content but also provide you with information about how well the class is understanding the lesson. Activities and questions should be thoughtfully designed to expose student thinking and understanding. For example, when a student gives a correct answer, you can probe with further questions: "What led you to that answer?" "What do you mean by . . .?" "What would come next?" "How else could you do that?"

Another way to develop content is to help students engage in research and problem solving, individually and in groups.

*Presenting New Content*   When students understand where a lesson is going, they are more likely to be with you at the end. Explain lesson objectives. If the lesson is complex, provide an outline to help students follow its organization and to keep them on course.

If students are to understand content from silent reading or from viewing a video, provide a content outline with a few items filled in and spaces for students to supply the rest. This task focuses their attention and helps motivate them to read or watch carefully. After a video, go over these items with the class, especially if the students will use the outline for further work or study. Alternatively, use the video as an opportunity to teach note-taking skills. Guide students in determining the questions they need to have answered, and then help them identify important information as the video progresses.

As you present a lesson, stay with the planned sequence unless an obvious change is needed. Avoid needless digressions, interruptions, or tangential information. Inserting irrelevant information into a lesson only confuses students about what they are expected to learn. Displaying key concepts, new terms, major points, and other critical information on a screen or board underscores their importance.

Presentations should be as focused and concrete as possible. Use examples, illustrations, demonstrations, props, charts, and any other means of adding substance and dimension to abstractions in the lesson. Avoid the vague expressions and

Shoe-New Business © 1980 Macnelly. Distributed by King Features Syndicate.

verbal time fillers that, at best, communicate little information and make presentations difficult to follow. Then allow students time and opportunity to process the information.

*Checking for Understanding*    Find out during the lesson whether students understand a presentation; do not wait until the next day. As content development activities unfold, ask students questions to verify their comprehension of main points. You can also ask students to provide a written response to key questions and then check some or all of their answers either orally or by examining the written work. Asking students to demonstrate comprehension at several points during a presentation not only allows you to verify their progress but also keeps students more involved in the lesson.

You can also check student understanding and emphasize main points by conducting an oral recitation after a presentation. Do this by asking a series of questions that recapitulate the lesson sequence and its major concepts. Be sure to involve many students in answering these questions so that you can identify the overall level of understanding in the class and can reteach what has not been satisfactorily learned. Again, remember to allow wait time to increase the number of students prepared to respond.

Other methods of checking for understanding include having students respond to your questions in these ways:

- Displaying the correct one of two or more possible answers by holding up prepared color-coded cards
- Using designated body movements (e.g., thumbs up or thumbs down, arms crossed or arms uncrossed)
- Folding a piece of notebook paper into fourths, using each of the eight sections to write a response, and holding up the appropriate section for you to see
- Writing answers or explanations in their own words and turning these papers in for your inspection
- Pairing with a designated neighbor and quietly explaining their answers to each other while you circulate and listen
- Keeping a journal or a learning log that includes responses to each lesson in a particular unit

*Classwork and Independent Work*    Often in whole-group instruction, students engage in assignments that build on presented material. *Classwork* is the portion of an assignment completed as a whole group immediately following content instruction. Most teachers use classwork to check students' understanding of the content and to identify any additional instruction needed. *Independent work* is that portion of the assignment completed by individual students, generally while the teacher moves through the class to check their progress. In the upper elementary grades, the portion of the assignment not completed in class typically becomes a homework assignment unless the materials or resources needed are available only in the classroom. (Procedures for independent work are discussed in Chapter 3.)

Good management of individual activities has several components. First, adequate content development must precede the independent student activity so that students can work productively on their own. Second, you must communicate clearly the requirements and objectives of the students' work and arrange for access to needed materials or resources. A good strategy is to begin the independent work assignment as a whole-class activity (e.g., working several of the exercises, problems, or questions together) before the independent work phase. This gets students started, gives them an opportunity to ask questions, and enables you to observe and correct common problems in a whole-class format rather than having to deal with the same problem with multiple individuals. Third, you should actively monitor the students' work so that problems are detected early and corrective feedback is provided.

Independent activities are best used for consolidating or extending prior learning rather than for acquiring new content. Therefore, be careful not to overuse independent activities; a rule of thumb is to devote at least as much time to content development as to independent work. Moreover, student engagement is more difficult to maintain in lengthy individual work activities. If you do find yourself assigning long periods of time to individual assignments, try breaking the activity into smaller segments and having a discussion or review between segments. The change in lesson format will help refocus attention and will give you an opportunity to check comprehension and clear up problems.

*Feedback*    Feedback can be provided during discussion, recitation, or checking and can occur before, during, or after content development. For example, in presenting new material, you may build on prior knowledge, and you might want to begin with a group discussion that leads to a new idea or problem to be solved. In addition, feedback is involved in student presentations, checking student work, demonstrations, and testing. Wherever these feedback activities occur in the instructional sequence, planning and management can make them more productive.

*Discussions* are helpful in encouraging students to evaluate events, topics, or results; to clarify the basis for their opinions; to help students become aware of other points of view; and to help them improve their oral expression skills. In discussions students are encouraged to express themselves, examine their opinions and beliefs, and understand other perspectives. Students may respond to each other rather than only to the teacher. The teacher's role becomes one of encouraging, clarifying, and using student ideas rather than evaluating their correctness.

Management of a discussion calls for a number of skills or traits, including warmth or friendliness (to promote security), conflict resolution, and encouraging expression of divergent points of view (to foster acceptance and openness). Avoid allowing a few students to monopolize the discourse; less verbal students should be included skillfully. Invite reticent members to speak from time to time by asking for their opinions or views of what has previously been discussed. Giving students opportunities to paraphrase, clarify, and elaborate on their own or other students' remarks helps keep a discussion moving and on target. Getting students to listen to each other rather than treating the discussion as a dialogue with the teacher is sometimes difficult. Therefore, it is important to emphasize that students should respond to each other as well as to the teacher's comments or questions.

Plan questions in advance. This can keep the discussion focused and productive. Similarly, encourage students to formulate their own discussion questions, especially in response to group or individual research projects. Whether discussions are student-led or teacher-led, ground rules for participation must be clear (e.g., raise hands, listen carefully, respect others' right to speak).

*Recitation* is a question-and-answer sequence in which the teacher asks questions, usually of a factual nature, and accepts, guides, or corrects student responses. The sequence of question/answer/evaluation is repeated frequently, with many students being asked to respond until a body of content has been covered. In effect, recitation is a form of checking that is done orally. It can be used as a skill drill or to review student understanding of a previous lesson or assigned reading. It can also be used to check spelling, knowledge of vocabulary words, or other factual recall.

When recitation is used to check understanding, it is important to address questions to all students, not just to those who are eager to answer. Calling on only those who volunteer can give you an inaccurate impression of what students know. Develop a systematic way to ensure that all students get a turn to answer. This can be done by using a checklist or a shuffled stack of name cards. It is helpful to ask a question, allow time for students to think, and then call on individual students. Sometimes teachers do not allow students enough time to respond, thus reducing opportunities for those who are slow to answer. Some experts recommend a "wait time" of several seconds before giving a prompt or calling on another student. Sometimes you can use choral or whole-group responses as a way of keeping everyone alert and active.

In *checking*, students evaluate the accuracy of their own classwork or homework. The checking activity is appropriate only when the judgment of correctness can be made easily. Checking provides quick feedback and allows the teacher to identify and discuss common errors on assignments. Careful monitoring during checking is important to be sure that students are doing it correctly. Students must be taught to check papers accurately, so it is important to explain the procedures as well as model them and allow students opportunities to practice. When student checking is used, you should collect the papers and examine them to remain aware of progress and problems. Note that grades are confidential. Checking can involve other students; however, all grades must stay between you and the individual student.

With *presentations* and *demonstrations*, students give a report to the whole group, demonstrate a procedure or skill, or summarize work done on a short- or long-term project. Presentations are more effective when guidelines are given ahead of time and students are allowed time for planning and practice. It's useful to discuss with students the kinds of audience behavior that are desirable. A good opener for a discussion of procedures is to ask students for suggestions about how they want others to behave or participate when it is their turn to give a presentation.

*Testing* has become a common activity in elementary school classrooms. Having directions for students in a fixed place or projected on a screen helps students know what is expected of them. Nevertheless, you will need to go over instructions carefully, including testing protocol, especially with younger children. Plan carefully for early finishers, and have a meaningful task available for them to do while others finish.

*Arranging Activities within a Lesson* In whole-group instruction, lessons usually consist of a series of activities. A common activity sequence in basic skill areas is this:

1. Checking or recitation
2. Content development
3. Classwork
4. Independent work, group work, or discussion

The first activity allows the previous day's assignment or homework to be corrected. If there was no homework, the teacher leads a review of prior content important for the day's lesson. During content development, new content or skills are taught. Following this, a short classwork activity is used to review the new content and to preview the new assignment. Then practice is provided through independent work, group work, or discussion.

The problem with this sequence is that it requires that the presentation of lesson content and the practice period be handled in two, usually lengthy, segments. A variation of the sequence that accommodates more complex content and that does not demand as much sustained attention is this:

1. Checking or recitation
2. Content development
3. Classwork or independent work, usually brief, with checking
4. Content development
5. Classwork, usually brief
6. Independent work, group work, or discussion

This sequence allows you to divide the lesson content into two parts, with practice and feedback following the first content development activity. Teaching new content in two parts with an intervening practice period helps students consolidate learning from the first part before they are asked to address new learning required in the second part. This sequence also allows you to check student understanding and to provide prompt feedback before moving on to more complex content. Furthermore, when individual activities are divided into shorter segments, student attention is usually easier to maintain. A challenge with this sequence is that it produces more transition points and thus greater potential for student disengagement. Usually these transitions can be managed without difficulty, however, because student movement, new materials, or greatly changed lesson focus is not required. The various activities blend together, usually without conspicuous transitions.

Of course, not all lessons fit either of the activity patterns just described. For instance, a science or social studies lesson may consist of a relatively long period of active student exploration or problem solving in small groups, followed by a whole-class content development discussion. Ongoing projects may entail long segments of individual seatwork or small-group work interspersed with short segments of whole-class or small-group instruction. Nevertheless, the two common patterns described here provide useful frameworks for building most teacher-directed lessons.

**Teacher-Led Small-Group Instruction.**    In this format, students are grouped together for instruction. In a teacher-led small group, the teacher works with small groups of students, one group at a time, while the rest of the class works independently. This mode of instruction is most commonly used for reading and frequently for mathematics. Its purpose is to accommodate a wide range of achievement levels in basic skill subjects. Because this format is used so extensively for basic skills, we will describe its features in detail.

A critical aspect of small-group instruction is that at least two different activities occur simultaneously. The teacher leads one group while students outside the group participate in a variety of independent activities. Because the teacher is actively involved with the small group, it is more difficult to monitor the behavior of other students and give them assistance. And because students may work independently for a long period, careful planning and extra effort are required to keep them involved in their work.

The first step in setting up effective small-group instruction is to plan for the out-of-group activities. You will need to give directions to the whole class at once: instructions for each assignment, a description of needed materials, and a suggested time for completing each activity. This list of assignments and timeline should also be posted, written on the board, or projected on a screen. Check whether students understand the directions by asking students in each group to repeat them before beginning.

Before calling the first group, monitor the beginning of independent work for a short time. After you are certain that students have started, signal the first group. During your work with the small group, monitor out-of-group students by scanning the room frequently. If you observe inappropriate behavior that is interfering with work, try to stop it with eye contact or some nonverbal signal, by calling the student's name once, or by reminding the student of what he or she should be doing. A "time-out" desk near you can also be used for persistent misbehavior: You can signal such a student to go to the desk for a while, without your having to leave the group.

Another consideration is how students needing help on an independent task can obtain it without interrupting you. Some teachers tell students to skip work they cannot do and go on to another activity until you are available. Others allow students to help each other, or they assign a few students (perhaps one for each table or group) the role of helper. This works best if students are seated in mixed-ability groups. Finally, students can sign up on the board or on a clipboard sheet to indicate the need for assistance when it is available. If you must leave the small group to help a student or to deal with a problem, be sure to give students in the group something to do. One student in the group may be able to lead the activity for a short time.

When work with one small group has been completed, delay calling the next group. Instead, take the opportunity to check the progress of the students who will be continuing individual assignments and help them with any problems they may have. Students who were off task while you were teaching the small group can be given delayed feedback at this time. Be sure to encourage and give positive feedback to students who are participating appropriately. The students who have left the small group and are moving to other activities should also be monitored to be sure they begin their work promptly. Then signal the next group to come for instruction.

Small groups are also used as an integral part of other teaching methods, such as cooperative learning, reciprocal teaching, and project-based learning. In cooperative learning activities (see Chapter 7), students work together to complete group and individual assignments. In reciprocal teaching, students take turns serving as small-group leaders during discussions of text material in order to practice summarizing, questioning, clarifying, and predicting. In project-based learning, students work in collaborative groups to develop solutions to "ill-structured" problems (i.e., problems having multiple possible solutions, unknown aspects, or requiring judgment and evaluation). Review Case Study 3.2 for considerations when planning group work.

## Planning for Clear Instruction

When you have an idea of the range and sequence of activities available to you, examine the content, concepts, and goals of the lessons and units that you will be teaching. One way to start is to review the unit and lesson in the teacher's edition of your textbook(s). Pay careful attention to suggestions for lesson development and activities. Study the exercises, questions, problems, and other activities in the textbook, and decide which items provide appropriate review of lesson objectives. Note examples, demonstrations, and key questions and activities to use in the development of the main concepts. Put yourself in the lesson. Try to anticipate problems students may encounter in the lesson or assignments. Check for new terms, and be ready to define them and present examples.

The textbook suggestions should not be limiting. Remember, you want your students to *understand* the content, not just retain it. Many educators talk about the importance of constructing knowledge, having students actively involved in making new information relevant to what they already know. This may be as simple as introducing a problem and exploring possible solutions or reframing a lesson through a thoughtful discussion of how it relates to individual experiences. You are targeting understanding, appreciation, and application.

Consider the interest the lesson is likely to have for students. Will you be enthusiastic about teaching this material to your class in this way? Your enthusiasm about the lesson is contagious and signals to students how you feel about its importance. If you find it interesting and exciting and you communicate this excitement to your class, students will probably respond with interest. However, if you find yourself unenthusiastic about a lesson or topic, chances are your students will share your feelings. Consider approaching the lesson in a different way. For example, rather than giving a lecture presentation of material, perhaps you can find ways for students to contribute through large- or small-group discussions that address the same issues.

Finally, organize your lesson parts into a coherent sequence. Outline the main components, and list any prompting/discussion questions. Then you will be well prepared for a clear lesson presentation.

## Technology in the Classroom

Using computers—whether for content development, research, or practice—requires awareness and planning. Few classrooms have as many computers as teachers would like, but almost all have at least one. Develop strategies to make technology a productive tool in helping students reach their academic goals. Unless your school has a computer lab, you will probably have to devise activities to be carried out at a computer station. As noted in Chapter 5, this requires that procedures for the use of the station be taught and rehearsed. In addition, you may want to appoint one or more student "computer experts," who can assist quietly while you continue with whole- or small-group instruction.

Having technology does not mean it is the appropriate tool for meeting a specific lesson's objectives. When technology is the appropriate choice, making the best possible use of shared technology can be a challenge. Useful strategies include using the Internet for research or setting up specific content software to reinforce skills. Email and word processing software may enable students to improve their organizational and writing skills. You may want to include study notes on a class Web page, learning game links, and instructional links to engage your students. Additionally, you might plan to provide content visually through projected slides, present online video of an animal in its habitat, utilize clickers for an in-class assessment, or develop a wiki with another class on a specific country of study.

To teach effectively with technology in the classroom, teachers develop more defined "hypertextual function" (Schussler, Poole, Whitlock, & Evertson, 2007), that is, they become more familiar with students, facile with technology, transparent in integrating students and technology with content, connective across learning areas, and have the necessary collegial support to maintain these interconnections. Simultaneously, researchers highlight the need for teachers to be aware of the aggressive marketing focus of technology (in particular, the Internet) toward children and to be advocates for students maintaining their privacy while becoming informed consumers of information obtained online (Seiter, 2005). Consider who will be using the technology, for how long, and with whom.

Internet access in the classroom makes it possible for students to find information more easily than ever before. Unfortunately, not all of the information available to them is appropriate. Certain precautions must be taken when including Internet use in your lessons. Many school districts have developed fair use policies for the technology they provide that include required signatures of all staff agreeing to supervise student online access. Most districts utilize Internet filters. Some school systems also require that parents give written permission before their child is allowed on the Internet. The teacher must find alternative ways for students without that permission to gather information. Children should be cautioned not to give their last names or any personal information over the Internet.

Visit Web sites (or use software) in advance to know the expected screen displays and to anticipate any student difficulties. Monitor students frequently as they access information on the Web. By giving them specific information to find and a limited time in which to find it, you can avoid many hazards. It is a good idea to set up guidelines for use at the beginning of the year. For example, have the students sign a contract that states, "I will use the Internet for school use only. If I knowingly search for inappropriate materials, I will lose the privilege of using the Internet for the remainder of the year." To eliminate the argument that a site was accidentally found, teach students to click the "back" button on the browser and get your attention immediately if they access an inappropriate site by mistake.

To make more efficient use of browsing time while students search for information, you may want to encourage them to print the resources they find. Teach them to skim headings for appropriate material and print a specified section of text. Alternatively, consider having students use the Search or Find function to identify the main idea of a section and scan the surrounding text for details, teaching them to take notes during the search.

When technology use is planned outside the classroom (e.g., in the library, at the computer lab), prior arrangements need to be made with the supervising teacher in those locations if students travel there without you. Provide written directions for your students to assist the supervising teacher in answering questions and problem-solving with them as needed. Review any necessary procedures with students for their movement to and from these locations.

Finally, as teachers, we must avoid allowing the immediacy of technology to interrupt the responsibility of teaching our students. Utilize your personal technology during your break times. Texting or talking on your cell phone during a lesson is not only a poor use of teaching time, but it also models lack of respect for your students, allows them to disengage with the content, and can encourage misbehavior to erupt. Checking the weather reports for potential storm warnings on a smart phone or texting the teacher of a student's sibling regarding a change in pick-up rides can be legitimate activities—but not in place of teaching your students.

# ■ Kounin's Concepts for Managing Whole-Group Instruction

A central theme in managing teacher-led activities well is the idea of activity flow—the degree to which a lesson proceeds smoothly, without digressions, diversions, or interruptions. Lessons with good flow keep student attention and prevent deviation because most of the cues for behavior during the lesson are focused on behaviors appropriate for the lesson. When lesson flow is jerky, with frequent interruptions and side trips, there is more competition for attention from cues external to the focus of the lesson. Therefore, there will be a greater tendency for students to disengage.

A series of classroom research studies by Kounin and his colleagues (Kounin, 1970; Kounin & Gump, 1974) identified several concepts that contribute to effective management of interactive group activities, leading to smooth activity flow. According to Kounin, activity flow is maintained through three types of teacher practices, summarized in Table 6.2. Within each class of behavior there are two or three related concepts. Look at how each is defined, and consider some examples.

## Preventing Misbehavior

Classrooms are complex settings. Many events can occur at the same time. One cannot always predict with certainty what will occur when. New teachers run the risk of focusing too closely on single events or on select areas of the classroom and missing the big picture. Understanding two of Kounin's (1970) concepts, withitness and overlapping, helps to prevent this mistake.

*Withitness* is the degree to which the teacher corrects misbehavior before it intensifies or spreads to more students and also targets the correct student when doing so. A teacher who is not "withit" either will fail to stop the problem until it has escalated and may require a major intervention or else will fail to catch the perpetrator and may instead target the wrong student. It is apparent that underlying aspects of withitness include good monitoring and prompt handling of inappropriate behavior, concepts that are discussed in detail in Chapter 8.

*Overlapping* refers to how the teacher handles two or more simultaneous events. Here are some examples: A visitor comes to the door in the middle of a lesson, a child from outside the group comes up to the teacher during reading group time, or several students get into a squabble while the teacher is busy helping other children across the room. A teacher who has good overlapping skills will handle both events in some way instead of dropping one event to handle the other or else ignoring the second event. To handle an interruption, for example, a teacher might tell the class or group to continue working or to get out some work, and then may deal with the interrupter. The squabble taking place away from the teacher might be handled by eye contact or a brief verbal directive while the teacher stays where he or she is.

Notice that a teacher who is withit and exhibits good overlapping skills is able to insulate lessons from the intrusions that student misbehavior or external interruptions might cause. Furthermore, by reacting promptly to problems (but not overreacting), the teacher is often able to use simple measures (e.g., eye contact, redirection, a quiet command) that do not interfere with ongoing activities or distract students very much. If a teacher is not withit or does not overlap when needed, lessons may be

**table 6.2** ■ How Effective Managers Maintain Activity Flow (Kounin, 1970)

| Issue | Skill | Definition | Example |
|---|---|---|---|
| Preventing misbehavior | Withitness | Communicating general awareness of the classroom to students; identifying and correcting misbehavior promptly and correctly | The teacher makes eye contact with a student who is about to "shoot a basket" with a wad of paper. The student puts the paper away. A student behind him, who has seen the interaction, decides he's not likely to get away with shooting a basket either. |
|  | Overlapping | Attending to two or more simultaneous events | The teacher is leading a class discussion when a student comes in late. The teacher nods to him, continuing the discussion. Later, when students have begun a seat-work assignment, she attends to him and signs his tardy slip. |
| Managing movement | Momentum | Keeping lessons moving briskly; planning carefully to avoid slowdowns | The teacher notices that the explanation of a relatively minor concept is taking too long and distracting attention from the primary focus of the lesson. The teacher makes a mental note to go more in-depth on this concept in a separate lesson the next day and moves on. |
|  | Smoothness | Staying on track with the lesson; avoiding digressions and divergences that can lead to confusion | While being responsive to student interests, the teacher avoids comments that tend to draw attention away from the key points of the lesson. |
| Maintaining group focus | Group alerting | Engaging the attention of the whole class while individuals are responding | Each student has a number that was drawn from a hat on the way into class. The teacher draws numbers and uses them to call on students during a fast-paced review. |
|  | Encouraging accountability | Communicating to students that their participation will be observed and evaluated | At the end of discussion and practice of a new skill, students are told to turn to a neighbor and explain the process to him or her. |
|  | Using high-participation formats | Using lessons that define behavior of students when they are not directly answering a teacher's question | While some students work problems at the board, students at their desks are instructed to check them by working the problems on paper. |

interrupted by student misbehavior and by the teacher's subsequently more visible and tardy reactions.

## Managing Movement

Whereas withitness and overlapping are accomplished by handling external interruptions and student intrusions into the flow of the lesson, movement management is accomplished by avoiding teacher-caused intrusions or delays. Good movement management is achieved through momentum and smoothness.

*Momentum* refers to pacing and is indicated by lessons that move along briskly. Teachers can cause slowdowns in momentum by dwelling on individual parts of a lesson, direction, or skill or by unnecessarily breaking an activity into too many parts. For example, teachers should provide a standard heading for assignments that can be used routinely rather than altering its form and having to explain it over and over.

*Smoothness*, as opposed to jerkiness, is epitomized in lesson continuity. A smoothly flowing lesson keeps student attention. If a teacher leaves a topic or activity to explore a side topic or to retrieve materials not prepared in advance, students may be distracted and miss the point of the lesson.

## Maintaining Group Focus

Classroom instruction involves teaching children in groups, often a whole class at a time. Doing so means that a teacher must be conscious of the group influence on the instruction. Like a conductor leading an orchestra, the teacher must elicit the performance of individuals and still provide signals and direction to the whole class. Group focus can be maintained through three techniques.

*Group alerting* means taking action to engage the attention of the whole class while individuals are responding. It can take the form of creating suspense, telling students they might be called on next, calling on students randomly, asking students not reciting to add to the answer, or using some new visual aid, display, or attention-getting strategy. Engaging in a dialogue with only one student and calling on students before asking questions are two examples of poor group alerting.

*Accountability* occurs when the teacher lets students know that their performance will be observed and evaluated in some manner. It does not require a letter grade or a score (although it might); it simply communicates some degree of awareness of how students are performing. For example, the teacher might ask everyone who knows an answer to raise a hand and then call on one or more of those students. The teacher could have all students write answers and circulate to check them. The teacher might also have students keep notebooks and check them from time to time.

*High-participation formats* are lessons that program the behavior of students when they are not directly involved in answering a teacher's question. Such lessons have a higher built-in rate of participation than do lessons that merely assume that students will sit and watch when other students respond. Higher-participation formats occur when students are expected to write answers, solve problems, read along, manipulate materials, or perform some other concurrent task.

Some activities lend themselves more to one type of group focus than another. When planning instruction, it is helpful to consider which of the three aspects to use. For example, during a demonstration that involves expensive materials, it might be difficult to use a high-participation format, but group alerting might be easy to incorporate.

Kounin's concepts for managing group instruction not only help identify key aspects of effective teaching, but can also be used to diagnose instructional problems and identify possible solutions. For example, if lessons seem to drag and student response is unenthusiastic, there may be a problem with group focus; a solution may be to work on alerting or accountability or to increase the degree of participation. Activities that take too long and that seem to get off track constantly may have a problem with movement management. Perhaps this teacher should check for slowdowns and jerkiness.

# ■ Transition Problems in Conducting Instruction

The interval between any two activities is a *transition*. Several management problems can occur during transitions, including long delays before starting the next activity, which can contribute to high levels of inappropriate or disruptive behavior. Transition problems can be caused by a lack of readiness by the teacher or the students for the next activity, unclear student expectations about appropriate behavior during transitions, and faulty procedures for transitions. Here are examples of transition problems, along with suggested ways of correcting them.

| Transition Problem | Suggested Solution |
|---|---|
| Students talk loudly at the beginning of the day. The teacher is interrupted while checking attendance, and the start of content activities is delayed. | Establish a beginning-of-day routine, and clearly state your expectations for behavior at the beginning of the day, reinforcing consistently. Practice this starting transition with a timer to build swiftness. |
| Students talk too much during transitions, especially after an assignment has been given but before they have begun working on it. Many students do not start their work activity for several minutes. | Be sure students know what the assignment is. Post it where they can see it easily. Work as a whole class on the first several exercises so that all students begin the lesson successfully and at the same time. Watch what students do during the transition, and urge them along when needed. |
| Students who go for supplemental instruction stop work early and leave the room noisily while the rest of the class is working. When these students return to the room, they disturb others as they come in and take their seats. They interrupt others by asking for directions and assignments. | Have a designated signal that tells these students when they are to get ready to leave, such as a special time on the clock. Have them practice leaving and returning to the room quietly. Acknowledge appropriate behavior. Leave special instructions in a folder, on the board, or on a special sheet at their desks for what they are to do when they return. Or for younger students, establish a special place (e.g., the reading rug) for returning students to wait and an activity for them to engage in until you can give them personal attention. |
| During the last afternoon activity, students quit working well before the end; they begin playing around and leave the room in a mess. | Establish an end-of-day routine so that students continue their work until the teacher gives a signal to begin preparations to leave; then instruct students to help straighten the room. |
| Whenever the teacher attempts to move the students from one activity into another, a number of students don't make the transition but continue working on the preceding activity. This delays the start of the next activity or results in confusion. | Give students a few minutes' notice before an activity is scheduled to end. At the end of the activity, students should put away all materials from it and get out any needed materials for the next activity. Monitor the transition to make sure that all students complete it; do not start the next activity until students are ready. |
| The teacher delays the beginning of activities to look for materials, finish attendance reporting, pass back or collect papers, or chat with individual students while the rest of the class waits. | Have materials organized ahead of time, and when transitions begin, avoid doing anything that interferes with your ability to monitor and direct students. |

These items summarize the major problems that occur in classrooms at and around transition times. If you feel that your class is wasting time or if you are having difficulty keeping control during transitions, the suggested solutions may prove helpful. If you still need assistance, ask a peer to observe and provide you with suggestions.

# ■ Chapter Summary

Students have many learning needs; therefore, teaching requires a variety of instructional plans. Planning for instruction includes establishing a daily schedule, deciding on specific content to cover and its sequence, maintaining a sense of both short- and long-range goals for students, varying the types of instructional activities (e.g., individual, small group, whole group), considering the use of technology, and helping students connect present with past learning as well as potential future use. Maintaining the lesson flow in progress also requires planning to prevent misbehavior, to manage movement, and maintain a group focus. Special attention to transitions within and across lessons prevents a number of potential problems. Effective classroom management and quality classroom instruction are interrelated; therefore, effective planning helps you to conduct instruction proficiently, which in turn maintains a learning-oriented classroom.

# ■ Further Reading

Bitter, G. G., & Legacy, J. (2008). *Using technology in the classroom* (7th ed.). New York: Pearson Education.

*This text gives an introductory explanation of technology and its use for teachers and students. The initial chapters are designed for those new to technology. Later chapters are helpful for those who are fairly fluent technologically.*

Borich, G. (2006). *Effective teaching methods* (6th ed.). Upper Saddle River, NJ: Pearson Prentice Hall.

*Practical yet theoretically substantive, this book provides teachers with effective teaching practices. To help prepare new teachers, the book includes significant discussion of standardized tests and exercises for Praxis test preparation. New to this edition are field-experience activities, portfolio-building activities, and classroom-observation activities.*

Fuchs, D., Fuchs, L. S., Mathes, P. G., & Simmons, D. G. (1997). Peer-assisted learning strategies: Making classrooms more responsive to diversity. *American Educational Research Journal, 34*(1), 174–206.

*Reporting a study on peer tutoring as a portion of planned reading instruction, the authors identify that students at low, average, and high levels of achievement all had achievement gains when involved in peer tutoring, in comparison to students who were not part of planned reading instruction involving peer tutoring.*

Price, K. M., & Nelson, K. L. (2007). *Planning effective instruction* (3rd ed.). Belmont, CA: Thomson Wadsworth.

*This work provides excellent descriptions of a variety of instructional methods, including steps in how to plan for their use.*

Wiggins, G., & McTighe, J. (2005). *Understanding by design* (Expanded 2nd ed.). Alexandria, VA: ASCD.

*This book outlines the process of planning from the end result of student understanding backward to the lesson at hand.*

www.apa.org/education/k12/classroom-data.aspx

*This module, "Using Classroom Data to Give Systematic Feedback to Students to Improve Learning," was designed by the APA Task Force on the Applications of Psychological Science to Teaching and Learning to maximize teachers' use of formative assessment to build toward student understanding, application, and appreciation.*

www.commoncraft.com

*This Web site explains "In Plain English" a number of technological terms and tools (e.g., wiki, blog, RSS, secure passwords).*

www.lburkhart.com

*This Web site includes useful suggestions about technology integration in the classroom for elementary, middle, secondary, and special needs students.*

www.lessonplanspage.com

*This Web site for educators, maintained by the University of Scranton, contains more than 2,500 sample lesson plans for all subjects (PreK–12).*

www.teachervision.fen.com

*This Web site for the Family Education Network has tips for teachers and a lesson planning center.*

# ■ Suggested Activities

1. Choose one of the two cartoons in this chapter, and describe what you know about planning and conducting instruction in the classroom that is represented in the cartoon.

2. Answer the following questions in conversation with a partner: How do you think students learn? How do you know when someone is learning? What is your own preferred

style of learning? How will these beliefs affect your choice of teaching strategies? How do they influence your philosophy of education? Consider how each suggestion supports or fails to support the kinds of learning you believe to be most important.

3. Consider Scenario 6.1. Select a grade-level situation, and respond in writing.

4. Read Case Study 6.1. How many examples (or nonexamples) of Kounin's concepts (pp. 114–118) can you identify in this description? (See the key to this portion of the activity in the Appendix.) Create a lesson outline that will improve the sequence of Mr. Case's instruction.

5. Case Study 6.2 illustrates problems that can arise in conducting instruction. Use the concepts in this and previous chapters to diagnose Ms. Lake's problems and provide suggestions for improvement. Compare your list with the key in the Appendix.

6. Teachers are sometimes caught between the need to cover a broad range of content quickly and the need to develop more specific content to deepen students' understanding. Interview several experienced teachers to get their ideas on how to meet this challenge.

7. In a single classroom, observe a couple of lessons with different formats of instruction (e.g., whole-group content development, centers, discussion, testing). Respond in writing to the following questions: What types of lesson formats did you see? How did these formats differ in arrangement, procedures, and advance planning? What management techniques did the teacher use across these differences?

8. Go to either www.lessonplanspage.com or www.teachervision.fen.com, and select a few lesson plans. How well are they organized around powerful ideas, long-range goals, and supporting objectives and activities? If you were to teach from one of these plans, what changes would you make? Why?

# SCENARIO 6.1

Imagine that you are teaching one of the following classes (A or B). Select from the lesson ideas provided, and discuss in writing how you might sequence them in planning the unit described and why the sequence you are choosing would be effective. What additional lesson ideas do you have that would include other instructional formats?

A. Second-grade class's upcoming unit on plant growth, parts, and seed distribution; class has science scheduled for three 30-minute sessions per week—unit to last 2 weeks. Lesson ideas include
- Walking field trip to the school's front flower garden to meet a local Master Gardener and to learn about and plant spring flowers.
- Science center activity of "planting" five varieties of beans in a zipper bag with a wet paper towel. Bags are then taped to the window for observation and journaling.
- Literature lectures for the whole class that begin with a poem or children's book to introduce plant parts, plant growth, seed distribution, and plant life cycles.
- Local landscaper as guest speaker to bring varieties of flowering plants and discuss plant caretaking.

- Small-group watching of online videos of plant growth, seed distribution, and the plant life cycle.

B. Fifth-grade class's upcoming unit on state military history; class has social studies daily for 25 minutes—unit to last 2 weeks. Lesson ideas include
- Guest speaker: retired local National Guard officer with Gulf War service.
- Student pairs taking online tour of state museum exhibit "[State] at War"
- Small-group exploration of assigned military engagement (e.g., American Revolution, Civil War, WWII, Vietnam) by state's units/soldiers. Individuals from differing groups are then partnered to create Venn diagram comparing and contrasting the state's service in differing engagements.
- Whole-group lectures with photographs, maps, and charts on the state's involvement in select military engagements.
- Reading through a chapter on military history in the district-adopted textbook on the state (as individuals, small groups, or whole class).

# ■ Case Study 6.1

## A MATH LESSON IN A FOURTH-GRADE CLASS

As Mr. Case is about to begin class after lunch, he makes eye contact with two students who are exchanging notes; the students quickly get out their class materials. "Let's begin by working some of the exercises at the end of the chapter; you will need a piece of paper with a heading." As students begin to get out their materials, Mr. Case calls out, "Oops! I forgot to tell you to bring money for tomorrow for the field trip. How many of you will be going?" After a brief discussion, students finish getting out their materials. Mr. Case says, "We'll go through these exercises orally, but I also want you to write the answers on your papers as part of today's classwork. I'll come around later and check your answers. Now, who can answer the first question? Hands please. Tyrone?"

Mr. Case conducts the lesson by calling on various students, some with hands up, others seemingly at random from the nonvolunteers. About halfway through the exercises, a student enters the room and says that he is new to the school and has been assigned to the class. Mr. Case goes to his desk, sits down, and says, "Okay, come here. I'll check out some of your books to you. I wish the school office wouldn't send children in the middle of the day. Where are you from, anyway? That's a nice shirt you are wearing."

After finishing with the student and sending him to a seat, Mr. Case leaves his desk and says to the class, "Now where were we? Oh, yes, question 7. Say, where did Kim and Lee go? I didn't give them permission to leave."

After several more minutes, Mr. Case calls a halt to the activity and says, "Now, I'd like us to discuss the test coming up this Thursday. Let's make sure that you are all clear on what will be on the exam and what you will need to do to get ready for it." After a pause he adds, "I almost forgot. Get your questions from before, and look at the next to the last one. We have to add an important point that was left out. . . ." After finishing the item, Mr. Case turns the topic back to the upcoming test: "Now, where were we? Oh, yes. I want to show you some items that will be similar to those on the test. Here's one." He writes it on the board, then pauses: "Well, I don't want to give away the test, do I?"

Without discussing the test further, he turns to another topic: "Just wait until you hear about the video we will be viewing tomorrow. I saw it on another teacher's Web posting during lunch, and she said that her students thought it was one of the most interesting, exciting stories they had ever seen!"

## ■ Case Study 6.2

### A SCIENCE LESSON IN A SIXTH-GRADE CLASS

Ms. Lake has been having great difficulty obtaining acceptable or even completed work from many of her sixth-grade students. They never seem to be able to follow instructions or directions, even for assignments in the textbook. Only the most able four or five pupils are actually doing good-quality work. Ms. Lake likes to challenge the students with new ideas to stimulate their curiosity and promote independent thinking. Although much of the class appears to enjoy her presentations, the students don't seem to be able to transfer their enthusiasm to their assignments. For example, in a recent science assignment, students were supposed to draw pictures illustrating stages in the evolution of birds from reptiles; most students did not perform satisfactorily. The lesson preceding this assignment included a five-item test containing questions on birds, reptiles, and vertebrates, reviewing some content covered during the preceding week. Students checked their own answers to this test in class and then passed them in. Although it was not a difficult test, most students got three or fewer items correct. After the checking activity, the teacher began a 20-minute presentation on the possible evolution of birds from reptiles. The following topics were discussed:

- The meaning of adaptation, with an example supplied by students.
- An example of environmental action in the local community. This topic was introduced by a student, and other students added comments.
- The possibility of life on other planets, including a discussion of the number of solar systems in our galaxy.
- A consideration of the question of why birds might have evolved from reptiles, with a student's answer, "To get away from enemies, they would take to the air," as the only reason given.
- The classification system of living organisms: kingdom, phylum, class, order, family, genus, and species.

At this point in the presentation, students were instructed to copy the classification system from the board. Ms. Lake also provided an example of classification, using the lion in the animal kingdom, vertebrate phylum, mammal class, and so on. Two similar examples were also presented and listed on the board. The teacher asked whether students understood and whether they had any questions. No questions were forthcoming, so Ms. Lake gave the assignment of illustrating the stages in the evolution of a reptile to a bird. Students were given 25 minutes and told, "Use some color in your picture, make it neat, and use three stages." As was the case with many of the assignments Ms. Lake gave, only a few students completed their work satisfactorily, although most seemed to make an effort to do some drawing, and many students checked frequently with Ms. Lake to see whether their pictures were acceptable.

What problems are evident, and what changes might Ms. Lake make to achieve more success in helping students complete assignments satisfactorily?

MyEducationLab

Now go to www.myeducationlab.com to:

- Take a Quiz to test your mastery of chapter objectives.
- Study chapter content with an individualized Study Plan.
- Deepen your understanding of particular concepts and principles with Classroom Management Simulations.
- Apply what you have learned in the chapter to your work with children in Building Teaching Skills exercises.

## CHAPTER 7

# Managing Cooperative Learning Groups

Students in Mr. Stockton's fourth-grade class are seated at small tables in groups of three or four. In previous lessons, each group drew a design for a bridge after studying types of bridges and assembling reports on famous bridges around the world. Each group is currently constructing a model of its own design, using materials such as Popsicle sticks and tongue depressors, paper, glue, string, and rubber bands procured by the group's "materials manager" from the classroom supply center. The students are engrossed in the activity and proceed without much direction from their teacher, who circulates among the groups, encouraging, asking questions, and making occasional suggestions.

> When Bryce leaves his group to complain to Mr. Stockton that DaLynn is wasting materials that their group needs to finish the bridge, Mr. Stockton asks Bryce whether he has talked to DaLynn about the problem. He suggests that Bryce bring up the matter with the other students in their group to see whether they can resolve the difficulty before seeking his help. When another group stops working, Mr. Stockton goes to their table and suggests that they review their construction according to a list of criteria developed in an earlier class discussion.

### Vignette Reflection

With a partner, discuss your responses to the following questions: What is Mr. Stockton's role in this lesson? What is the students' role? What procedures does he already have in place? What preparations did he have to make for this specific lesson?

Mr. Stockton is using a form of instruction called *cooperative learning groups*. As the name implies, the method involves organizing students into small groups in which students complete assignments cooperatively, assist each other, solve problems, share materials, and participate in their own discussions. Teachers who use cooperative learning groups do so because they believe that the method increases learning and involvement. Many teachers also value the increased independence of students that results from an emphasis on group planning and decision making. These teachers describe their roles as being more facilitators than directors of group activities. Finally, teachers value the social skills and problem-solving abilities that students learn through frequent group work. These important life skills will serve students well in social settings in or out of school.

Using cooperative groups requires some modification of traditional managerial routines. A number of the procedures that you developed for managing work and behavior in whole-class and individual formats also apply to cooperative groups, but you will have to modify some of your procedures for talk and movement. In addition, your managerial tasks of pacing activities, monitoring, and giving feedback to students become especially important. Most important, you must teach your students the skills necessary for working effectively in groups.

# ■ Research on Cooperative Learning

Substantial research on cooperative learning has focused on its effects on achievement and other outcomes of interest, such as interpersonal relations, motivation, and student attitudes toward learning (Johnson & Johnson, 1994; Nastasi & Clements, 1991; Slavin, 1995). Explanations of the positive benefits of cooperative groups usually point to the students' increased engagement with the content as an important factor. Compared to large-class or individual work formats, small groups have greater potential for participation, feedback, and mutual construction of meaning among students. The group format encourages students to become active participants rather than passive recipients of information. Other explanations suggest that lower-achieving students profit from their peers' explanations, and high achievers benefit from constructing explanations for other students. All students can develop interpersonal skills through group tasks with a common goal. Furthermore, all can benefit from the support they receive in a cohesive group. Such support can help create positive norms for achievement and learning.

Although cooperative groups can improve learning and other outcomes for students, these results are by no means ensured simply by grouping students. Research has identified a number of strategies that you can use to promote the effectiveness of cooperative groups (Emmer & Gerwels, 2002; Gillies, 2007; Lotan, 2006). Such actions include teaching students how to work in groups, practicing the role of facilitator, carefully choosing and pacing academic activities, and promoting interdependence along with individual responsibility. Characteristics of more effective cooperative group lessons also include some form of daily accountability (versus later or no evaluation of individual or group performance), teacher monitoring of and feedback to groups, and the use of manipulative materials (Emmer & Gerwels, 2002).

The importance of these and other actions depends in part on your goals and the nature of group-based academic tasks. Some teachers use groups as the primary means of instruction and develop projects and an integrated curriculum to deliver much of their academic content. Other teachers use groups primarily as a supplement to whole-class and individual instruction in one or a few subject areas, relying on groups during the classwork portion of lessons to provide short practice activities. Whichever approach you adopt, you will find the strategies described in the remainder of this chapter to be helpful. You will, however, have to tailor them to your own application.

## ■ Examples of Group Activities

*In Ms. Liu's second-grade class, students work in pairs with a chart and a bag of plastic coins of various values. The chart has 10 rows, with columns headed by "Penny," "Nickel," "Dime," "Quarter," and "Half-Dollar." Ms. Liu asks the pairs to fill in the chart with coins to total a particular amount. After about 15 minutes, Ms. Liu has some of the pairs demonstrate their results using the overhead projector, and she leads a conversation about the many ways the same dollar amount can be achieved.*

*Mr. Garcia uses groups of three for reading comprehension activities. Students rotate in the roles of reader and questioner, depending on the day. Some days, before the activity begins, Mr. Garcia conducts a short whole-class discussion about how to ask and answer questions in the group. During the 20-minute activity, the teacher observes each group for 2 or 3 minutes, occasionally giving feedback or making a suggestion.*

*Ms. Dodd's fourth-grade class has been studying the culture and customs of the Quileute people. During one activity later in the unit, students choose tribal roles to dramatize in a "freeze frame." Each group of four or five students plans their dramatization to depict an important activity, such as whaling, in the Quileute culture. Ms. Dodd monitors, answers questions, and makes suggestions as she circulates among the groups during a 30-minute planning and rehearsal period. Afterward, each group enacts the freeze frame for the class. A follow-up discussion of each role play is conducted to clarify the depicted concepts.*

*Ms. Richardson's fifth-grade science class works in groups to build models of a go-cart, using wooden wheels of various sizes, sticks, rubber bands, paper clips, and other materials. In a sequence of three lessons, students explore various constructions to try to create self-propelled models that will travel various distances. Ms. Richardson encourages the groups to discover the effects of friction and wheel sizes, how to generate power, and how to transfer motion using an axle. Each student records observations in an individual notebook, but the construction is a group activity.*

### Vignette Reflection

Please discuss your responses to the following questions with a partner: What would students find attractive about the lessons depicted in these vignettes? What actions do these lessons require of the teachers to make sure they are effective? How are these lessons different from whole-group instruction? How might whole-group instruction be involved in these lessons?

The examples presented in these vignettes indicate the range of group activities possible in several content areas of the elementary curriculum. However, getting multiple groups to operate smoothly and productively requires planning by the teacher and preparation of the students. Try to visualize these groups in action, and imagine the repertoire of behaviors students need in order to engage successfully in the activity. Consider also how the physical setting of the classroom must be arranged to accommodate group activities. Note that the teacher's role during the group activity is less focused on giving information and more concerned with monitoring and giving feedback. This doesn't mean that teachers who use groups don't engage in teacher-led content development activities or use individual work exercises. Such activities are used, to varying degrees, along with group work.

We turn next to the procedures, routines, and teaching strategies that will help you manage group-based activities effectively.

# ■ Strategies and Routines That Support Cooperative Learning

## Beginning to Use Cooperative Learning Groups

Whether you begin to use groups at the start of the year or wait until later, you should address several matters. It is important that the physical arrangement of the classroom support the use of groups, especially if you intend to use them extensively. You should also teach the desired procedures for the groups as initial group tasks because you want a successful experience to set the stage for subsequent group activities. Group composition is important; students must be able to work constructively with each other and aid each other's learning. Additionally, you must plan how to teach the group attention signals needed for effective communication mid-lesson. Finally, it is critical to balance building group interdependence and simultaneously developing individual student accountability.

**Room Arrangement.**   If you plan to make extensive use of groups, arrange seating in groups rather than having students move to group seating each time the format is used. Some classrooms are equipped with tables. In the absence of tables, desks can be pushed together to form groups. To facilitate monitoring, seating should be arranged to permit your unrestricted movement among the groups. Remember also that groups will be talking among themselves as they complete projects. Try to arrange groups to minimize distraction from other groups' noise. Teachers often begin group activities with pairs of students and increase group size as students become familiar with the experience, but seating arrangements can still accommodate larger numbers, such as table groups of four.

In some classrooms, it is necessary to move from whole-class arrangements to small groups. In that case, mark the location of tables or desks in each arrangement, using masking tape on the floor. Many teachers have found that putting slit tennis balls on the bottoms of chair and table legs makes for quieter, quicker movement. Teachers can also mark the location of groups by hanging symbols or signs over their sites in the classrooms.

Storage of student materials is an integral part of room arrangement. Store materials for easy group access either at the group site in a collective container or in a location where a "materials manager" from each group can obtain them efficiently. Keeping the containers stocked is your responsibility as facilitator or can be designated as a classroom job. Individual materials can be kept in desks, on open closet shelves, or in a bookcase. Some teachers place a small box or bin in the middle of each table for materials to be used by everyone in the group. This eliminates the need for borrowing and reduces the need for trips to out-of-group storage areas (see also Chapter 2).

**Procedures and Routines.**   Don't assume that because students follow the rules during whole-class and independent work activities, they will automatically do so during group work. Instead, be prepared to teach students your specific expectations for talk and movement during group work. Teachers often report that when they begin using groups, they are bothered by the increased noise level. After a while they get used to it and are less anxious when they realize that the noise is coming from engaged, involved students. Nevertheless, to prevent excessive or extraneous noise, you should discuss with students your expectations about talk and give them guidelines. One common guideline is the use of "12-inch" voices. Another is to speak quietly enough so that students in nearby groups can't hear or aren't distracted. Using "whisper voices" does not work well as a guideline because groups usually can't work efficiently and conduct discussions while whispering. If noise becomes excessive, you can use a group attention signal to decrease noise to an acceptable level. If noise continues to be a problem, groups can work silently (communicating through written notes only) for the remainder of the session.

Discuss your expectations for appropriate behavior during movement and transitions. Emphasize the importance of everybody working toward the group's success. For example, provide a guideline such as "Stay with your group" or "Take care of out-of-group business promptly" to limit unnecessary wandering and visiting. Some movement is needed, of course, when students obtain materials.

Some teachers change group composition for various activities, resulting in movement during transitions between the activities. Such transitions can be real time wasters and make it difficult to start the next activity. An efficient routine is to announce the beginning of the transition, state the expectation, and tell students how much time they have to make the transition (e.g., "All of you must bring your materials and be in your group in 1 minute"). Continue to monitor throughout the transition to cut down on stragglers. You can also give students an expectation about what they are to do when they arrive at their group's location (e.g., "Sit in your seat and put your supplies—book, paper, pencil, and so on—on the table," or "Start work on your project right away").

In instances where the room must be rearranged for cooperative learning groups (e.g., where you share the classroom with another teacher), plan ahead to speed these transitions by marking the desired locations of the desks. Teach and practice movement into groups as you would any other procedure. As you teach group procedures, ask students for their views on what makes groups work well together; then incorporate their ideas in your guidelines for good group participation and cooperation.

**Forming Groups.**   At the beginning of the year, before you know your students very well, it may be instructive to allow students to choose partners for a few initial activities. Limit the length and scope of these activities, and monitor closely to make sure that no child feels left out. Your initial use of groups may involve pairs only, having the students simply check each other's work or discuss a question or problem. You might also use pairs to work on a class exercise or to practice spelling words or number facts. When pairs are used in such straightforward ways, most students do not have to move to new locations, and the activity is brief, placing fewer demands on the students and on you.

As groups are used more extensively, frequently, and with increasing levels of accountability, group membership becomes more critical. Teachers usually form groups ahead of time and seat students accordingly rather than have students move to new locations for group work, although that is not always the case. Different groups might be formed for math, for example, than for reading and social studies. It is helpful to have more than one grouping option planned in advance.

When assigning students to groups, a main consideration of most teachers is to represent in each group a range of achievement in the subject. A second concern is often to place a leader in each group (see the section on leadership skills later in this chapter). Teachers also try to avoid personality conflicts. Students who are argumentative often work best in groups that have a student with good leadership abilities, including social skills. Gender, English language fluency, artistic ability, and other traits can also be utilized to vary group composition to meet age- or grade-appropriate needs or to match the group task assigned.

Some teachers avoid placing in the same group students who are at extremes in achievement levels in the content area. For example, they would not place a very high achiever and a very low achiever in the same group, instead seeking less variation and pairing a midrange achiever with a very low achiever. These teachers' concern is that the pace of work and the discourse patterns in the groups with very high-achieving students may be inappropriate for and intimidating to the lower-performing students, resulting in their withdrawal and task avoidance. In groups having midrange achievers, the pace and vocabulary are more likely to encourage the lower achievers' participation. This principle obviously depends on the degree of social and explanatory skills possessed by the various students.

No hard-and-fast rules can be stated about how long groups should stay together. Some teachers change group membership frequently, as often as every few weeks. Most leave students in the same groups for longer times but shift membership at least a few times each year. Some teachers allow students to form their own groups for special activities or projects or as a change of pace, but rarely do they allow self-selected groups for an extended time, except for a special project. An alternative grouping technique is to group the students by interest. Place several topics or types of activities on the board. Have the children write down their first, second, and third choices. Collect the choices, and assign students to groups based on their first or second choice.

After groups are formed, they should be monitored for signs of conflict. Don't be too quick to step in with a solution, but do ask groups to address such problems. Giving students responsibility for dealing with group problems can create an opportunity for learning. As students acquire group skills and experience success in working together, conflict usually diminishes. When conflicts cannot be resolved in a reasonable time within a group, however, most teachers choose to move antagonistic students to new groups. Later in the year, when such students have become more adroit at cooperating, they might be given an opportunity to work together again.

## Group Attention Signals

When your students work in groups, you may have to stop their work to provide additional directions or to make a transition to another activity or task. You may also have to provide feedback to the whole class, modify some aspect of the assignment, or provide additional instruction. Also, noise may rise to unacceptable levels, requiring that you intervene. In all of these cases, you must interrupt students who are already engaged in a task or who are interacting with each other, making it difficult to gain their attention. The solution to this problem is to use a signal.

Efficient signals for group attention require that the students make an overt response, which interrupts whatever else they may be doing:

> The teacher says, "One, two, three," clapping as she does so. Students respond, "Eyes on me," and "Look at the teacher."

> The teacher says, "Thumbs up if you can hear me," "Fold your hands if you can hear me," or "Clap if you can hear me."

Each of these signals gains student attention by requiring that students substitute a behavior, thus effectively stopping the prior activity. These signals are especially useful when students are working with manipulatives, which might distract them from attending.

Sometimes a signal may be used to pace students through a transition between activities. A signal is especially helpful when the transition involves the movement of students from one location to another. The following signals may be used for such transitions, as well as to gain student attention:

> The teacher claps rhythmically, first twice, then three times. Students pick up the clapping rhythm: After the teacher claps twice, they clap in unison three times.

> The teacher turns off the light, then begins clapping and counting, "Ten, nine, eight, seven, six, . . . one, zip." Students pick up the count as they complete the prior activity, clap, and repeat "zip" in unison with the teacher, "zipping" their lips at the end.

Bell ringing and a simple oral direction such as "Stop, look, listen" are useful signals when students are not as interactively engaged, thus requiring a less dramatic or intrusive stimulus to get their attention. Teach several signals to avoid overworking one of them and to give you some options. Finally, avoid interrupting students unnecessarily. Present information or directions ahead of time or post them on a board to minimize the need to break into ongoing student activities. When appropriate, give reminders to individual groups rather than to the whole class.

## Promoting Interdependence within the Group

Positive interdependence has occurred when either the group's product or the individual's performance is enhanced by the actions of the group members. In addition to improving performance, interdependence builds group cohesion and helps create group norms that support learning. Interdependence can be fostered in a number of ways:

- Each student can be responsible for contributing a unique component to the group's product. For example, students might do research on different aspects of a topic for a group report.
- Each student chooses a specific part of a topic to teach to the rest of the group. Or in groups of four students, pairs work together to prepare information for the other two students in the group.
- In groups of two, students work as drill partners to help each other learn.
- The teacher assigns roles to students (e.g., reader, checker, recorder, materials manager) to ensure that each student makes a contribution to the group's activity.

- Group assignments (e.g., projects, reports, performances, constructions, oral group presentations) can be given a group grade, recognition, points, or some other reward.

## Individual Accountability

When group assignments are the outcome, establishing group accountability—for example, by giving the group's product a grade or by asking the group to report orally—may not be sufficient for some students, who may be content to loaf or ride other students' coattails. Group members may also miss content if some of the group's members dominate the task. Individual accountability in the context of a group-based assignment may be increased in several ways:

- Require that individual students perform an identifiable portion of the group assignment.
- Ask groups to turn in a list identifying each student's contribution to the final product.
- Ask students to record observations in individual notebooks that you will collect and grade at various times.
- Have students turn in individual work along with the group's product.
- Require that students keep a daily record of their individual work in spiral notebooks.
- Let students know that when their group reports to the class, each student should be ready to explain his or her work.
- Have selected students report individually on their group work.
- Give students a quiz based on the group assignment.

You can foster individual responsibility when you set expectations: Stress to students that even though they are working on a group assignment, each member is responsible for learning the material. Tell them that it's important for all members of a group to help the others understand what they are learning, and for each person to contribute. Finally, when you monitor group work, note participation by individual students. If some are not contributing, try to determine why not; then take corrective measures such as redirecting those students. When simple interventions don't work, teachers often ask the group to help solve the problem, or they may have a conference with the student to try to assess the situation and to work out a solution.

Maintaining individual responsibility in a group setting is not easy. Adding individual assessments on top of group assessments may increase the amount of time the teacher must spend on planning and preparation as well as evaluation. Moreover, focusing on individual accountability may deflect attention from group outcomes. Procedures for accountability, therefore, should be planned carefully and amended as necessary until you develop a balance between accountability needs and available time and energy. If difficulties cannot be resolved, reconsider whether cooperative learning is the best format for the content you are teaching.

# ■ Group Tasks

The quality of the tasks you develop and assign to groups is of significance to their ability to complete them successfully. Initially, you will want to plan tasks that help groups focus on learning the procedures of working together as well as developing group work skills.

> *Mrs. Walker focused on one group work skill per week until her fifth graders developed an effective repertoire by the end of the first six weeks of the school year. During the first week, she emphasized participating during group work; the second week, she focused on remaining on task. Subsequent weeks were devoted to cooperating, encouraging, explaining, and active listening. Mrs. Walker introduced each skill in a whole-class discussion, soliciting examples, suggestions, and a rationale from her students. During the first week, she displayed a five-point rating scale for "participating" and indicated what she would be looking for as students worked in groups. At the end of several group activities that week, she engaged students in a discussion about the skill, asked them to review their performance, and shared her assessment of student participation with the individual groups. In each subsequent week, Mrs. Walker added a new scale, so that groups received feedback about their progress in acquiring the skills.*

### Vignette Reflection

Respond to the following questions in conversation with a partner: Why might Mrs. Walker have chosen the sequence she did for these group work skill lessons? How did her pacing impact the students' understanding of these skills and their importance to group work? What other group work skills might she want to practice with her class?

## Initial Group Tasks

Students who don't have much experience with working in groups will have to develop their skills in uncomplicated tasks rather than in complex projects. It's important not to rush into group work before you have built a foundation of practice and skills. Beginning groups find tasks easier in simpler formats with uncomplicated procedures, such as the ones described next. After your students have had success in some of these initial group tasks, they will be ready for more complex group formats and assignments.

- **Drill partners.** Partners practice material that must be memorized.
- **Reading buddies.** Students read to each other. The teacher can build on this after a while by asking students to summarize or make up questions for their partners.
- **Summarizing.** Partners take turns retelling directions, content, or other material in summary form.
- **Checking.** Students compare answers and resolve discrepancies. Each student must be able to explain the answer.

■ **Reviewers.** Students review for a quiz or test or prepare for an oral report by working together to develop questions. They ask and answer each other's questions.

## Teaching Group Work Skills

A good way to begin the teaching process for group work skills is to have a whole-class discussion about what is needed to work cooperatively. To build a rationale for working together, some teachers like to broaden the discussion to include home, playground, and neighborhood as well as classroom groups, and to discuss the character and life skills needed. Eventually, of course, the discussion has to address concrete behaviors that constitute good social, explanatory, and leadership skills in groups.

**Social Skills.**   Active listening includes listening to others without interrupting, being able to summarize others' ideas, incorporating them into the ongoing discussion, and using them constructively in completing the group's assignment. Sharing materials and taking turns are also necessary for effective cooperation. Another important social skill is giving support, which includes accepting differences, being friendly, and encouraging others. Students who lack social skills may insist on doing things their way, may argue frequently, ignore or put down another student's contributions, or fail to participate in the group's work.

The ability to work in a group depends on social skills, so teachers usually emphasize their development and reinforce appropriate use of social skills throughout the year. They may even teach certain phrases for students to use in summarizing, questioning, or expressing disagreement.

**Explanatory Skills.**   Explanatory skills are an important aspect of group work, and they are critical to the development of academic outcomes. Indicators of explanatory skills are comments that describe a problem, assignment, or goal. Student comments might also identify steps to be accomplished or followed to complete a task, as well as reasons for the steps. Students might summarize the work they have done or plan to do. If a group assignment includes answering questions, students can give their answers and explain how they arrived at them.

Another important component of the explanatory process is seeking explanations from others. This may involve students' describing what they do and do not understand and asking for help from other group members. Such requests are unlikely to occur unless other students in the group practice good social skills. To encourage students to seek help, the teacher might say, "No one knows everything. If there's something you don't understand, it's smart to ask for help from the group. And if someone asks for help, the friendly thing to do is to give a good explanation."

Interactions about content are essential to the process of constructing meaning. They enhance comprehension and are critical to learning. Most students need encouragement to engage in these behaviors because conversations about content are not a natural part of their interactions. Some ways to encourage them include these:

- Model for students several ways of summarizing and clarifying using available text material. Then ask students to practice in pairs, alternating roles of explainer and listener.
- Ask students to turn to a partner and explain something (a process or a concept); then have the partner "explain back" what he or she heard.
- Have each student in the group write one question; then have the members of the group answer it.
- Conduct role plays of asking for help and explaining; demonstrate and discuss the examples portrayed.
- Lead a discussion about how to give a good explanation and how to ask for help.
- Have students write their group's ideas on a chart and present them to the class.

**Leadership Skills.**   When a group has someone who steps up and says, "Let's figure out what we need to do to get this job done," it has someone who is practicing a leadership skill. Desired attributes include demonstrating initiative, planning, and enthusiasm. Good social skills also complement this repertoire, as does basic competence in the content relevant to the group's task. Teachers can help students develop leadership skills by assigning roles such as presenter or discussion leader, which give students the opportunity to demonstrate initiative and gain confidence. Such roles should be defined clearly and the tasks delineated. Roles should be rotated so that every student gets an opportunity for practice.

Most teachers value leadership skills highly and try to form groups with at least one student who exhibits them "naturally." It is also wise to help the natural leader learn to take direction from the assigned leader when it is that student's turn. Although leadership skills are developed over time and students possess them in varying degrees, all students can make some progress toward learning and achieving them.

Some group skills can be taught by assigning roles to individual students in a group. Roles such as materials manager, recorder, discussion leader, encourager, discussant, or reporter entail the use of specific skills. By assigning some of these roles to students, teachers encourage them to practice new behaviors. Rotating the roles among group members permits all students to gain experience in the skills. Using roles also helps promote interdependence among the group members because each student has a unique job to perform for the group. Roles that are frequently used can be written on cards, along with key behaviors, and laminated. Posters with role descriptions can also be displayed in easy-to-see locations until students have mastered the basics.

Posting desired group behaviors, providing students with examples, and modeling desired group behaviors are important and should be accompanied by practice and feedback. Remember that it takes many weeks for some students to become comfortable with the new demands of group participation. Be patient. Rather than reviewing all desirable group skills, pick one and spend time discussing it. Let students practice it, and give them feedback as they work in groups. Introduce other skills in subsequent days or weeks.

As in the vignette of Mrs. Walker, the use of scales is one way to focus students on specific components of group work. Another way is to conduct whole-class discussions about group work activities. Begin with a request that students evaluate an aspect of their group work, indicating what went well and what could be improved. Or they might be asked to describe how someone in their group performed one of the group skills effectively. Students might also describe what makes it difficult to perform a particular skill and how that problem might be overcome. Getting students to talk about their group experience is one of the best ways to help them develop good monitoring and self-regulation skills.

# ■ Monitoring Student Work and Behavior

Good monitoring of group work requires that you be on your feet and walking among the groups, scanning the rest of the class, just as you do when monitoring any classroom activities. Try not to spend too much time with any one group at the expense of another. Goals for monitoring include keeping track of individual performance, behavior, and growth in academic areas, as well as group performance and skills. A complicating factor is the extent to which individual versus group performance must be distinguished.

The way teachers keep track of student work in groups depends on the nature of the group activity. When individual assignments are used and the group's function is to support individual learning, monitoring academic performance is completed by circulating among the groups and noting individual performance. You can also collect the individual assignments and check them. Critical to the effective utilization of groups for the support of individual learning is the quality of interaction among students—that is, providing explanations and demonstrations for each other rather than simply giving answers or ignoring peers' questions. Remember that the best way to teach appropriate helping behaviors is to model them yourself.

An effective monitoring technique is the use of a clipboard that contains student names and space to record ratings or notes about performance and behavior during group activities. When this technique is used, it encourages teachers to obtain information about all students, not just the active, visible ones. The information can be used later to give feedback to groups and individuals or to add to performance evaluations. The use of this strategy as seldom as once or twice a week can add important information about individuals and supplement other types of monitoring.

With group assignments, the focus of monitoring shifts to the group's collective progress, along with individual performance. If you provide checkpoints and time limits, you will not only give yourself monitoring milestones, but also help students self-monitor. Asking groups to report to you on their progress, plans, or difficulties also provides information about comprehension that you might not obtain through observation alone. It may be additionally beneficial to include an individual component in a collective assignment. For example, ask students to record individual observations, solve a problem, or write a summary of their contribution to the group's project. Not only do such data increase your information about each student's achievement, but the procedure improves individual accountability.

Group work skills are an important concern when monitoring (see the previous section). As is the case with academic skills, students vary in their understanding and use of cooperative behaviors. Posted checklists and a careful program of teaching students important group work skills go a long way toward helping the students self-monitor, but you should also pay attention to the extent to which individuals and groups operate appropriately. Students sometimes complain about group grades because they feel that they have contributed more than other group members to the group's product. At the beginning of each group assignment, spend time explaining to the class how individual and group progress will be assessed, and structure and monitor group tasks carefully to see that all students are participating.

Teachers use various indicators to determine satisfactory group functioning. Because students usually have a specific task to perform in the group, it is not difficult to determine whether they are engaged in a suitable activity. When students are talking with each other about the task and performing behaviors needed to complete an assignment such as writing, assembling materials, practicing, or constructing, teachers can easily identify appropriate, on-task behavior. Teachers also watch for signs that individual students may be uninvolved or disengaged. Momentary off-task behavior can usually be ignored, but if it is prolonged, intervention may be needed. Another indicator is the level and nature of emotionality that students exhibit. Students' tense, angry, or hostile behaviors suggest frustration or potential conflicts that could escalate and therefore call for early intervention to prevent the development of more serious problems.

# ◼ Interventions for Groups

Interventions for groups are closely tied to the monitoring features just described. The most common interventions are simple, easy to use, and brief. During the initial stages of group work, when students are acquiring group skills, it is especially important that appropriate behaviors be identified and supported. Interventions with students who aren't practicing good group behaviors can sometimes be addressed as a group problem: "Roberto isn't participating yet. What can the group do to let him know that it supports his participation?" At other times, discussing the situation with the individual student may be the best way to encourage attempts to practice group behaviors. Students who persist in inappropriate behaviors may be given a short time-out (such as 1 or 2 minutes, initially) or sent to work alone for a longer time if they don't respond to milder interventions. Other interventions for individuals are described in detail in Chapter 10.

At times, teachers find that using rewards is helpful as an extra motivational tool to encourage students to practice appropriate group skills or to improve the participation of undermotivated students.

> *Mr. Galvan used a weekly raffle system, rewarding students with "tickets" for desirable group behavior. A group could also receive bonus tickets when all of its members did well on an assignment. Students initialed their tickets, and at the end of the week, Mr. Galvan drew four or five from a box; winners received small toys or privileges as prizes.*

*Ms. Frank gave points to groups for desirable behaviors, such as getting ready or cleaning up promptly, helping and sharing, or listening and explaining. She awarded points during group work, for example, by telling a group, "The way you have been explaining your ideas to each other has helped your group demonstrate active listening. You have earned a group point." She also awarded points during wrap-up discussions with the whole class, noting that she observed good examples of desirable behavior during group work. She kept a tally of points for each group on the board; when a group reached a set number of points, its reward was to eat lunch with Ms. Frank in the classroom.*

## Vignette Reflection

Discuss with a partner your responses to the following questions: How might the use of rewards help these groups succeed? How might the rewards motivate students? What dangers might there be with using rewards in this setting?

Judicious use of rewards can direct student attention to important behaviors and make it more likely that students will employ them. Group rewards, moreover, can strengthen cohesiveness through a common goal and the shared positive feelings that result when the group succeeds. However, as noted in Chapter 8 in the discussion on intrinsic motivation, extrinsic rewards should be a supplement to more natural consequences of student accomplishment, such as recognition, positive feedback, other forms of praise, and the satisfaction that accompanies learning and goal attainment. As long as these consequences are abundant, the use of additional group and individual reinforcers should not interfere with intrinsic motivation.

When interventions are needed for noncompliance or misbehavior, conferences with students can be used more readily during group work than during whole-class activities. The teacher can meet individually with one student or a group because other students are engaged in the group activity. Such conferences typically last for a short time—less than a minute—and consist of feedback to the student or group, along with redirection and a plan for changing the behavior. A brief conference allows the teacher to offer an alternate behavior and to provide feedback on the spot, rather than delaying it so long that it would prove ineffective.

Teachers engage groups in a conference when a group process has broken down. Examples include groups in which students don't ask for or give assistance constructively, make poor progress toward the group's goal, or encounter a problem that they aren't able to overcome. Teachers often describe their role as that of facilitator or mediator in this type of conference. Although the teacher may provide feedback about the problem and a reality check for the group's perceptions, students are encouraged to solve the problem themselves. Strategies teachers use to facilitate a solution include asking the students to identify the problem, asking them to suggest alternatives, asking for reactions and comments, and calling for the group to select one different approach to try. As a last resort, teachers may offer a solution or change group membership if the problem proves intractable.

# ■ Student Goals and Participation

Students should be told the purpose of their group work and given direction about how they are to proceed, consistent with the task they are to accomplish. Cohen (1994) makes an important distinction in the nature of group tasks. She summarizes research indicating that the nature of a teacher's directions depends on the degree to which the group's task is structured. For outcomes that are well defined and for which there is a limited range of suitable strategies (e.g., completing a worksheet, performing a specific laboratory procedure, answering comprehension questions, reviewing material presented in a text or by the teacher), teachers can give explicit instructions about steps to follow and can monitor the groups for satisfactory progress. On such tasks, the teacher might prepare a list of steps that should be followed and then display it on a board or handout. A student can be assigned to monitor, noting when a step has been completed, or the whole group can be asked to keep track of its progress.

However, when the task is less structured, the nature of the product and steps to achieve it are not as evident, nor is there an easily identifiable strategy. Teachers then must be less directive about how the group proceeds. The teacher might delegate some responsibility to the group to decide on its procedures and to select appropriate resources. Typically, the goal of such group tasks includes higher-order thinking and problem solving. Too explicit a set of directions about how to proceed might stifle the types of thinking such a task is intended to promote.

Suppose a teacher's goal in assigning the development of a group report is to promote critical thinking and problem solving about the topic. If the teacher is highly directive about how the group is to function and what resources it can use, the students may simply try to develop a report that satisfies *pro forma* the assignment requirements. If, however, the teacher's directions offer the students latitude, and if responsibility is delegated, there is a better chance that students will draw on their own creativity and be more engaged in the group process. Effectively utilizing cooperative groups requires attention to designing and assigning tasks in ways that allow groups to excel.

# ■ Chapter Summary

Use of cooperative learning groups in the classroom can increase student participation and engagement and simultaneously teach content and interpersonal skills. However, such groups can also be sources of difficulty if not managed effectively. Managing cooperative learning groups requires monitoring, facilitating, and guiding in order to intervene as needed. Teacher interventions support group problem solving and assist student development of group work skills. These skills include social skills (e.g., sharing, active listening), explanatory skills (e.g., demonstrating, summarizing), and leadership skills (e.g., planning, delegating). Like the beginning of the school year, the initial use of cooperative learning groups requires thorough planning that includes preparation for room arrangement, group structure, group tasks, group skill instruction, student participation, communication, the roles of individual students, the development of group coherence, and rewards for individuals as well as groups.

# ■ Further Reading

Cohen, E. G. (1998). Making cooperative learning equitable. *Educational Leadership, 56,* 18–21.

> *Status differences among students reduce the participation and learning of lower-status students. Cohen provides some practical strategies teachers can use to improve lower-status students' opportunities, including teacher emphasis on the multiple abilities needed to accomplish many group tasks and altering student expectations about the competence of lower-status students.*

Gillies, R. M. (2007). *Cooperative learning: Integrating theory and practice.* Los Angeles: Sage.

> *The author presents numerous case studies and a thorough description of cooperative learning and strategies for implementation. The book brings together a range of powerful teaching strategies connected to students taking responsibility for their own learning and the learning of others.*

Johnson, D. W., & Johnson, F. P. (2005). *Joining together: Group theory and group skills* (9th ed.). Boston: Allyn & Bacon.

> *This text presents a broad, integrative overview of group dynamics in a well researched, readable, and experiential format. It introduces the theory and research findings on how to make groups effective and build skills required to apply that research to practice.*

Slavin, R. E. (1995). *Cooperative learning: Research, theory, and practice* (2nd ed.). Boston: Allyn & Bacon.

> *This authoritative book provides a good overview of cooperative learning approaches along with a careful description of research. The author has done extensive research and development in this field, and this book provides a thorough review of his and his colleagues' work.*

clte.asu.edu/active/usingtps.pdf

> *Susan Ledlow of the Center for Learning and Teaching Excellence at Arizona State University provides an overview of the Think-Pair-Share cooperative learning structure. It can be used for higher-level thinking as well as for basic review and recall. The steps and potential extensions are spelled out in this brief article.*

www.co-operation.org

*This Web site for the Cooperative Learning Center at the University of Minnesota gives detailed information about cooperative learning and how it is accomplished.*

# ■ Suggested Activities

1. Return to the vignettes of Mr. Stockton, Mrs. Walker, Mr. Galvan, and Ms. Frank across the chapter. Discuss with a partner what unique management was required for these teachers' use of cooperative learning.

2. Observe in a classroom using cooperative learning. As you do so, note room arrangement features and routines that support group learning. Use the Checklist at the end of the chapter as an observation guide.

3. Choose a lesson (from observation, online, or a teacher's edition) that was designed for an individual or whole-class instructional format. Identify ways to use cooperative learning groups to teach that lesson. Discuss the modifications you would make to incorporate concepts presented in this chapter.

4. In a group, discuss problems associated with fostering individual responsibility in a group-based task, as well as how to give feedback to individuals about academic performance and individual behaviors in the group setting. What are some workable, efficient strategies for enhancing responsibility and providing feedback?

5. Reread Case Study 5.2, which illustrates one teacher's approach to introducing cooperative groups at the beginning of the year. Compare your ideas for *a* and *b* with the key in the Appendix.
   a. Note concepts described in this chapter that are evident in Ms. James's procedures and strategies. What functions do the associated procedures and strategies serve?
   b. Are any areas discussed in this chapter not present in Ms. James's classroom during the first three days? Would you suggest introducing them? Why or why not?
   c. Ms. James teaches in a departmentalized fifth-grade math class. What changes might be appropriate for earlier grades? for different content areas?

6. Review plans for cooperative group lessons by going to the Web. To find examples of cooperative group lessons, type "sample cooperative group lesson plans" in a search engine. Share a favorite lesson plan with colleagues. What management issues could arise if you were to teach this lesson? Get feedback from others in your group.

7. Supporters of the use of cooperative learning emphasize the interdependent nature of social life, including work and family settings. They also emphasize the social nature of learning and the importance of interaction in constructing meaning. Some educators and commentators, however, have expressed concerns about overreliance on groups, arguing that group learning wastes time, especially that of gifted students who must help their less able peers. These critics also dislike the focus on group rather than individual

performance. What is your position on these issues? Should groups be used more or less frequently in your teaching field? to accomplish which goals? How do your responses reflect your philosophy of education?

# ■ Checklist: Planning for Cooperative Group Instruction

| Check When Complete | Item | Notes |
|---|---|---|
| | **Beginning Cooperative Learning Groups** | |
| ☐ | A. How will student seating be arranged? | _____ |
| ☐ | B. How will individual and group materials and supplies be stored? | _____ |
| ☐ | C. What are your expectations for student movement to, from, and during group work? | _____ |
| ☐ | D. What expectations about talk will you communicate to students? | _____ |
| ☐ | E. How will you form groups? | _____ |
| ☐ | F. What group attention signals will be used? | _____ |
| ☐ | G. Will students have specific roles? | _____ |
| ☐ | H. How will you build group interdependence? | _____ |
| ☐ | I. What initial tasks will groups do? | _____ |
| ☐ | J. Do any group work skills have to be discussed, modeled, or practiced? | _____ |
| | **Monitoring Student Work and Behavior** | |
| ☐ | A. Will group work have individual products, group products, or both? | _____ |
| ☐ | B. How will individual or group work be assessed? | _____ |
| ☐ | C. How will you monitor student behavior and work during group activities? | _____ |

☐    D. How will students receive feedback about individual and group performance?

_____

☐    E. How will students receive feedback about their behavior in groups?

_____

**Interventions for Groups**

☐    A. How will you encourage good group work skills?

_____

☐    B. How will you redirect struggling groups?

_____

☐    C. How will you redirect individual students?

_____

---

## MyEducationLab

Now go to www.myeducationlab.com to:

- Take a Quiz to test your mastery of chapter objectives.
- Study chapter content with an individualized Study Plan.
- Deepen your understanding of particular concepts and principles with Classroom Management Simulations.
- Apply what you have learned in the chapter to your work with children in Building Teaching Skills exercises.

**CHAPTER 8**

# Maintaining Appropriate Student Behavior

As you have seen in the preceding chapters, good classroom management depends on careful planning of the classroom's organization, rules, procedures, initial activities, and instruction. This planning and preparation will pay large dividends when the students arrive. However, being ready is not enough. To sustain their good behavior throughout the year, you will have to be actively involved in maintaining student cooperation and compliance with necessary classroom norms, rules, and procedures. You cannot assume that students will behave appropriately just because you carefully taught them what was expected of them. In primary grades, children are in the early stages of learning going-to-school skills, so you will need to pay constant attention to prompting good behavior. Even in the intermediate grades, children need teachers who encourage good behavior by implementing their rules, procedures, and consequences consistently.

In particular, don't be lulled into complacency by the good behavior of your students at the beginning of the year. Most elementary classes are quiet and subdued on the first day or two of school. Without your careful attention to *maintaining* good behavior, even a class that begins very well may ultimately become disruptive and difficult to control. The following example illustrates such a class.

*Ms. White carefully discussed her classroom rules and procedures with her fifth-grade class at various times on the first several class days, and students were generally well behaved. However, at the start of the third week, problems are beginning to occur. While leading a whole-class discussion, Ms. White stands at the front board to jot down important points. When she turns to write on the board, students at the back of the room begin talking quietly among themselves. During quiet work time, some pass notes, throw paper wads, and wander around the room. If Ms. White reprimands students for talking, they say they do not understand what to do and are asking for help from others. If she allows students to help each other, before long everyone is talking, few are working, and the noise level increases.*

*At first, students raised their hands for permission to speak. Later, some students called out comments, and rather than ignore the contributions, Ms. White began to accept them when they were substantive. Now, more and more students have become loud and distracting. Because discussion activities do not seem to work well, Ms. White has begun to reduce the amount of time spent on these activities and to assign more individual work.*

*During reading instruction, Ms. White meets with students in small groups while the rest of the class works on individual assignments. While working with the small group, Ms. White is interrupted more and more frequently by students who are having problems with individual assignments. At other times, her small-group instruction is interrupted by misbehavior outside the group. At the end of the small-group instruction period, Ms. White frequently is dismayed to see what little progress students have made on their independent work.*

### Vignette Reflection

With a partner, discuss your responses to the following questions: Beyond what Ms. White might have read in the previous chapters, what is she still missing? What actions or inactions on her part are potentially leading to student misbehavior? What suggestions might you offer to her?

Problems such as those occurring in Ms. White's class often have a gradual onset, developing over several weeks or even months. It is usually possible to avoid these problems, but to do so you must first understand why they occur and what you can do to prevent them. Because they develop gradually, their causes are not always apparent to the teacher or even to an observer unfamiliar with the history of the classroom. This chapter explores four important guidelines that will help Ms. White—and you—to prevent or handle the onset of misbehavior:

- Monitor student behavior and academic progress carefully.
- Be consistent in the use of procedures, rules, and consequences.
- Manage inappropriate behavior promptly.
- Maintain a positive climate with an emphasis on reinforcing appropriate behavior.

## ■ Monitoring Student Behavior

To monitor classroom behavior effectively, you must know what to look for. Two categories of behavior are especially important to monitor:

1. Student involvement in learning activities
2. Student compliance with classroom rules and procedures

Shoe–New Business © 1981 Macnelly. Distributed by King Features Syndicate.

Student involvement is indicated by many behaviors, including attention during presentations and discussions and satisfactory progress in individual work and other assignments. Student compliance with classroom rules and procedures is easy to monitor if you have clear expectations for behavior and have effectively taught them to the class.

Monitoring behavior during *whole-class presentations* requires that you stand or sit where you can see the faces of all students and that you scan the room frequently. During your presentations, try to move around and develop "active eyes." If you notice a commotion involving several students and you have no idea what is going on, this is a sign that you have not been monitoring closely enough. This happens easily when teachers focus their attention on a limited number of students (usually those seated in the middle rows or tables and at the front desks) or when they "talk to the board." In either case, the teacher does not have a very clear perception of overall response to the presentation, nor is the teacher fully aware of what may be occurring at the periphery of the classroom.

When instructing a *small group* of students while the remainder of the class is engaged in individual work, sit where you have an unobstructed view of all students. Don't become so absorbed in working with the small group that you lose track of the other students. Look up frequently, and be alert for problems. After finishing with one group, circulate around the room, and provide needed assistance before calling the next small group.

Monitoring *cooperative groups* can present special challenges. To be sure each group understands your expectations, move quickly from group to group as students begin to work. Then return and spend more time with each group, listening and occasionally contributing as a group member. Remember to move through the class for a quick scan between each visit with a group. In this way, you can gather information about the group's progress, provide a model for participation in a group, help guide discussions to higher levels, and still maintain a grasp of the larger picture.

When students are working on *individual assignments* and you are not instructing a group, monitor the class by moving around the classroom and checking each student's progress periodically. You will, of course, help students who request assistance; however, you should not just "chase hands," or you will not be aware of the progress of other students. One way to prevent having to chase hands is to establish a procedure by which students can ask questions of members of their group or their neighbors. This can free you to work with other students.

It is difficult to monitor progress on assignments from your desk or from any other fixed location, so don't spend too much time in one place. If you must work at your desk for an extended time, get up periodically, and circulate around the room, looking at each student's work. If you must spend a long time (more than a minute or two) helping an individual student, avoid doing it at the student's desk unless you can monitor the rest of the class from that position. If the student's seat is in the middle of the room, for instance, half of the class will be behind you. In such a case, call the student to a small-group worktable, to your desk, or to some other location from which you can easily see the other students. Finally, when you work at your desk or at any other location, don't let students congregate around that area. They will obstruct your view of the class, and they will probably distract students seated nearby. Instead, call students to you one at a time.

A critical monitoring task is *checking assignments*. Collect them regularly, and look them over, even when students check their own work in class. Keep your grade book current so you will be able to detect students who skip assignments. If you give a long-term assignment, check progress regularly. You may even give a grade or assign points toward a grade at these times. In upper elementary grades, students can keep a checklist of assignments and due dates.

Because an important part of monitoring is *checking student progress* and understanding, build into your assignments ways to monitor these areas. For example, ask small groups to report on their progress; have individuals make and update daily or weekly work plans; follow up individual work time with brief discussions of concepts and with oral checks for understanding (see also Chapter 6).

# ■ Being Consistent with Procedures and Consequences

In the classroom, consistency means retaining the same expectations for appropriate behavior at all times and for all students. If students are expected to work silently during independent work on Monday, the same procedure must be in effect on Tuesday and the rest of the week. Penalties should be applied consistently. If the penalty for missing assignments is losing one's place on an honor list, the teacher must make sure that all students who skip assignments receive the penalty. This procedure should be followed even when it is inconvenient to administer and in spite of the pleading of individual students for exceptions. Obvious inconsistency in the use of procedures or in the application of penalties can cause confusion about what is acceptable behavior. Students then frequently test the limits by not following the procedure or by repeating whatever behavior evoked the penalty. These events can rapidly escalate and force the teacher either to abandon the procedure or to tolerate high levels of inappropriate behavior. Because neither outcome is desirable, you should avoid the problem by learning to be consistent from the start. Of course, it is important to recognize there are occasions when the most reasonable course of action is to make an exception to a rule or procedure. For example, a deadline for an assignment may be extended when a student has a death in the family, or a procedure for lining up in alphabetical order might be ignored during an emergency. Note that using certain procedures routinely for some activities but not for others is not inconsistent. For example, you may require that no students leave their seats without permission during discussions or presentations, but you may allow them to get materials, sharpen pencils, or turn in papers as needed without permission during individual work time. Differentiate between these activities when you teach these procedures to the students.

Maintaining a consistent policy for student talk can be complicated by the need for student interaction during some activities. For example, during small-group activities, task-appropriate, student-to-student interaction is encouraged, whereas in some independent work assignments, student talk has to be limited. During other independent work activities, students may need to talk to help each other. Such apparent inconsistency can be confusing. One way to manage the varying expectations for talk is to introduce the activities gradually, provide a rationale, and explain the expectations clearly for each activity type. For instance, begin the year with a "no talking" procedure for independent work; once students are acclimated to this policy, introduce independent activities with relevant on-task talking permitted, and provide a signal that identifies when talking is allowed. You might post a sign with the names of common activities that have "talk" expectations (e.g., groups, independent seat work, study pairs) and then use movable arrows labeled "on-task talking," "quiet voices," or "silent work."

Undesirable inconsistency usually arises from three sources: First, the procedures or rules as presented are not reasonable, workable, or appropriate. Second, the teacher fails to monitor students closely and detects only a fraction of the inappropriate behavior, creating the appearance of inconsistency. Third, the teacher may not feel strongly enough about the procedure or rule to enforce it or to use the associated penalty. If you find yourself being inconsistent in ways that cause problems, consider these alternatives:

1. Reteach the procedure. Take a few minutes to discuss the problem with the class and to reiterate your desire that they follow the procedure. Then enforce it consistently.
2. Modify the procedure or consequence, and then reintroduce and use it consistently.
3. Abandon the procedure or consequence, and possibly substitute another in its place. Note: Options 2 and 3 are not valid for schoolwide procedures, such as obtaining a tardy slip before entering class late. As part of a faculty, your role is to be consistent with the stated rules and procedures. If you disagree with these, follow the designated paths for voicing your opinion and offering alternative suggestions.

Your choice of alternatives depends on the circumstances and the importance of the issue to your classroom management system.

# ■ Managing Inappropriate Behavior

Inappropriate behavior must be handled promptly to keep it from continuing and spreading. Behaviors that you should be concerned about include lack of involvement in learning activities, prolonged inattention or work avoidance, and obvious violations of classroom rules and procedures. Lack of involvement prevents you from assessing students' understanding of content and/or allows students to stay disconnected from the learning community. Prolonged inattention makes it difficult for the students to learn and to complete assignments, and violations of rules and failure to follow procedures create many problems we have already discussed. These behaviors should be dealt with directly but without overreaction. A calm, reasoned tone or approach is more productive and less likely to lead to confrontation. The following alternatives are recommended:

**1.** Make eye contact with or move closer to the student. Use a signal, such as a finger to the lips or a head shake, to prompt the appropriate behavior. Monitor until the student complies.

**2.** If the student is not following a procedure correctly, a simple reminder of the correct procedure may be effective. You can either state the correct procedure or ask the student whether he or she remembers it.

**3.** When the student is off task—that is, not working on an assignment—redirect his or her attention to the task: "Sammy, you should be writing now," or "Cynthia, the assignment is to complete all of the problems on the page." Check the student's progress shortly thereafter to make sure he or she is continuing to work.

**4.** Ask or tell the student to stop the inappropriate behavior. Then monitor until it stops and the student begins constructive activity.

Sometimes it is inconvenient or would interrupt the lesson flow to respond to minor misbehavior immediately. If the behavior is not disruptive, or is not likely to spread to other students, make a mental note of the problem, and continue the activity until a more appropriate time occurs. Then tell the student that you saw what was happening, and discuss what the appropriate behavior should have been.

The four response options just outlined are easy to use, cause little interruption of class activities, and enable students to correct their behavior. However, when a student persists in an unacceptable behavior, other alternatives should be used. If the rest of the class is working appropriately and does not need your immediate attention, a brief talk with the student may be sufficient. If that doesn't settle the matter, or if an immediate conference is not desirable or feasible, stop the child's behavior, and assess whatever penalty is appropriate. Some teachers use a time-out desk or chair as a holding area for erring students. Note that these four response options apply to relatively minor forms of misbehavior. Additional measures for dealing with more disruptive problem behaviors are described in Chapters 9 and 10.

# ■ Maintaining a Positive Climate

This chapter emphasizes maintaining appropriate behavior by monitoring students effectively, applying rules and procedures consistently, and promptly using nonintrusive interventions when possible to maintain activity flow and student involvement in lessons. We now want to emphasize the importance of keeping a positive perspective and avoiding overdwelling on misbehavior or inadequacies. Sometimes teachers get caught in the trap of seeing only faults and problems and overlooking the better features of students' behavior. Instead of rejoicing when 29 students are involved in learning, we complain about the one student who is off task.

> *Mr. Acerbic's fourth-grade physical education class could do nothing right. Although most of the students initially participated willingly in the class activities, students never seemed to perform quickly or well enough for their teacher. "Come on, you horseflies, quit buzzing and listen up," he would yell when he heard talking. Laps around the gym were given for even slight infractions, such as brief inattention; there always seemed to be three or four students making the rounds at any given time. Instead of feedback about good performance, criticism was usually given for inadequacies. Although students took the constant carping in stride, they displayed little zest for the class.*

### Vignette Reflection

Discuss with a partner your responses to the following questions: What is the result of Mr. Acerbic's approach? How might students interpret his actions? What might improve the situation?

Although poor performance should not be ignored—students need specific, corrective feedback to know what they need to improve—it is important that the climate for learning be positive. Students should look forward to the class. They should expect to learn, to receive assistance when they encounter difficulty, and to feel supported in their efforts. Teachers can foster such a climate by communicating positive expectations to students, by praising good performance, and, at times, by using additional rewards.

The teacher's expectations can be communicated in a variety of ways, some obvious and others subtle. (For a thorough description of this, see Chapter 2 in Good & Brophy, 2008.) Teachers can do the following:

- Identify appropriate instructional goals, and discuss them with students so that students are clear about what is expected.
- Communicate acceptance of imperfect initial performance when students struggle to achieve new learning.
- Insist that students complete work satisfactorily.
- Convey confidence in students' ability to do well.

- Display an encouraging "can do" attitude that generates excitement and self-confidence.
- Refuse to accept excuses for poor work.
- Compliment effort as well as success.
- Avoid comparative evaluations, especially of lower-ability students, which might cause them to conclude that they cannot accomplish the objectives.

By communicating positive expectations, you lay the foundation for students to attempt new tasks and reach new goals. When students know that their teacher believes them to be capable, they are more likely to try harder.

Appropriate praise creates a positive climate for learning. When used well, the teacher's praise can be uplifting and provide great encouragement to students. The most powerful type of praise provides students with information about which aspect of their performance is praiseworthy and demonstrates that the teacher is impressed with the quality of their work. In other words, effective praise provides both informative feedback and genuine approval. It can also accompany suggestions for improvement (i.e., constructive criticism) without loss of effect.

For students from about the third grade and up, public praise that focuses on accomplishment works better than praise for effort. When teachers praise students for working hard, many older elementary students are likely to assume that the teacher thinks they aren't very able. When you know that a student put forth considerable effort and you want to acknowledge it publicly, be sure the praise also includes an emphasis on the student's achievement. "Gloria, all of your hard work paid off—your project was beautifully done. The organization of ideas and the extra details in the descriptions were outstanding!" Likewise, praise should be deserved and should not be too easily obtained. Public praise of a student for success on an easy task can communicate to the rest of the class (and the student who was praised) that the teacher believes he or she has little ability.

It is a good idea to look for private ways to provide praise. Written comments on papers, tests, and other assignments and personal notes offer excellent opportunities for quality praise. Private conversations, conferences with parents, notes home, and informal contacts also offer opportunities for praising students. Private praise avoids some of the complications of public praise and permits the teacher to include a greater variety of performances and behaviors as the focus of praise. Further discussion of the uses of praise can be found in Emmer (1988) and Brophy (1981).

# ■ Improving Class Climate Through Incentives and Rewards

Extra incentives and rewards can help build a positive climate. The improvement in class climate occurs because the incentives add interest or excitement to the class routine while directing attention toward appropriate behavior and away from inappropriate behavior. Moreover, students are then more likely to respond positively to the teacher, contributing to a mutually supportive pattern of interaction.

Rewards can have beneficial effects at some times, but they can have negative effects under certain circumstances. The following sections cover different types of rewards and incentives as well as cautionary guidelines regarding potential negative effects on student motivation.

Before using an added incentive, consider several factors that might affect its appropriateness and effect. Check your school or district policies because sometimes certain incentives are prohibited, and you would not want to promise a field trip or party only to find out that it was not allowed. Your rewards should target the behaviors you would like to encourage. Rewards too easily earned or too difficult to achieve lose their motivational effect. A major consideration in the use of rewards is their feasibility. While some rewards require a great deal of planning, record keeping, or other preparation, others require little preparation or effort. Start with simple rewards, and add to them as you see the need. Avoid using complex systems that distract you and your students from a focus on learning.

Be careful not to create incentives that only the most able students can achieve. Systems that encourage excessive competition for scarce rewards discourage students who don't believe they have much chance to be successful. The examples in this section and in the activities at the end of the chapter include a variety of types. Combine these ideas with those of other teachers and your own experience to create rewards for use at various times of the year.

## Recognition

Recognition rewards involve a means of giving attention to the students. Individual students, groups, and the entire class can all be rewarded through recognition. Examples are displaying student work; awarding a certificate for achievement, for improvement, or for good behavior; and orally citing accomplishments. Recognition rewards may be given on a weekly or monthly basis using a system such as "Super Stars of the Week," a class honor roll, or "Good Worker's Award." Be sure to explain the basis for awards—for example, good attendance, hard work, or citizenship. The more specific you can be when describing the desired behavior, the more likely it is that you will obtain that behavior.

Some teachers encourage competition among work teams or other groups. These competitions may be simple and short (e.g., in a first-grade class, the teacher might say, "Let's see which table is ready first!"); at higher grade levels, competitions may run for a week, a month, or a grading term and may be based on behavior or a specific academic task. If competition among groups is encouraged, this fact should be kept in mind when the teacher forms the groups. Group composition should be balanced so that all groups have an equal chance to succeed.

## Activities

Permitting or arranging for students to do something special or enjoyable constitutes giving an activity reward. Sometimes you can let students choose what this might be. If they have a voice in what the activities are, they are more likely to "buy in." Examples of activities for individuals are privileges such as free-reading time, game time, visits to the school library, extra time on the computer, or appointment as a room monitor, game leader, or special helper.

Some whole-class activities that might be used as incentives include watching a video, 15 minutes of extra recess, playing a game, listening to music, having a popcorn party, or no homework. A group activity reward should be made contingent on specific desirable behaviors; if the group cooperates, they receive the incentive. If not, they lose some or all of the time in the activity. Because the purpose of using an activity reward is, in part, to promote positive climate building, don't let one or two students spoil the fun for the rest of the class. A chronically uncooperative student can be invited to participate but can be excluded from the reward if he or she persists in noncompliance. In most cases, positive peer pressure encourages such a student to cooperate without the teacher's having to resort to exclusion.

## Symbols

Elementary teachers use a variety of symbols to communicate a positive evaluation of student work. Examples include letter grades and numerical scores, happy faces, checkmarks, stars, and stickers with an appealing design. At all elementary grade levels, the teacher's positive evaluation and written comments are a source of satisfaction for students. For younger children especially, this reward should be provided as soon as possible after they complete a task and on a daily basis. Assignments in the early grades can usually be checked quickly, so there is no reason to delay feedback. One effective procedure for checking assignments such as worksheets, writing, or math is to have the children place them on a corner of their desks when finished. As you circulate through the room, you can check completed assignments and place a symbol on the paper to praise good effort, correctly done work, or neatness.

In the upper grades, where assignments are more complex or somewhat lengthy, you are more likely to collect assigned work to check it and record the grades in your grade book. Acquire a box of stars or other stickers, or buy hand stamps with a happy face or other symbols to supplement your numerical or letter grades. Be liberal in your use of them; reward improvement and good effort so that

Shoe-New Business © 1980 Macnelly. Distributed by King Features Syndicate.

all students have access to these incentives. Obviously, you should not reward poor performance, but do give feedback and encouragement so the student can improve.

In addition to their use for daily feedback, symbols are also used on report cards. Elementary-grade children, even first graders, place a positive value on high grades (or "lots of E's"), and it is not uncommon to hear young children comparing report card grades. However, most first or second graders are not likely to have a clear conception of a specific relationship between daily work and long-term grades. Consequently, report card grades are not particularly useful incentives for encouraging young children to complete daily work. In the upper elementary grades, however, students are better able to understand a connection between their effort on daily assignments and the grades they receive in particular subjects. Therefore, it is a good idea to explain your grading policies to these children so they will understand that the value you place on good effort and performance on daily work will translate into a report card grade. However, do not expect report card grades to be the major source of motivation for most students; plan to rely more on the daily use of symbols, positive feedback to students, and other rewards.

## Material Incentives

Material incentives are objects of value to students. Examples include food, a pencil or eraser, discarded classroom materials, games, toys, and books. You must consider your own financial circumstances as well as school policy before deciding to use such rewards. It is best to spread the honors around and include a good portion of the class. Do not give awards only for outstanding achievement; have awards for improvement, excellent effort, good conduct, and so on.

## Caution in the Use of Rewards

Some researchers (e.g., Deci, Koestner, & Ryan, 2001) have urged caution in the use of extrinsic rewards by pointing out that in many cases their use erodes students' intrinsic motivation to engage in the activity that is rewarded. Rewards that are expected, tangible, and related to task performance can interfere with both the *process* and the *quality* of learning. In general, these rewards have a negative effect on a student's inner motivation and cause a shift of attention away from the content to be learned, the challenge to a student's natural curiosity, and a desire to be competent. Explanations of this dampening effect on motivation usually focus on the thinking processes that occur when individuals are given rewards: "This must be an unpleasant or boring task, because I'm being offered a reward to do it." Or the student may feel as though the reward is being used to control behavior rather than to encourage learning. Frequent use of these types of rewards may result in passive learning and undermine creativity instead of supporting the teacher's goal of developing self-regulation, deep understanding, and appreciation of knowledge and skill.

Teachers need to differentiate between rewards given to control or shape behavior and those that are designed as feedback on student competence or that support a sense of mastery (Reeve, 2006). If the teacher's objective is to control

student behavior through prizes or other extrinsic rewards, students may comply with specific standards. However, they may not develop a sense of self-regulation or an appreciation of the need for competence; instead they may be working primarily for the reward.

Not all rewards are perceived to have this dampening effect. Awards tied to progress, competence, or a sense of mastery may actually increase inner motivation and validate a student's sense of personal ability (Cameron, 2001). Praise, symbols, or prizes should be tied as specifically as possible to positive behavior. The informational aspect of the reward is also important and nurtures students' inner motivation.

No purpose is served by rewarding activities that are already highly interesting to students. In fact, the evidence suggests that to do so reduces motivation. However, many classroom tasks are not highly interesting, especially those in which extensive repetition is needed to produce skilled performance and learning. When student motivation flags, external incentives may be necessary to maintain engagement. When rewards are used, they should support students' engagement and self-management rather than emphasize teacher control over student behavior (Reeve, 2006). For example, the message the student receives should be "You did a great job!" rather than "Do it my way, or you don't get a reward."

Finally, the teacher can counteract the potentially negative effects on intrinsic motivation by pointing out to students the usefulness of the skill to be learned, by choosing materials and activities that have high potential for sustaining interest, and by modeling and demonstrating personal interest in and enthusiasm for the task.

## ■ Chapter Summary

Once good classroom management has been established, it must be maintained on a daily basis. Four guidelines help sustain good student behavior by preventing or halting student misbehavior: (1) monitor student behavior and academic progress carefully; (2) be consistent in the use of procedures, rules, and consequences; (3) manage inappropriate behavior promptly; and (4) maintain a positive climate by reinforcing appropriate behavior. Monitor by attending to student action, interaction, or inaction via visual scanning, careful listening, and frequent movement around the room. Be sure to check students' behavioral compliance and their academic comprehension.

Teachers provide consistency by holding the same expectations for all students for the duration of a given activity. Procedures, rewards, and penalties all require consistent application. Inconsistency in these areas undermines student–teacher relationships and invalidates the entire classroom management system. Consistency promotes a positive classroom climate in which appropriate student behavior is reinforced. Classroom rewards can include student recognition (e.g., honor roll, first to line up), special activities (e.g., extra recess, teacher helper), symbols (e.g., smiley faces), and material incentives (e.g., books, stickers). Teachers can avoid the potential harm to student intrinsic motivation that accompanies the use of rewards by using them prudently, selecting a variety of tasks/events to reward, and utilizing rewards for feedback rather than control.

When students misbehave, teachers manage the situation effectively when they respond directly, calmly, and in a reasoned fashion. Suggestions for responding to misbehavior include using nonverbal cues for the student to change behaviors, reminding the student of the expectation, asking the student to stop the behavior, and monitoring until the student complies. Maintaining effective classroom management is a continual process.

# ■ Further Reading

Akin-Little, K. A., Eckert, T. L., Lovett, B. J., & Little, S. G. (2004). Extrinsic reinforcement in the classroom: Bribery or best practice. *School Psychology Review, 33*, 344–362.

*The authors review the history of research on the use of rewards, with special attention to the debate over their effects on motivation. Their conclusion is that detrimental effects are minimal and that use of extrinsic rewards should not be equated with bribery. The authors provide suggestions for the appropriate use of rewards in educational settings.*

Brophy, J. E. (2004). *Motivating students to learn* (2nd ed.). Hillsdale, NJ: Erlbaum.

*This very readable book addresses teachers directly and offers strategies and principles to use in motivating students to learn. Based on the author's research on motivation and effective teaching practices, the book identifies parts of the literature that are most relevant to teachers, summarizes research in everyday language, and provides helpful examples with an eye toward the complexities of the classroom setting.*

Hansen, J. (2010). Teaching without talking. *Phi Delta Kappan, 92*(1), 35–40.

*In this brief article, the author encourages teachers to consider their nonverbal communication being extended to students. She offers suggestions for utilizing these interactions in supportive, nondistracting ways to encourage student participation and learning.*

Jennings, P. A., & Greenberg, M. T. (2009). The prosocial classroom: Teacher social and emotional competence in relation to students and classroom outcomes. *Review of Educational Research, 79*, 491–525.

  *The authors propose a model of classroom climate that emphasizes the role of the teacher's social and emotional competence. They provide a literature review that supports connections of student social, emotional, and academic outcomes to effective classroom management, healthy student–teacher relationships, and teacher social–emotional competence.*

Mueller, C. M., & Dweck, C. S. (1998). Praise for intelligence can undermine children's motivation for performance. *Journal of Personality and Social Psychology, 75*(1), 33–52.

  *Through a series of six studies, the authors demonstrate that students who receive positive feedback based on their effort continue to exert effort in learning. These students associate struggles with a lack of effort, therefore exerting more. Students who receive positive feedback based on their intelligence seek to continue looking smart and may choose activities with less challenge. These students associate struggles with lack of ability and, therefore, may not make further attempts.*

Reeve, J. (2006). Extrinsic rewards and inner motivation. In C. Evertson & C. Weinstein (Eds.), *Handbook of research on classroom management: Research, practice, and contemporary issues* (pp. 645–664). Mahwah, NJ: Erlbaum.

  *The author provides a comprehensive review of research on the use of rewards, with an emphasis on supporting student autonomy and engagement rather than behavior control. Principles underpinning the appropriate use of rewards are clearly described, and numerous suggestions for teachers are presented.*

www.apa.org/education/k12/using-praise.aspx

  *This module, Using Praise to Enhance Student Resilience and Learning Outcomes, was designed by the APA Task Force on the Applications of Psychological Science to Teaching and Learning to help teachers use praise to encourage students to maintain a learning focus despite struggles and to enhance students' learning outcomes.*

# ■ Suggested Activities

1. Return to the opening vignette of Ms. White. Discuss with a partner your responses to these questions: How would you assess the monitoring in this class? What are the results? What recommendations would you make to Ms. White? (Focus your discussion on consistency, managing misbehavior, and building a positive climate.)

2. Write a response to the following prompts: What does "appropriate" behavior mean to you? Imagine your own classroom. When students are behaving appropriately, what will it look and sound like? How much movement do you find acceptable? How does your philosophy of education influence what you define as "appropriate"?

3. Interview a practicing teacher on maintaining student behavior. Include in your conversation questions about school and/or district policies that affect that teacher's use of rewards, as well as how faculty consistency across a school affects schoolwide procedures.

4. Review the checklists at the end of Chapters 3 and 4, and identify the rewards you intend to use with your major conduct and accountability procedures. By planning ahead, you will be better able to explain these incentives and be consistent in their use.

5. Read Examples 8.1 through 8.4, and consider how you might adapt these descriptions of reward systems to your own classroom. Analyze each example using the following questions as the starting point:

   a. What teacher and student roles are encouraged?

   b. Is the system primarily intrinsic or extrinsic?

   c. Is the system cooperative or competitive?

   d. What kind of classroom environment is the system likely to foster?

*Example 8.1: Shoot for the Moon* Mrs. Li used a reward system called "Shoot for the Moon" to give feedback to second-grade students for behavioral and academic performance. She decorated a large bulletin board with blue paper, a large round moon, a few clouds, and a title, "Shoot for the Moon." Each child's name was written on a small construction paper spaceship. The spaceships were lined up at the bottom of the bulletin board at the start. At the beginning of the year, Mrs. Li discussed with her class the kinds of behaviors that would result in the movement of each spaceship closer to the moon. Daily completion of assignments and good behavior in the classroom, at lunch, and on the playground would result in the spaceship's moving 2 inches closer to the moon. For bad behavior (such as misbehavior in the lunchroom or during instruction, not working in class, or not turning in an assignment), a student's spaceship would be moved 1 inch away from the moon. When students reached the moon, they were rewarded by being able to keep their spaceships decorated with a star. The teacher then started another spaceship for them at the bottom of the board. Sometimes students were required to reach the moon by a certain deadline to get a special reward, such as a privilege or a popcorn party. Mrs. Li was consistent in rewarding appropriate behavior each day and in penalizing inappropriate behaviors, and she occasionally rewarded individual students for being especially quiet or helpful or for improving their work or grades. This worked well with students who had particular behavior or academic problems.

*Example 8.2: Regular Feedback* Ms. Harmony's first-grade class functioned smoothly and productively without many obvious rewards and penalties. Although she only occasionally rewarded individuals or groups with public compliments, Ms. Harmony maintained a high level of student involvement by using interesting, well-paced lessons and assignments with a high level of student success and by promptly returning assignments and giving students feedback regarding their work. She dealt with inappropriate behavior by brief verbal correction of students or short private conferences with individuals inside the classroom. Often she simply mentioned what the student should be doing if all the rest of his or her work was finished. Ms. Harmony made extensive use of telephone contacts with parents to inform them of their children's progress and particularly to identify when a student was not completing assignments satisfactorily. She did this frequently during the first few months of the school year, with long-lasting results.

*Example 8.3: A Token Exchange System* Mr. Young used a variety of strategies, some simple and some elaborate, for encouraging appropriate behavior in his third-grade class. Throughout the year, he used a system in which the class as a whole earned blue chips for good behavior and red chips for poor behavior. When a monthly goal for the number of blue chips was reached, the class was rewarded with a treat or special privilege. Goals and rewards escalated during the course of the year. During each day, blue chips were dropped into a container for various appropriate behaviors—2 for good behavior during the time a visitor was in the room, 10 for each satisfactory class-wide cleanup, 1 for each student who had completed his or her individual contract work by the end of the day, and so on. Red chips were dropped into the container for excessive noise, throwing trash on the floor, bad behavior on the way to lunch, or other transgressions. Shaking the can that contained the chips was often used to signal that there was too much talking or misbehaving and that failure to become quiet would result in another red chip. At the end of the day, red chips were counted, and an equal number of blue chips were deducted from the blue chip collection.

In addition to the chip system, Mr. Young complimented good workers aloud, sometimes let best-behaved or best-prepared students line up first, put names of cooperative students on the board under a "Super People" title, and awarded happy faces to students who did all of their work that day.

*Example 8.4: Token Reward System in Grade 4* In Ms. Woodmore's class, students were issued a "bank account" on the first day of school. Each day they were able to earn three dollars to deposit: one dollar for being at school on time, one for turning in all work for the day, and one for receiving no more than one warning about misbehavior. At the end of the day, Ms. Woodmore recorded the number of dollars each student had earned. On the last day of the marking period, Ms. Woodmore held an auction. Students bid, based on the accumulated dollars in their accounts. Items for sale at the auction included prizes donated by parents, books, pens, free homework passes, computer passes, and a pizza lunch to be shared with a friend. There were enough prizes in the auction for every student to get a prize. Dollars not spent could be rolled over to the next six weeks.

6. Reread Example 8.4, and review what research has to say about expected, tangible, and task-contingent rewards. What message is Ms. Woodmore sending regarding her expectations of her students' academic and personal behavior?

7. In Problem 8.1 Ms. Greene is encountering problems maintaining her management system. Use the information in this and previous chapters to diagnose her problems and to suggest what she can do to improve student behavior. Refer to the key in the Appendix for other suggestions.

# PROBLEM 8.1

## Misbehavior in a Second-Grade Class

Ms. Greene's second-grade students never seem to settle down. Regardless of whether the children have been assigned independent work or are supposed to be paying attention to a presentation, some degree of commotion or noise is always present. During the first few days of school, the class seemed well behaved and was seldom out of order, and almost all of the children were cooperative and did their work. Gradually, however, more and more inappropriate socializing, loud talk, call-outs, and other interruptions occurred, even from previously quiet students.

During Ms. Greene's presentations to the class, students are frequently inattentive, and she is able to complete lessons only with difficulty. Sometimes she even stops lessons short because the children are so difficult to control. At times, the only way she can restore a semblance of quiet is to start writing names on the board and assigning detention. However, even that tactic doesn't work for long because so many students are inattentive that the list of names gets very long and not being on the list becomes something of a social stigma.

During a recent reading-group period, three students talked continuously while Ms. Greene was working with one of the small groups. Two other children wandered around the room, and a half-dozen others made frequent trips to the drinking fountain, restrooms, and hamster cages.

What has gone wrong in this class? How might Ms. Greene attempt to gain better cooperation from her students?

---

### MyEducationLab

Now go to www.myeducationlab.com to:

- Take a Quiz to test your mastery of chapter objectives.
- Study chapter content with an individualized Study Plan.
- Deepen your understanding of particular concepts and principles with Classroom Management Simulations.
- Apply what you have learned in the chapter to your work with children in Building Teaching Skills exercises.

**CHAPTER 9**

# Communication Skills for Teaching

Throughout this book we have emphasized classroom management's preventive and instructional aspects. Not all problems can be prevented, however, and sometimes unobtrusive handling of inappropriate behavior during instruction is not sufficient. The approaches described in this chapter provide additional means for dealing with persistent problems. This example illustrates such a situation:

> During the past several days, Debra and Diane have been increasingly inattentive in Ms. Harris's fifth-grade class. Their off-task behavior has included whispering with other students and each other, teasing boys seated nearby, and displaying exaggerated boredom with class discussions. Ms. Harris first asked the girls to stop bothering the class, and when that had no effect, she moved the girls to different seats. However, Debra and Diane continued to disrupt by passing notes and calling out loudly to one another.

We will not second-guess Ms. Harris by wondering whether she had communicated expectations clearly or had taken action promptly enough; let us suppose that she had, in fact, practiced good preventive management skills, but the students misbehaved anyway. No strategy works all the time! What options are now available to Ms. Harris to deal with the situation? Possible approaches include the following:

- Ignore the problem and hope it goes away.
- Refer the students to the principal.

- Call the students' parents, and ask for their help.
- Apply a consequence, such as detention or some other punishment.

Each of these approaches has advantages and limitations. Ignoring the problem requires little effort and might work if the students are mainly seeking the teacher's attention. The description does not, however, suggest that this is a likely reason for the behavior, and ignoring may only allow it to intensify and spread to other students. Referral has the advantage of taking little of the teacher's time, at least in the short run; it also temporarily removes the disruptive students, and it can have deterrent value. However, it may do nothing in the long run to deal with the problem the students are causing in the class, and although referral may sometimes be a reasonable approach to serious misbehavior, it can easily be overused and erodes the teacher's classroom authority.

A telephone call to parents sometimes works wonders and is usually worth a try. However, parents cannot always stop misbehavior. They do not, after all, accompany their children to your class, nor do they control the cues that are eliciting the misbehavior. Punishing the students by assigning detention or withholding some desirable activity or privilege is another possible reaction. Punishment, as discussed in Chapter 10, can stop misbehavior temporarily and can deter other students. But punishment can have the disadvantages of creating hostility or resentment and of trapping the teacher and students in a cycle of misbehavior–reaction that leads to power struggles. By itself, punishment does little to teach the students self-control and responsibility.

Because each of these approaches has limitations, you need additional means of coping with problems. This does not mean that approaches such as ignoring, referring, applying consequences, or involving parents will be supplanted. It does mean that communication strategies should be added to your repertoire to deal with problems that cannot be corrected with minor interventions and to help students learn to take responsibility for their own behavior.

In addition to being helpful in dealing with students whose behavior is creating a problem for the teacher or for other students, using communication skills can assist students who are themselves experiencing problems. Teachers frequently become aware of student problems caused by factors both inside and outside the classroom. Sometimes teachers can help students by being good listeners and by encouraging the students to consider alternative ways to solve problems or to adapt to difficult situations.

We use the label *communication skills* for the set of strategies described in this chapter to emphasize that the approach focuses on communicating clearly and effectively with others in order to help bring about a change in their behavior, in their thinking, or in the situation that has caused the problem. But communication also means being open to information, so teachers also have to be good listeners and try to understand the students' (or parents') concerns and feelings. To become an effective communicator, three related skills are needed:

1. **Constructive assertiveness:** Describing your concerns clearly, insisting that misbehavior be corrected, and resisting being coerced or manipulated.

2. **Empathic responding:** Listening to the other person's perspective and reacting in ways that maintain a positive relationship and encourage further discussion.
3. **Problem solving:** Resolving problems in mutually satisfactory ways; working with the student (or parent) to develop a plan for change.

These three elements are derived from a variety of sources, including Kottler's *Students Who Drive You Crazy* (2002), Glasser's *Reality Therapy* (1975), Alberti's *Assertiveness* (1977), Zuker's *Mastering Assertiveness Skills* (1983), and others. The treatment of communication skills in this chapter is an introduction; if you are interested in further reading, one or more of these books would be helpful.

Although this chapter's treatment of assertiveness, empathic responding, and problem solving focuses on their use with students, the skills are also helpful when dealing with parents—especially during parent conferences—and with other adults. Thus, the skills described here have a variety of applications and can improve your effectiveness in handling many classroom and school-related situations.

## ■ Constructive Assertiveness

Assertiveness is the ability to stand up for one's legitimate rights in ways that help ensure that others cannot ignore or circumvent them. The adjective *constructive* means that the assertive teacher does not deride or attack the student involved. Assertiveness is a general characteristic or attribute that can be used in a wide variety of settings or as a set of skills that are more situation specific. Some individuals are assertive in a variety of settings (e.g., with strangers, on the job, at parties, in school), whereas others lack assertiveness in many social situations.

Even if you are not generally assertive, you can learn to use assertive behaviors while you are teaching. In fact, doing so may generalize to other situations as you become more confident of your skills. People who are very unassertive—who feel extremely nervous whenever they are expected to lead a group, are unable to begin conversations or to make eye contact with others, accede to inappropriate demands readily, are unable to ask others to respect their rights—find teaching uncomfortable and have particular difficulty with discipline. Such people can help themselves in several ways, especially by reading about assertiveness and practicing some of the skills, preferably in situations that are not too uncomfortable, until they begin to develop more confidence. Alternatively, overly aggressive individuals—who respond to questions with threats, use sarcasm and humiliation to manipulate others, hold intimidating postures, do not acknowledge the rights of others—use their position to control rather than teach students. These individuals can learn to manage their aggression by finding other outlets to release stress (e.g., exercise, playing an instrument). It is also possible to obtain professional help, such as from a counseling center, or to enroll in a course or workshop on assertiveness training. A good training program usually includes cognitive restructuring to reshape negative thought patterns that interfere with appropriate social interaction, anxiety-reduction exercises, anger management, and/or skills training and practice to develop more effective behaviors.

The elements of assertiveness include

- A clear statement of the problem or issue
- Unambiguous body language
- Insistence on appropriate behavior and resolution of the problem

Assertiveness is not

- Hostile, timid, or apathetic
- Argumentative or pleading
- Inflexible

Assertiveness lies on a continuum of social response between aggressive, overbearing pushiness and timid, ineffectual submissiveness. Assertiveness skills allow you to communicate to students that you are serious about teaching and about maintaining a classroom in which everyone's rights are respected. Assertiveness does not limit or hamper teachers' and students' caring for one another. The following aspects of constructive assertiveness have special importance for teachers.

## Stating the Problem or Concern

Student misbehavior usually causes problems for teachers by making it difficult to conduct lessons, slowing down activities, subverting routines that help a class run smoothly, and distracting other students from their work. When misbehavior persists, the teacher must let the student know what the problem is, from the teacher's point of view. Sometimes just a simple description of the problem results in students' changing their behavior because they become more aware and begin to monitor themselves better. Stating the problem has two parts: (1) identifying the behavior and (2) describing its effects, as in the following examples:

"Loud conversations in the library corner distract other students."

"Please raise your hand so that I can call on you."

"Wandering around the room disturbs the class."

"Calling other students names causes hard feelings."

By focusing on the behavior and its effects, you can reduce the potential for student defensiveness and keep open the chance for a satisfactory resolution to the situation. Conducting the conference privately (e.g., at a table separate from the class, after class, or during a conference period) lessens the potential for embarrassing the student in front of peers and reduces the likelihood of a confrontation or power struggle that challenges the teacher's authority. However, sometimes you will be forced to act immediately.

Notice that the problem descriptions do not label students or their behavior; that is, students are not accused of being bad, rude, and annoying or behaving in an inconsiderate and stupid manner. Such labeling, whether of a student or the student's behavior, impedes behavior change by suggesting that a student's behavior is a permanent characteristic that the student might accept as valid. Notice also that statements rather than questions are used. Quizzing students (e.g., "Why are you talking?" "Do you think you should be calling someone that name?") invites defensive, sarcastic, or oppositional responses that can lead to arguments.

## Body Language

Constructive assertiveness with students needs the visual reinforcement of appropriate body language in three areas. The first is making eye contact when addressing the student, especially when describing the problem and when calling for behavior change. Note that there is a difference between eye contact that communicates seriousness or resolve and an angry, hostile glare. Breaking eye contact from time to time relieves tension. A second area of assertive body language is maintaining an alert posture and body orientation toward the student (but not so close as to be threatening). Maintaining an erect posture, either standing or sitting, and facing the student communicate your attention and involvement in the conversation. A third area is matching your facial expressions with the content and tone of your statements (e.g., not smiling when making serious statements).

## Obtaining Appropriate Behavior

Assertiveness requires that the teacher not be diverted from insisting on appropriate behavior. Students may engage in diversionary tactics in several ways: by denying involvement, by arguing, and by blaming others (including the teacher). When dealing with such tactics, remember: There are many reasons, but no excuses, for misbehavior. Although it is possible that others contributed to the problem, the student must accept responsibility for his or her own behavior. Listen carefully to understand the student's point of view, but in the end, if the student's behavior is interfering with your ability to teach, the behavior must change. Thus, if a student begins to argue or to deny responsibility for the behavior, avoid being sidetracked; the bottom line is that the student's behavior is not acceptable, whatever the reason for it.

Being an assertive teacher means that you let students know your concerns and wants in a manner that gets their attention and communicates your intent to carry through with consequences and to deal with the situation until it is resolved. You don't have to lose your sense of humor or treat students impolitely. A little humor can reduce tension, and treating students with courtesy models the kind of behavior you expect of them. Developing a level of assertiveness that is comfortable for you and understanding how your behavior is perceived by others are important; working through the activities at the end of this chapter will help.

# ■ Empathic Responding

Another important communication skill is responding empathically to students. This skill shows that you are aware and accepting of the student's perspective, as well as willing to seek clarification of it when necessary. Empathic responding helps keep the lines of communication open between you and your students so that problems can be understood and resolved in mutually acceptable ways. Such skills are especially appropriate when a student seems excessively concerned, under stress, or otherwise upset. As a teacher, you have to be able to respond in a manner that helps students deal constructively with those emotions or at least avoids further discomfort or distress. Empathic responding can also be used as a part of the problem-solving process when dealing with students who must change their behavior. In such situations, students may be resistant and express negative feelings; the teacher's empathic response can then help defuse these reactions and increase the acceptance of a plan for change.

Empathic responding complements constructive assertiveness. Whereas assertiveness allows teachers to express their wants, empathic responding solicits and affirms the student's viewpoint. The use of empathic responding skills does not imply that misbehaving students are entitled to "do their thing" without regard for others; rather, the purpose is to understand and take into account the student's views in order to reach a satisfactory solution. When the teacher shows some openness toward the student's perspective, there is a better chance that the student will make a commitment to change. Conversely, a teacher who shows no interest in the student's feelings is more likely to encounter defiant behavior and an unwillingness to cooperate or to accept responsibility.

Compare the following two episodes.

### Episode A

STUDENT:  I'm not staying. You can't make me.
TEACHER:  You'll have to stay after school. You haven't completed your work.
STUDENT:  No, I can't stay.
TEACHER:  That's life. If you don't serve your time now, it's doubled. That's the rule.
STUDENT:  (*Angry*) I'm leaving.
TEACHER:  You'd better not.
STUDENT:  I'm going! (*Student leaves.*)

In Episode A the teacher's response does nothing to resolve the situation. It's likely that the student is aware of the consequences of skipping detention, so the argument only provokes a confrontation, which the student wins, at least temporarily, by leaving.

Here is another way to handle the same situation:

**Episode B**

STUDENT:   I'm not staying. You can't make me.
TEACHER:   It's true, I can't. It's up to you.
STUDENT:   I can't stay.
TEACHER:   Staying after school is a problem for you?
STUDENT:   I have to be at home right away.
TEACHER:   So it would be a problem for you to get home late.
STUDENT:   Right, we're going somewhere after school today.
TEACHER:   That's a difficult situation. Would you like to talk about what you could do?
STUDENT:   Okay.

In Episode B the teacher avoids arguing with the student and instead acknowledges the student's concern and invites further discussion. The student responds to the teacher's approach by stating his or her concern more explicitly. Notice that the teacher's role in this conference is that of listener or helper rather than opponent. Notice, too, that the teacher does not offer to solve the student's problem by dropping the detention penalty. Instead, the student is led to consider what options are available. Of course, there is no guarantee that the situation will be resolved to everyone's satisfaction. But the approach at least offers the possibility of resolution and avoids the confrontation that occurred in Episode A. Further, it maintains the student's responsibility for dealing with the situation rather than giving the student yet another excuse for avoiding responsibility.

Empathic responding has several advantages. It provides the teacher with a way to deal with a student's strong emotions without taking responsibility for solving the student's problems. At the same time, the strategy helps defuse an emotionally charged situation. By not reciprocating with a similar emotional intensity, the teacher avoids fueling the student's fire.

One consideration of empathic listening skills is choosing the right time and place to use them. It would be awkward to respond empathically to every expression of emotion or opinion during class activities. Such reactivity would cause slowdowns and undermine your students' attention. How frequently and in which circumstances you use these skills depends on a variety of factors, including opportunities, your goals and values, and how competent you feel. At least you should develop your skills so you are able to respond empathically in situations in which the use of the skills is helpful. Responding effectively requires practice and observation. Working through the activities at the end of the chapter can help. Empathic responding has two components: listening skills and processing skills.

## Listening Skills

Listening skills enable a teacher to acknowledge or accept a student's feelings or ideas. At a minimal level, the listener merely indicates attention. Sometimes an interested look encourages the student to continue speaking. Other examples of nonverbal listening behaviors are nodding, making eye contact with the speaker, and other body language that communicates openness to discussion. Verbal encouragement is indicated by utterances such as "Um hm," "I see," and the like. At other times, a little more encouragement may be needed. A child who expresses feelings of rejection or discouragement and who needs reassurance may be seeking a pat on the shoulder or a hug. The teacher can invite more discussion with statements such as, "Tell me more," "What do you think?" and "You've listened to my opinion—I'd like to listen to yours."

## Processing Skills

Processing skills allow you to confirm or clarify your perception of the student's message. Consider the following exchanges, and identify the teacher response that would be most likely to lead to further discussion:

> STUDENT:  I can't do this assignment.
> TEACHER: (A):  You're having difficulty?
> TEACHER: (B):  Come on, try harder—you'll get it done.

> STUDENT:  (*Tearful*) I hate Angela. She's not my friend anymore.
> TEACHER: (A):  It's upsetting to lose a friend.
> TEACHER: (B):  Don't be silly. She's your best friend. Just tell her you're sorry.

In these exchanges, the A responses are more accepting of the student's feelings, whereas the B responses ignore the student's emotional tone and tend to block further communication. The B comments are judgmental and suggest a solution without obtaining enough information about the situation and without giving the student the opportunity to deal with his or her own problem.

To process a student's comments, you can repeat or summarize what the student has said. If the student has given multiple messages or a confusing array of statements, select what seems to be most important and paraphrase it. This paraphrase can simply be stated back to the student, or you can "reflect" or "bounce back" the paraphrase as a question. Whichever you do, the student will usually either acknowledge the correctness of your perception or offer clarification or elaboration. Consider the following exchange in a short after-school conference:

> STUDENT:  I hate this place. School is stupid!
> TEACHER:  Would you like to talk about it?
> STUDENT:  I just don't like it here.
> TEACHER:  There's something about school that bothers you.
> STUDENT:  (*Crying*) Yes. Sean and Billy laugh at me.
> TEACHER:  (*Puts arm around student*) You feel sad because they're making fun of you?
> STUDENT:  Yes.
> TEACHER:  Can you tell me about that?
> STUDENT:  They call me stupid and dummy.

TEACHER:    It hurts a lot to be called those names. Are you worried that they really think that about you?

STUDENT:    No. I'm not dumb.

TEACHER:    You're not, and I'm glad you don't think so. I don't think so either. Would you like to talk about what to do when someone calls you a name or makes fun of you?

In this example, the teacher uses a variety of responses with an unhappy student and progresses to the point at which the student can express, at least partially, the basis for the feelings. The teacher then offers to help the student learn how to deal with the problem. Although it is not realistic to expect that major problems will be resolved by a single empathic exchange, it is not unusual for the sharp edge of negative emotions to be blunted and for the conversation to end on a positive note. At the least, the student knows that an adult cares enough to listen, and the teacher is in a better position to guide the student in the future.

The skills of empathic responding—both listening and processing—have been presented in the context of interactions with an individual student, but they are also helpful when problems arise in group settings. Using these tactics helps prevent teachers from responding defensively when students react emotionally or express a problem during class. These skills also buy time for the teacher to consider alternatives for dealing with a problem. In addition, listening and processing skills are useful for leading group discussions and for interacting with parents.

Although empathic responding skills are very helpful in some situations, they are not the primary means of dealing with students who are acting out, breaking class rules, or interfering with other students. Such misbehavior has to be dealt with using approaches discussed in Chapters 8 and 10 and in the other sections of this chapter. However, listening and processing skills will support these other measures.

## ■ Problem Solving

Problem solving is a process used to deal with and to resolve conflicts. Conflicts arise between teachers and students because different roles give rise to different needs and because individuals have different goals and interests. In a crowded classroom, diverse paths can cross, and individuals can find themselves at odds with one another. If conflict arises, teachers need a way to manage it constructively so that teaching and learning can continue in a supportive classroom climate. An effective means of accomplishing this is the problem-solving process, in which the teacher works with the student to develop a plan to reduce or eliminate the problem. Steps in the problem-solving process include (1) identifying the problem, (2) discussing alternative solutions, and (3) obtaining a commitment to try one of them. Depending on circumstances, problem solving may include attempts to identify the causes of the problem and may specify the consequences of following or not following the plan. Because it generally requires more than a brief intervention, problem solving is usually conducted during a conference with the student it concerns. Often, the skills of constructive assertiveness and empathic responding are helpful in reaching an agreement for solving the problem.

Problem-solving conferences are usually reserved for chronic situations that have not yielded to simpler remedies. Action must be taken to stop the behavior because allowing it to continue would interfere with your ability to teach, with other students' opportunities to learn, or with the student's long-term functioning in your class or school. Consider three examples:

1. *Brad likes to be the center of attention. Whenever you ask a question, he calls out the answer without raising his hand and with no regard for the fact that you have already called on another student. Although you have reminded him of correct behavior and have tried to ignore his call-outs, the behavior continues to interfere with your class discussions.*

2. *Alice and Alicia never seem to clean up materials, supplies, or their work areas when they have finished a project or assignment. They resent your reminders and insistence that they observe class procedures, and unless you monitor them closely, they avoid all responsibilities. Lately they have been arguing and complaining whenever they are asked to complete a task. Their foot-dragging seemed trivial at first but has become a constant source of irritation.*

3. *Terrence has skipped his last three arithmetic assignments even though you allowed ample time in class to work on them. He seems to have a lackadaisical attitude about academic work and uses his time in class for goofing off whenever he can get away with it. Twice last week he was kept in from recess to work on his missing assignments, but he did not finish them and resented the loss of his midmorning break. During the previous grading period he had several unsatisfactory grades on his report card, and skipping assignments is sure to prevent his making satisfactory progress in learning arithmetic skills.*

Each of these examples illustrates a situation that has reached a stage at which a problem-solving conference might be useful. In each case, routine interventions have not changed the student's behavior; in each case, more of the same teacher response is likely to result in a continuing power struggle or in a deterioration in the student's ability to behave constructively.

What is evident in the three examples is that the students are not accepting responsibility for their behavior. It may be that what is needed is a stronger consequence (i.e., a penalty) that is clearly tied to the misbehavior. In fact, this strategy can be an alternative discussed with the student during a problem-solving conference. But until the student makes a commitment to change the offending behavior, the use of punishment will probably be perceived as coercive and controlling rather than as a natural consequence of the behavior and thus may do little or no good. It also appears that the basis of the problem in each of the three examples is not totally clear. Why won't Brad wait his turn? Why can't Alicia and Alice follow simple cleanup procedures? Is Terrence having difficulty understanding the content, or is some external problem the source of his reluctance to do his work? Giving the students a chance to discuss their situations might provide insights that would lead to better solutions. It would also permit the teacher and students to become more aware of each other's perceptions and possibly prevent the development of additional problems.

A problem-solving conference involves three steps.

**STEP 1: Identify the problem.** You can begin the discussion by stating the purpose of the meeting and asking the student to express his or her viewpoint. Obtaining the student's views gives you useful information for later steps and also enables you to gauge the student's degree of cooperation and understanding of the situation. An alternative opening is to describe the problem yourself and ask the student for a reaction; this alternative is especially needed when dealing with young children, with students having limited verbal skills, and with evasive and dissembling students. Unless the student's attitude is cooperative, you must be assertive in expressing your concerns. As explained earlier, this can be done by describing, without labeling, the behavior of concern and the problem it is causing. You may also have to stress that the problem will not be allowed to continue and that something must be done to solve it.

Glasser (1975) recommends asking students to evaluate whether their behavior is helping or hurting them or has good or bad effects. The logic is that a student who understands and admits that a behavior has negative consequences is more likely to participate in the search for and commitment to a solution. A student who denies responsibility or who sees no harmful effects seldom makes a meaningful commitment to change. It may be helpful to ask such a student what might happen if the behavior continues.

During this initial phase of the conference, students may react defensively or emotionally and may try to avoid responsibility by blaming others, arguing, citing extenuating circumstances, and so forth. When such behavior occurs, you must decide whether the student's reactions are primarily for the purpose of evading responsibility or whether they have some validity. If the latter is the case, you can use listening and processing skills to respond. This communicates your willingness to hear the student's point of view and may increase subsequent cooperation. By modeling such desirable behavior, you encourage its use by the student. A disadvantage of using empathic responding during this phase of problem solving is that the student's excuses, arguments, and extenuating circumstances may simply be a means of avoiding responsibility. Because you do not want to get sidetracked from the issue that brought the student to the conference in the first place, be sure to tie the student's concerns to the main issue after they have been expressed. When the problem has been identified and agreed on, the conference can move to the next step.

**STEP 2: Select a solution.** One way to begin this phase is to invite the student to suggest a solution to the problem. If the student is unable to do so, you can offer one. Whenever possible, it is best to have two or more alternatives so that options can be compared and the most desirable one chosen. Frequently, the student's solution will be stated negatively, focusing on simply ending an undesirable behavior. Although this is a step in the right direction, it is best to include a positive focus as well by suggesting a plan for increasing desirable behavior. Thus, you should be ready to work with the student's ideas and to suggest modifications.

If you are the one who suggests a solution, seek the student's reaction to check whether the plan is understood and accepted. Also, evaluate the plan's appropriateness: Is it realistic? Will it significantly reduce the problem? Does it call for changes in other students or in the classroom environment, and are such changes feasible? Can it be evaluated readily? Occasionally a student may try to avoid responsibility by proposing a solution that places the burden for change on the teacher or on other students—for example, to design more interesting lessons or to get other students to "leave me alone." Consider such changes to the extent they are appropriate and reasonable, but don't allow a student to shift responsibility to others—unless, of course, that is where responsibility for the problem lies. A reasonable response is, "Yes, such changes would help, but what will you contribute?" Once a mutually agreeable solution is reached, you are ready for the third step.

> **STEP 3: Obtain a commitment.** In this step, the teacher asks the student to accept the solution and try it for a specified period, usually with the understanding that it will be evaluated afterward. The student's commitment can be given orally or in written form, as in a "contract." Sometimes contracts are printed with an official-looking border, seal, and script, with space for the student's and the teacher's signatures and for listing contract terms and consequences for following or not following the plan.

Whether consequences are specified in case the plan is not followed will depend on the severity of the problem and whether it is a first conference or a follow-up for a broken contract. Some teachers like to give students a chance to correct their behavior without resorting to penalties, the rationale being that long-range cooperation is better when the teacher uses the least controlling or coercive approach. However, if the student is not making a reasonable effort to comply with the plan, or if the misbehavior is dangerous or too disruptive to be allowed to continue, spelling out the consequences may be needed to get the student's attention and to communicate the seriousness of the situation: "You will have to choose between following our agreement and discussing your behavior with our principal and your parents."

If the plan fails to solve the problem, you'll have to either follow through with whatever consequence was stipulated or work with the student to alter the plan and produce a more workable solution. A major consideration is the amount of time and energy you can or should devote to pursuing the plan versus using a referral, a detention, or some other consequence available in your school. To get another perspective on the problem, you might also consult with a counselor, an assistant principal, or another teacher before taking further action.

When problem-solving conferences fail to make progress (e.g., the student does not make a sincere commitment to a plan or simply does not cooperate), the teacher should evaluate his or her assertiveness and empathic responding skills before concluding that the problem-solving approach does not work with that student. Poor assertiveness skills—hostile, critical, or attacking behaviors or timid, tentative responding—interfere with the problem-solving process. An excessively assertive, hostile style reflects a reliance on power and cuts off communication. An unassertive, timid style abdicates authority and is easily ignored; the teacher is not seen as credible, and the student may simply not believe that the teacher will insist on correct behavior or will follow through with consequences.

A constructively assertive teacher, however, captures the student's attention and communicates seriousness of intent in changing the situation. Empathic responding communicates a willingness to listen to the student's point of view and permits the teacher to clarify and react to a student's statements without closing off further discussion. Such skills are especially needed during problem-solving discussions because they allow the teacher to deal constructively with defensive behavior. They also help to clarify solutions as they are discussed, and they improve the chances of obtaining a sincere commitment to change.

When you use these skills, be patient and give them a chance to work. Teachers often use a problem-solving approach after a situation has become chronic or for behavior that has been established over a long time. In such cases you cannot expect miracles; change may occur only gradually and imperfectly. However, problem-solving conferences can be helpful in many cases and should be a component of your set of management and discipline skills. Exercises on problem solving are presented in activities at the end of the chapter.

## ■ Talking with Parents

Constructive assertiveness, empathic responding, and problem solving can be useful strategies in your interactions with students, and they can also be effective in working with parents. In Chapter 5 we presented suggestions for involving parents; those initial steps can help lay the foundation for good home–school communication and foster a good working relationship with parents. Additionally, we offer the following suggestions to help conferences with parents go more smoothly.

- Express your appreciation for parents' efforts to rearrange their schedules to meet with you. Use their time wisely by being prepared and organized.
- Schools and teachers may intimidate parents who had difficulty in school. Their anxiety may be expressed as anger, avoidance, or defensiveness, so realize that parental reactions may be more a reflection of the parent's state of mind than something you said or did.
- Parents whose child is exhibiting behavioral or academic problems are especially sensitive to being blamed. Keep the focus on choices the student is making and what can be done to encourage better decisions.
- Approach parents as team members. You both have a common goal: the best interests of their child. The point of the conference is to find ways to work together.
- Whenever possible, document your concerns. Have examples of the student's work available, or have notes regarding behavioral issues. If the student is not turning in assignments, give parents the assignment sheet showing the due dates.

- Stick to descriptions of behavior rather than characterizations of students (e.g., "Barbara calls other students names" rather than "Barbara is a bully"). Characterizations are more likely to put parents on the defensive.
- Respect parents' knowledge of their child. Parents often have insights about what behavior is typical for the student and may be able to suggest alternative ways of dealing with a problem.

The secret to successful parent–teacher conferences is planning. If you have back-to-back conferences, provide a place for the next arrivals to sit and wait. Arrange chairs for all participants in a circle, a semicircle, or around a table. Decide which issues need to be addressed with the parent(s). Bring documentation and a collection of the child's work over time to support those issues. Have the child's grades written on a separate piece of paper; showing the entire grade book may infringe on another child's right to privacy.

Begin the conference by describing some of the child's strengths. During the meeting, avoid "teacher talk," acronyms, or technical terms the parents may not understand. Encourage comments and questions. If possible, include the child in all or part of the conference. Keep a written record of suggestions, concerns, and plans of action. End the conference by reiterating any responsibilities that have been assumed. Thank the parents for supporting their child's education.

# ■ Chapter Summary

When the planning and preparation aspects of classroom management do not prevent misbehavior, it becomes necessary to communicate directly with students regarding their behavior. Three communication skills can help resolve conflicts. The first is constructive assertiveness: a communication tool wherein the teacher states concerns about the misbehavior, describes the effects that will result if it continues, and mandates a change in behavior. With this assertive form of communication, the nonverbal aspects of the conversation should be calm, professional, and confident.

The second skill is empathic responding: a response that focuses on listening to the underlying issues prompting the misbehavior. In this way, teachers affirm students' feelings, inviting them to continue the conversation. This form of communication requires that the teacher show both listening (e.g., attentive posture, asking follow-up questions) and processing skills (e.g., avoiding judgment, summarizing, hearing between the lines). The third response is problem solving, a type of communication in which teacher and student together (1) identify the problem, (2) select a solution, and (3) obtain a commitment (e.g., contract). Problem solving does not always result in a solution in a single cycle; rather, repeated iterations may help the teacher and student come to a joint agreement.

These three communication skills are equally helpful in communicating with other members of the schooling community, such as parents. When communicating with parents, teachers should approach them as team members, finding ways to value their input. Communication with parents is an valuable tool in an effective classroom management system.

# ■ **Further Reading**

Berger, E. H., & Rojas-Cortez, M. R. (2011). *Parents as partners in education: Families and schools working together* (8th ed.). Englewood Cliffs, NJ: Prentice Hall.

> *This is a useful handbook for understanding important aspects of home–school relations. It provides a comprehensive look at parent–school partnerships and offers practical suggestions to aid collaboration between teachers and parents. It includes topics such as diverse families, the exceptional child, programs to enrich parent–school involvement, and communication necessary for partnerships.*

Greene, J. O., & Burleson, B. R. (Eds.). (2003). *Handbook of communication and social interaction skills.* Mahwah, NJ: Erlbaum.

> *A comprehensive reference work, this book has chapters describing research, theory, and applications on topics such as interpersonal conflict, nonverbal communication, impression management, emotional support, and intercultural communication.*

Hill, C. E. (2009). *Helping skills: Facilitating exploration, insight, and action* (3rd ed.). Washington, DC: American Psychological Association.

> *This textbook outlines a three-stage model of helping and presents basic skills used at each stage, emphasizing the role of affect, cognition, and behavior in the change process.*

Jennings, P. O., & Greenberg, M. T. (2009). The prosocial classroom: Teacher social and emotional competence in relation to student and classroom outcomes. *Review of Educational Research, 79,* 491–525.

> *The authors propose a model of classroom climate that emphasizes the role of teacher social and emotional competence. Connections to student social, emotional, and academic outcomes are identified for effective classroom management, healthy teacher–student relationships, and teacher social–emotional competence.*

Kottler, J. A. (2002). *Students who drive you crazy: Succeeding with resistant, unmotivated, and otherwise difficult young people.* Thousand Oaks, CA: Sage (Corwin Press).

> *This book blends theory and research with examples from practicing teachers, counselors, school administrators, and students. It offers tools for dealing with frustrating, hostile interactions.*

www2.scholastic.com/browse/teach.jsp

> *This Web site is a good resource for teachers. Enter "parent conferences" in the search line to pull up a variety of ideas for planning and conducting meetings with parents.*

# ■ Suggested Activities

## ACTIVITY 9.1: PUSHING BUTTONS

Everyone is sensitive to or self-conscious about some aspect of personal image or background. Height, weight, appearance, content knowledge, experience, ethnicity, marital status, and acceptance or respect are among the areas that may be a source of insecurity or concern. Because teaching is so public, and because children and adolescents are astute observers of teachers' reactions, teachers often reveal much about themselves as they react when students find the right "button" to push. Think about a characteristic that represents a source of insecurity for you, and discuss your responses to the following questions with a partner: What area of teaching represents a source of insecurity to you? What can you do to minimize the negative effect of that insecurity or, better still, turn it into a plus? How might your communication with students be affected if a student "pushes your button" in that area? What insecurities might students be indicating with their misbehaviors?

## ACTIVITY 9.2: DEVELOPING ASSERTIVENESS SKILLS

This activity provides situations for practicing assertiveness skills. For each situation described, prepare an assertive response. Use the following sequence of steps one at a time with the situations until you are comfortable with the approach. Then combine the steps into a fluid statement with the remaining situations so you have the experience of responding to situations.

**STEP 1:** Write out a statement that describes the problem clearly or that insists your or classmates' rights be respected. Compare and discuss your statements with a partner. Revise your statement if you wish.

**STEP 2:** Use role-playing to portray the situation, with you as the teacher and someone else as the student. During the role play, try to use appropriate body language (including eye contact and facial expression) to support your intervention.

**STEP 3:** Get feedback from observers regarding your use of assertiveness skills. Use the Assertiveness Assessment Scales on page 183 to assess your own behavior, and check out your perceptions by comparing your self-ratings to those of observers. Be sure to discuss any discrepancies and any problems you experienced in enacting an assertive role. Repeat Step 2 until you feel comfortable with your handling of the situation.

It is not necessary to continue the role play to a complete resolution of the situation. The purpose is only to provide experience in enacting assertive behaviors. The person playing the student role should respond as naturally as possible.

*Situation A.* Scott often visits the class pet, a hermit crab, when he should be completing independent work. His paths to the pencil sharpener, trash can, small-group table, and other destinations all seem to involve the aquarium. As you are monitoring the class's work, you see Scott reaching in the aquarium.

*Situation B.* Alyson and Maria are supposed to put the equipment away, but they have left much of it strewn about the gym. Now they are heading for the door in anticipation of the end-of-recess bell.

*Situation C.* Victor has not been working on his assignment. You caught his eye, but he looked away and has continued to talk to nearby students. As you move around the room checking other students' progress, he begins to make a paper airplane.

*Situation D.* As you walk down the hallway, you hear two students trading insults ("Your mama ... !"). The students are not angry yet, just fooling around, but several other students are gathering, and you think they may encourage the two students to fight.

*Situation E.* As you begin class, you observe Daphne eating a cupcake, in violation of the rule prohibiting food in the room. When she sees that you notice her, she stuffs the cupcake into her mouth and gets another one out of the package.

*Situation F.* During your current events discussion, Susan and Kris trade notes and laugh noisily. You sense that other students' attention is being captured by the duo's antics, and you begin to be annoyed by having to compete for the class's attention.

*Situation G.* When you were absent yesterday, your fourth-grade class gave the substitute teacher a difficult time. According to the note she left for you (with a copy sent to the principal!), many students refused to work at all, four or five students left for the restroom and didn't return until lunchtime, and a paper and spit wad fight raged most of the afternoon. As the morning bell rings, you enter the room to greet your class.

## ACTIVITY 9.3: RECOGNIZING LISTENING RESPONSES

Each of the following dialogues depicts a statement and a variety of teacher responses. In each case, decide which response is closest to a listening response; that is, which one invites further discussion, best reflects the student's idea or feeling, and/or allows the student an opportunity to find his or her own solution? Check your accuracy against the key in the Appendix.

1. STUDENT: School stinks.
   a. Don't use that type of language.
   b. You seem upset about school.
   c. Come on, things aren't that bad.
   d. That attitude will get you nowhere.

2. STUDENT: I can't understand fractions. Why do we have to learn this stuff?
   a. You'll need it to get into college.
   b. Just keep at it. It'll make sense after a while.
   c. Something isn't making sense to you?
   d. I'm not available to help you until after school.

3. STUDENT: I don't want to sit near those boys anymore.
   a. Sorry, but seats have been assigned.
   b. If they're bothering you, I can move you.
   c. Didn't you talk to them about it?
   d. What is the situation?

4. PARENT: My child is very upset and needs more help or she won't be able to pass. She says she doesn't understand anything.
   a. Please go on. I'd like to hear more about this.
   b. She needs to pay closer attention in class.
   c. She's very anxious, but actually she'll do just fine. She only needs to review more before tests.
   d. Most students find my explanations to be quite clear. Is there something going on at home?

5. TEACHER NEXT DOOR: My class is going to drive me up a wall. They have been impossible lately!

a. Have you considered being more assertive with them?
b. I know. Everyone in this wing can hear them.
c. You sound frustrated.
d. You think they're bad, you should have my group.

## ACTIVITY 9.4: PRODUCING EMPATHIC RESPONSES

You will have to work with a colleague during this activity; take turns role-playing the student and the teacher. The person role-playing the teacher should practice empathic responding skills, and the student should try to behave as naturally as possible. It is assumed that the dialogue is occurring at a time and place that permit this type of exchange and that the teacher is interested in allowing the student to describe the problem. These assumptions will not always be true, of course. You could not deal with these issues in the middle of reading groups, for example, nor will you always have the time to deal in this way with every student problem. In this exercise, avoid giving solutions for the student's problem; instead, concentrate on using listening and processing skills to encourage the student to talk about the situation and think through the problem.

*Situation A.* Teresa is an ESL student who is doing well in math and science. However, she has displayed difficulty with writing skills. With tears in her eyes, she approaches you after class with a writing assignment that you have given an unsatisfactory grade. "I thought I did okay on this."

*Situation B.* David, a bright student, offers you some advice: "This class would be a lot more interesting if we didn't have to do all these worksheets. Couldn't we choose our own work sometime?"

*Situation C.* While the rest of the class is at work on an assignment, Barry closes his book, throws away his assignment sheet, and slides down in his seat disgustedly.

*Situation D.* For the second time this week, SueAnn has not turned in an assignment. Last week she "forgot" to bring her homework twice. Later, you remind SueAnn that assignments are important. "I don't care," she responds.

*Situation E.* Armand, a new student, has been having trouble making friends. Lately he has been getting into arguments with some of the more popular boys and has been teasing a few girls, apparently to gain attention. However, he has not succeeded in breaking into the social scene. After class one day he says to you, "I wish I could go back to my old school."

## ACTIVITY 9.5: PROBLEM-SOLVING EXERCISES

Use role-playing to practice the problem-solving steps—identify the problem and its consequences, identify and select a solution, obtain a commitment to try it out—with the following situations. In situations in which the student is the one primarily experiencing the problem, assume that the teacher's initial listening response is received positively by the student so there is a basis for continuing the discussion and for the teacher's assisting the student in thinking through a solution. In cases in which the student's behavior is affecting the teacher's ability to teach or is interfering with other students' rights, the student may initially be reluctant to participate in this type of discussion, and the teacher will have to use assertiveness skills to overcome this resistance. In addition to these situations, you can use some of the situations presented in Activities 9.2 and 9.4 for further practice.

*Situation A.* Bob and Ray are noisy and distracting when they clown around and vie for other students' attention. Reminders and penalties have only fleeting effects on their behavior. Therefore, you decide to have them come in for a conference.

*Situation B.* David is good-natured as long as no demands are placed on him. However, when reminded that class time is for learning and for working on assignments, he becomes defiant and insists that it is his right to do whatever he wishes as long as he "don't hurt no one."

*Situation C.* Lucy is a bright student but often turns work in late; frequently it is incomplete. She is able to pass your tests, however, and could easily be a top student if she were prompt and better organized. Recently, you sent her parents a progress report because of missing assignments, and Lucy and her mother have come in for a conference to discuss the situation. Her mother wonders whether you will allow Lucy to make up the missing work to avoid her receiving failing grades.

## ACTIVITY 9.6: DIALOGUE ANALYSIS

Discuss the following two vignettes, expanded from the examples provided in this chapter's problem-solving section. To what extent did the teachers use the problem-solving steps as well as constructive assertiveness and empathic responding? Were those skills appropriately used? What other approaches might the teachers have tried for dealing with these problems? What are the advantages and disadvantages of those approaches?

## ■ Vignettes

These two examples illustrate the use of a problem-solving conference for problem situations described earlier in this chapter.

### Dialogue 9.1: Brad

TEACHER: Brad, I asked you to stay to talk with me because of a problem we've been having during discussions. Often, when I ask a question, you call out the answer without waiting to be called on. Do you agree that this is happening?

BRAD: I guess so.

TEACHER: Can you tell me why this is a problem?

BRAD: I suppose it doesn't give others a chance.

TEACHER: That's absolutely right. I have to be able to find out whether other boys and girls understand what we are discussing.

BRAD: What if they don't know?

TEACHER: You mean, if nobody raises a hand or tries to answer?

|          |                                                                                                              |
|---------:|--------------------------------------------------------------------------------------------------------------|
| BRAD:    | Yeah, then can I answer?                                                                                      |
| TEACHER: | Do you suppose that some people might need more time to think about what they are going to say?               |
| BRAD:    | I guess so. But it's boring to just sit and wait for someone to think if I already know it.                   |
| TEACHER: | It is difficult to wait and be patient. But I must be able to teach the whole class and to conduct the discussions for everybody. Can you think of any way that we could handle this so that I can call on others and you can still have your fair turn? |
| BRAD:    | I suppose I could raise my hand.                                                                              |
| TEACHER: | That would be a big help. I would really appreciate that. I think you have some good ideas and should have plenty of chances to answer. Brad, how often would you like to speak during our discussions? |
| BRAD:    | I don't know. (*Pauses*) Three or four times, I guess.                                                        |
| TEACHER: | That would be fine. How about if I guarantee you four times during each discussion? You raise your hand to respond and keep track of the times you answer. If I don't call on you sometime, you know you'll get your chances later. |
| BRAD:    | Okay.                                                                                                        |
| TEACHER: | How about our trying this for the rest of the week, and then we'll talk again and see whether it solves our problem? |
| BRAD:    | Okay.                                                                                                        |

## Dialogue 9.2: Alice and Alicia

|          |                                                                                                              |
|---------:|--------------------------------------------------------------------------------------------------------------|
| TEACHER: | Girls, I asked you to stay for this conference because I've been having to take more and more of my time to get you to clean up and to keep work areas neat. I wonder what you both think about this problem. |
| ALICE:   | I don't know.                                                                                                |
| ALICIA:  | I don't think we're so bad about it.                                                                         |
| TEACHER: | It has become very frustrating to me. Do you remember that I had to remind you and wait for the jobs to be done? |
| GIRLS:   | Yes.                                                                                                        |
| TEACHER: | Whose job is it to pick up materials and put things away?                                                     |
| GIRLS:   | Ours.                                                                                                       |
| TEACHER: | Do you think we can find a way for those jobs to get done? Do you have any suggestions?                       |
| ALICIA:  | I could just do it without being asked.                                                                      |
| TEACHER: | Okay. That is a good idea. Do you have any other suggestions?                                                 |
| ALICIA:  | We could ask someone to help us.                                                                             |
| TEACHER: | That is an interesting idea. Do you know someone who wants to clean up your things?                           |
| ALICIA:  | I don't know. Probably.                                                                                      |
| TEACHER: | Would you like to help someone else clean up or put things away?                                             |
| ALICIA:  | Sure, it'd be fun.                                                                                           |
| TEACHER: | How about you, Alice?                                                                                        |
| ALICE:   | Okay.                                                                                                        |
| TEACHER: | Well, then I have an idea. How about if I let you both be my room helpers this next week. As soon as you finish your own cleanup, you can help me with jobs that I need to have done. How would that be? |

GIRLS: Yeah!

TEACHER: Okay. Let's try this out. Tomorrow, when you have cleaned up, let me know. Then I'll tell you what you can do to help me. How does that sound?

GIRLS:: Sure! Okay.

TEACHER: I'm glad we had a chance to plan this, because now I have two room helpers, and we will have our problem solved.

# ■ Assertiveness Assessment Scales

When using the following scales, note that a midrange rating represents an appropriate degree of assertiveness. When rating your own or another teacher's behavior as either nonassertive or hostile, circle the descriptive term that best reflects the basis for your judgment, or write a note on the scale if the descriptors don't adequately capture your perception.

| | Unassertive | Assertive | Hostile |
|---|---|---|---|
| | 1 _____ 2 _____ | 3 _____ | 4 _____ 5 |
| *Eye contact* | Teacher avoids looking at student. | Teacher maintains eye contact with student. | Teacher glares at student; stares student down. |
| | 1 _____ 2 _____ | 3 _____ | 4 _____ 5 |
| *Body language* | Teacher turns away, gestures nervously, trembles. | Teacher faces student; alert posture but not threatening. Gestures support statements. | Teacher crowds student, points, shakes fist threateningly. |
| | 1 _____ 2 _____ | 3 _____ | 4 _____ 5 |
| *Message* | Obsequious, self-denigrating; excuses student behavior; pleads with student. | Clearly states the problem or insists that the behavior stop. Makes own feelings known, may use humor to relieve tension. | Name calling, labeling, blaming, threatening, being sarcastic, preaching, lecturing. |
| | 1 _____ 2 _____ | 3 _____ | 4 _____ 5 |
| *Voice features* | Tremulous, whiny, hesitant, broken, or too soft. | Appropriate volume, natural sounding, varied for emphasis. | Voice too loud; shouts, yells. |
| | 1 _____ 2 _____ | 3 _____ | 4 _____ 5 |
| *Facial features* | Smiles inappropriately; nervous twitches and tics. | Expression suits message. | Excessive affect; contorted, disgusted, enraged expression. |

# ACTIVITY 9.7: PARENT–TEACHER CONFERENCES

Consider the following scenarios of potential parent–teacher conference topics/situations. In groups of three (one as teacher, one as parent, one as observer), role-play the potential conversation. Rotate these roles with each new situation. After the role play, the observer should lead a group conversation in response to the provided questions.

*Situation A.* Ms. Charles, a second-grade teacher, is meeting with a parent, Mr. Akim, for the standard end-of-the-first-grading-period parent–teacher conference concerning his daughter, Maya. At the end of the school day yesterday, Ms. Charles sent home a request for parents to choose their desired meeting times. Mr. Akim returned the note this morning, indicating a 4:00 time desired. Since two parents requested that same time, Mr. Akim was assigned a 3:40 conference but received no communication about that change from the teacher. Mr. Akim is paying for his two school-age children to be with child care during both this conference and the one scheduled with his other child's teacher at 4:20. After dropping his children off with the sitter, he arrives at 3:55 for the anticipated 4:00 conference.

*Situation A Questions:* What are the possible outcomes of this situation as it is? How might Ms. Charles salvage this conference? What suggestions might you offer to Ms. Charles to prepare for the next parent–teacher conference?

*Situation B.* Mr. Tetch, a fifth-grade teacher, is Justin Roberts's homeroom teacher. He is meeting with Justin's mom, Ms. Roberts, at her request. The parent plans to share her concerns over her son's declining grades in math and social studies, to ask for suggestions about how she can support his learning in these areas, and to see if there are any situations in the classroom that might be serving as obstacles for Justin's learning in these subjects. Mr. Tetch does not know why Ms. Roberts has requested the conference but, prior to their meeting, has gathered the following information: his grade book, some examples of Justin's classwork, the class seating chart, and the same materials from a fifth-grade team teacher, Ms. Gray, who is Justin's math and social studies teacher.

*Situation B Questions:* How was Mr. Tetch prepared for this conference? In what ways was he not prepared? What additional action(s) might be required following their conversation? How can Mr. Tetch best represent Ms. Gray in her absence?

*Situation C.* Kalia's mom, Ms. McCann, did not have a good schooling experience and is not confident in school settings. She is meeting with Kalia's third-grade teacher, Ms. Pratt, at the teacher's request. Kalia has been showing severe difficulties in reading, and Ms. Pratt would like to talk with Ms. McCann about their family history with reading and a course of help for Kalia. In this conference Ms. Pratt would also like to recommend testing Kalia for both dyslexia and qualification for special education services.

*Situation C Questions:* How could Ms. Pratt help put Ms. McCann at ease? What documentation might Ms. Pratt want to have with her at this conference? How might Ms. McCann's insecurity at school influence the actions taken for Kalia?

---

**MyEducationLab**

Now go to www.myeducationlab.com to:

- Take a Quiz to test your mastery of chapter objectives.
- Study chapter content with an individualized Study Plan.
- Deepen your understanding of particular concepts and principles with Classroom Management Simulations.
- Apply what you have learned in the chapter to your work with children in Building Teaching Skills exercises.

# CHAPTER 10

# Managing Problem Behaviors

In this chapter, we describe strategies for dealing with some problem behaviors you may encounter. Although previous chapters described preventive measures as well as tactics for managing inappropriate behavior, it is helpful to consider a full range of approaches. We hope that you will not encounter problems, especially serious ones, in large numbers. However, as you work with students, you will undoubtedly face difficult situations that must be resolved to preserve the climate for learning or to assist a student in developing behaviors more compatible with group life and learning. The aim of this chapter is to pull together and organize a wide variety of strategies from which you can select. By having a broad array of approaches to draw on, you will be better able to choose one that fits your specific conditions. Having alternatives in mind is very useful, too, in case your first plan doesn't work.

We hope this chapter's concern with behavior problems will not be taken as a grim comment on the teacher's role. In particular, this extensive list of strategies should be considered within the context of the other chapters in this book. We have advocated generally for a positive, supportive climate with heavy reliance on preventive measures. Within that framework, however, you must be ready to deal with problems when they arise. With a variety of strategies at hand, you can tailor your approach to fit the situation, keep interruptions to the instructional program to a minimum, and promote positive behavior.

This chapter's focus is on problem behaviors rather than problem students. Only a small percentage of students exhibit maladaptive behaviors with such consistency and to such a degree that they warrant being labeled emotionally disturbed or behaviorally disordered. With a few students you may have to "teach" acceptable behavior. Most students do, however, behave inappropriately on occasion; we think it is much more constructive in the long run to help students learn how to behave rather than assume they are restricted in their capacity to make good choices.

On occasion, problem behaviors result from stressors the student is experiencing at home or elsewhere (e.g., abuse, a death in the family, parental unemployment, serious illness, or divorce). If a student's behavior changes, or if inappropriate behavior persists after reasonable attempts to deal with it have been made, a discussion of the situation with a parent, guardian, school counselor, or social worker is in order. Sometimes the student's previous teacher can provide additional information. When you talk with the student about what is happening, use listening skills (see Chapter 9) to try to understand the situation. Be empathic, but help the child understand that acting out will not help the problem. By all means, follow up if you discover that a situation outside the classroom is affecting the child's behavior.

## ■ What Is Problem Behavior?

The concept of problem behavior is broad. Rather than enumerate all possible misbehaviors that might occur in classrooms, it is more manageable to consider categories.

### Nonproblem

Brief inattention, some talk during a transition between activities, small periods of daydreaming, and a short pause while working on an assignment are examples of common behaviors that are not really problems for anyone because they are of brief duration and don't interfere with learning or instruction. Everyone is the better for their being ignored. To attempt to react to them would consume too much energy, interrupt lessons constantly, and detract from a positive classroom climate.

### Minor Problem

This category includes behaviors that run counter to class procedures or rules but that do not, when occurring infrequently, disrupt class activities or seriously interfere with learning. Examples are calling out or leaving one's seat without permission, reading or doing unrelated work during class time, passing notes, eating candy, scattering trash around, and talking during independent work or group work. These behaviors are minor irritants as long as they are brief in duration and are limited to one or a few students. You would not give them much thought except for two reasons: Unattended, they might persist and spread; if the behaviors have an audience, not responding might cause a perception of inconsistency and potentially undermine an important aspect of the overall management system. Also, if students engage in such behavior for an extended period of time, their learning is likely to be adversely affected.

## Major Problem Limited in Scope and Effects

This category includes behaviors that disrupt an activity or interfere with learning but whose occurrence is limited to a single student or perhaps to a few students not acting in concert. For example, a student may be chronically off task. Another student may rarely complete assignments. A student may frequently fail to follow class rules for talk or movement around the room or may refuse to do any work. This category also includes a more serious but isolated violation of class or school rules, for example, an act of vandalism or hitting another student.

## Escalating or Spreading Problem

This category includes any minor problem that has become commonplace and thus constitutes a threat to order and the learning environment. For example, when many students roam around the room at will and continually call out irrelevant comments, content development activities suffer; social talking that continues unabated even when the teacher repeatedly asks for quiet is distracting to others; and talking back and refusing to cooperate with the teacher are frustrating and may lead to a poor classroom climate. Frequent violations of behavioral guidelines cause the management and instructional system to break down and interfere with the momentum of class activities.

# ■ Goals for Managing Problem Behavior

In dealing with problem behavior, several types of goals must be considered. You have to judge the short- and long-term effects of any management strategy you choose. In the short term, the desired results are that the inappropriate behaviors cease and the students resume or begin appropriate behaviors. In the long run, it is important to prevent the problem from recurring. At the same time, you must be watchful for potential negative side effects and take steps to minimize them. Also, you should consider the effects on the individual student(s) causing the problem as well as the effect on the whole class.

*Joel is talking and showing off to a group of students during independent work.*

### Vignette Reflection

Discuss with a partner your responses to the following questions: What happens next if the teacher uses a sarcastic put-down? stands close to Joel? asks for Joel to return to work? yells at Joel? ignores the behavior? How might the combination of some of these responses play out?

The ideal strategy is one that maintains or restores order in the class immediately without adversely affecting the positive learning environment; in addition, an ideal strategy prevents a repetition of the problem and results in subsequent appropriate behavior in similar situations. In practice, classrooms are busy places, and you rarely have sufficient time to mull over the various options and their effects whenever a problem arises, especially in the midst of a crisis. If only there were a "pause" button on classroom events! The need for prompt reaction should not, however, deter us from evaluating the results of our efforts and from seeking alternative approaches, especially when our initial efforts do not meet with success. It is therefore useful to have a repertoire of strategies to apply to various problem situations.

# ■ Management Strategies

This section includes useful strategies for dealing with a variety of classroom behavior problems. The first several strategies can be utilized without much difficulty, require little teacher time, and have the great virtue of being relatively unobtrusive. They have much to recommend them because they do not give undue attention to the misbehavior and do not interfere with the flow of instructional activity. As we move down the list, we encounter strategies that are more direct attempts to stop the behaviors and to do so quickly; however, the strategies have more negative features. They demand more of the teacher's time, they may have unintended consequences on students, or they interrupt class activities. A general principle helpful in selecting a strategy is to use an approach that is effective in stopping the inappropriate behavior promptly and that has the least negative impact. The theory is that minor problems should usually be dealt with by limited interventions. As problems become more serious, the limited interventions may be ineffective in quickly ending the disruptive behavior, and thus a more time-consuming or intrusive intervention may be required. With every level of problem and strategy chosen, however, you must be consistent and fair with all students.

Most elementary schools have prescribed procedures for dealing with certain types of major problems and sometimes even minor ones. For example, teachers' responses to events such as fighting, use of obscene language, stealing, vandalism, and unexcused absence are likely to be directed by school (or district) policies. Therefore, a beginning teacher must learn what policies are in force and follow them. When no specific policy is established for particular problems or when teachers are given latitude in their responses, the alternatives listed later in the chapter can be helpful.

We describe here classroom strategies that have a wide range of application, but the list is not exhaustive. Readers interested in additional ways of coping with behavior problems will find these resources helpful: Emmer and Stough (2008), Myles and Simpson (1994), Poland and McCormick (1999), and Shukla-Mehta and Albin (2003). Additionally, the *Handbook of Classroom Management* (Evertson & Weinstein, 2006) has many excellent chapters that describe strategies for managing problems.

## Simple Interventions

**Use Nonverbal Cues.**   Make eye contact with the misbehaving student, and give a signal such as a finger to the lips, a head shake, or a hand signal to direct the student to desist. Sometimes lightly touching a student on the arm or shoulder helps signal your presence and has a calming effect. Never touch a student when you are angry, though, and avoid touching students when they are angry. Touching in these cases is likely to escalate the situation. Touching is often covered by school or district policy. To avoid the appearance of inappropriate physical contact, keep touch within appropriate contexts (e.g., celebrating student success with a high five, consoling a crying child with a hug), on appropriate body parts (e.g., hands, shoulders), and in appropriate locations (e.g., not behind closed doors with an individual student).

**Get the Activity Moving.**   Often student behavior deteriorates during transition times between activities or during dead time when no apparent focus for attention is present. Students leave their seats, talk, shuffle restlessly, and amuse themselves and each other while waiting for something to do. The remedy is obvious: Move through the transition more quickly, and reduce or eliminate the dead time. This strategy entails planning activities so that all materials are ready and adhering to a well-conceived lesson plan. Trying to catch and correct inappropriate behaviors during such times is usually futile and misdirected. Just get the next activity under way, and direct students to the desired behaviors.

**Use Proximity.**   Move closer to students. Combine proximity with nonverbal cues to stop inappropriate behavior without interrupting the instruction. Be sure to continue monitoring the students at least until they have begun an appropriate activity.

**Use Group Focus.**   Use group alerting, accountability, or a higher-participation format (see Chapter 6) to draw students back into a lesson when attention has begun to wane or when students have been in a passive mode for too long and you observe off-task behavior spreading.

**Redirect the Behavior.**   When students are off task, remind them of appropriate behavior: "Everyone should be writing answers to the chapter questions," "Be sure your group is discussing your project plan," or "Everyone should be seated and quiet unless you have been given permission to leave your seat or talk." If only one or two students are engaged in inappropriate behavior, a private redirection will be less likely to interrupt the activity or to direct attention toward the incorrect behavior. A redirection strategy that works well with younger children is the use of public praise for appropriate group and individual behavior. For example, if several students are talking and inattentive at the beginning of a new activity, the teacher could identify students who are behaving correctly: "I see many students who are sitting quietly, ready to begin. . . . I really appreciate the boys and girls who are ready for our next activity. John is listening, Donica is being very quiet. Oh, good, Demetrius, Richard, and Corby are ready. . . ." In most cases, off-task students quickly come around.

**Provide Needed Instruction.**   Especially during individual or group work, off-task behaviors may reflect poor comprehension of the task. Check the work, or ask brief questions to assess understanding; give necessary assistance so students can work independently. If many students can't proceed, stop the activity, and provide whole-class instruction. Next time, be sure to check comprehension before starting the independent work activity.

**Issue a Brief Desist.**   Tell the student(s) to stop the undesirable behavior. Make direct eye contact, and be assertive (see Chapter 9). Keep your comments brief, and monitor the situation until the student(s) comply. Combine this strategy with redirection to encourage desirable behavior.

**Give the Student a Choice.**   Tell the student that he or she has a choice: either to behave appropriately or to continue the problem behavior and receive a consequence. Be sure to describe the desired behavior. Telling a student to "behave appropriately" does not communicate clearly what the desired behavior should be. For example, suppose a student has refused to clean up properly after completing a project: "You may choose to clean up now; if not, you are choosing to stay in during recess until your area is clean." To a student who continues to distract nearby students: "You may choose to work quietly on your assignment at your seat, or you will have to sit in the time-out area to do your work." The purpose of stating the consequence as a choice is to emphasize the student's responsibility for his or her behavior. Also, making the consequence clear increases the chance that the student will choose to self-regulate.

## Moderate Interventions

These strategies are more confrontational than the limited interventions just described and thus have greater potential for eliciting resistance. In cases in which the student's behavior is not especially disruptive, it is desirable to use a simple intervention or to issue a warning to the student before using these moderate interventions. That approach permits the student to exercise self-control and may save the teacher time and effort.

**Withhold a Privilege or Desired Activity.**   Students who abuse a privilege (e.g., being allowed to work together on a project, sitting near friends, or having the freedom to move around the classroom without permission) can lose the privilege and be required to earn it back with appropriate behavior. For teachers who allow quiet talking during independent activities, removing this privilege can be an effective way to limit unproductive social behavior. Other teachers allow a class to choose as incentives a favorite activity or a short period of free time on one or more days each week. Time lost from such activities can then be a strong deterrent to inappropriate behavior at other times. Although withholding a privilege is a form of punishment, it usually has fewer side effects than punishment that requires directly applying an aversive consequence.

**Isolate or Remove Students.**    Students who disrupt an activity can be removed to another area of the room, away from other students. It is helpful to have a carrel with sides, or at least a desk at the back of the room facing away from other students, to discourage eye contact with someone in the time-out area. If no suitable place is available, the student may have to have time-out in the hall outside the door, although not if your school has a policy prohibiting this because of the problem of adequately supervising the student.

Time-out is a variation on the preceding consequence in that it takes away the student's privilege of participating in the activity. It is a good idea to allow excluded students to return to the activity in a short time, as long as their behavior in time-out is acceptable. Some teachers prefer to let them retain some control over the return, using a direction such as, "You may come back in 5 minutes if you decide that you can follow our class rules." Other teachers prohibit the student from returning until the activity is completed or until the teacher has a brief conference with the student.

A problem with time-out is that some students may find it rewarding. They receive attention when it is administered, and it allows them to avoid an activity they dislike. When this occurs, you should switch to another strategy. Another problem is that a student may refuse to go to the time-out area. Usually this is a temporary problem; if you are firm, ignoring the student's protests and continuing with the activity, the student will go eventually. One way to move a recalcitrant body is to offer a choice: "You can either take time-out or walk to the principal's office. It's your decision."

Time-out has another risk. Its use clearly identifies a student as someone who is excludable, and it may result in implicit labeling by the teacher, by other students, or by the excluded student. If used frequently with a particular student, it may cause resentment and anger. Therefore, be sure to provide opportunities for such students to resume full participation in the class and use other strategies to promote appropriate behavior at the same time.

**Use a Penalty.**    Sometimes a small amount of repetitious work is required as payment for inappropriate behavior. For example, in physical education, students may be required to run an extra lap or do push-ups. In math, students may work extra problems. The advantage of this type of consequence is that it can usually be administered quickly with a minimum of the teacher's time and effort. A disadvantage is that the task is being defined as punishing, and therefore the student's attitude toward the content may be negatively affected. Another problem with the use of penalties is that their ease of use can lead to overuse, detracting from the overall climate.

**Assign Detention.**    Another penalty commonly used is to require that the student serve a detention, whether at lunch, during recess, or before or after school. Because of the logical relationship between the problem and the consequence, this penalty is often used for misbehaviors that involve time (e.g., extended goofing off and time wasting, behavior that interferes with instruction or work time). Other common uses of the penalty are for repeated rule violations and for frequent failure to complete assignments. You may have to supervise the detention in your room, or your school might have a detention area with an assigned monitor. The time in detention need not be lengthy, especially for misbehaviors that are not severe or frequent; a 10- or 15-minute detention is often sufficient to make the point.

An advantage of detention as a penalty is that it is disliked by most students, and they want to avoid it; at the same time, it is administered away from other students in the class and thus does not give undue attention to the behavior. Also, it is a common punishment, so extensive explanations and unusual procedures aren't needed. Finally, the teacher can sometimes use a little of the detention time to hold a conference with the student and perhaps work out a plan for improving the situation.

A disadvantage of detention is that it does take the teacher's time, especially when he or she must supervise it. Even when the school has a detention room, the teacher must write a referral. Also, students may not have access to transportation to or from school at the time of the detention. Another disadvantage is that students might be able to avoid detention, at least in the short run, simply by not showing up. Thus, the teacher or the school must have a backup plan, such as doubling the time. Moreover, records must be kept, and often additional time is required to deal with such students.

**Referral to the School Office.**    Many schools have a system of referral to an assistant principal, who then deals with the student. Sometimes referrals are built into the school's discipline plan for specific behaviors such as fighting or vandalism, but teachers also have wide latitude to refer a student for noncodified transgressions, such as disrespect, rudeness, and insubordination. Often a first-referral consequence is limited to detention or a warning, with subsequent referrals resulting in further detention, a parent conference, or, for serious or persistent infractions, suspension for one or several days. To deal with the student fairly and appropriately, it is essential that the

© ZITS Partnership, King Features Syndicate.

administrator be made aware of the basis for referral. Thus, the teacher usually fills out an office referral form or sends an email to the assistant principal who is handling the referral.

Advantages of the office referral are that it can be an effective limit for students who do not respond to other approaches, and it does not take much teacher time, at least in the short run. It may also allow the teacher to short-circuit an emerging problem that is awkward to settle publicly. Disadvantages include that its usefulness depends on others for its effectiveness, it requires frequent external support, and it demonstrates that the teacher does not have final authority. Additionally, frequent use of this strategy often demonstrates to administrators that a teacher is not doing his or her job. As a strategy for handling in-class problems, it is not a realistic option in most schools.

Another concern with disciplinary referrals is their potential for discriminatory use. Some research (cf. Skiba & Rausch, 2006) has shown that African-American students are more likely than white students to receive disciplinary referrals, an effect that is evident even after controlling for student socioeconomic status. In addition, the research indicates that teachers are more likely to refer African-American students for behaviors that are subject to interpretation, such as disrespect and excessive noise; white students are more often referred for behaviors that violate clearly defined prohibitions, such as vandalism and use of obscene language. Other researchers who have examined disciplinary practices in multicultural schools (cf. Gay, 2006) have noted that African-American students' communication styles tend to be more dramatic, animated, and confrontational than those of students from other racial and ethnic groups. Teachers may misinterpret these students' communications as rude and inappropriate for the classroom, and attempts to correct the students may lead to resentment and misunderstanding. It is plausible, therefore, that some portion of the more numerous disciplinary referrals received by African-American students is a function of overreaction by teachers to their communication styles. In fact, to avoid inadvertent discrimination through classroom management, teachers are encouraged to consider how their classroom management can be made culturally relevant. For more detail on culturally responsive classroom management (CRCM), see Weinstein, Tomlinson-Clarke, and Curran (2004).

We suggest that you be sparing in your use of office referrals. Try to use other, less intrusive interventions, and refer only when the problem is growing more serious and out of control. If you do use a referral, consider the possibility that you are reacting to a student's communication style rather than to a specific type of misbehavior. However, once you have made the referral, follow up with the appropriate administrator and the student to be sure there is a satisfactory resolution to the problem.

## More Extensive Interventions

When students do not respond to simple or moderate interventions, more extensive interventions are required to prevent their behavior from continuing to disrupt classroom activities and interfering with their own and others' learning. In such situations one or more of the following strategies may be helpful. This section describes strategies that are more involved and more time-consuming but may be more effective with the given student(s).

**Use Problem Solving**   Problem solving, described extensively in Chapter 9, is not discussed here. However, four other strategies, which share features with problem solving, are sufficiently distinct to warrant separate presentations.

*Use a Five-Step Intervention Procedure*   Jones and Jones (2010) recommend following five steps when dealing with disruptive student behavior.

STEP 1: Use a nonverbal signal to cue the student to stop.

STEP 2: If the behavior continues, ask the student to follow the desired rule.

STEP 3: If the disruption continues, give the student a choice of stopping the behavior or choosing to develop a plan.

STEP 4: If the student still does not stop, require that the student move to a designated area in the room to write a plan.

STEP 5: If the student refuses to comply with Step 4, send the student to another location (e.g., the school office) to complete the plan.

The five-step intervention process requires students to complete a form for the plan (see Figure 10.1). When the approach is introduced to students, preferably at the beginning of the year, the teacher explains its purpose and how to fill out the form. Role-playing the use of the five steps is recommended, both to teach the procedures and to provide a positive model of their application. It is helpful to laminate a couple of examples of appropriate plans so students have models.

Advantages of this five-step approach include its emphasis on student responsibility and choice. Also, a graduated response to the problem allows the teacher to intervene nonpunitively at first and thus provides a means of settling the matter quickly, with a minimum of disturbance to the ongoing activity. The steps are simple and straightforward, which promotes consistency by the teacher; students, in turn, are aided by the structure and predictability of the approach.

A disadvantage of the system is that movement from Step 1 to Step 5 can occur very rapidly, and intermediate strategies may be necessary to avoid excessive reliance on sending students out of the classroom. In addition, some students, especially in early primary grades, have difficulty writing an acceptable plan by themselves. Also, some misbehaviors (e.g., hitting, destroying school property) do not fit a graduated response and instead require immediate action. Finally, setting up the system and meeting later with students to discuss their plans and then monitoring implementation require at least a moderate investment of time.

*Use the "Think Time" Strategy.*   Designed to help students learn self-control and to prevent a reciprocally escalating sequence of student noncompliance–teacher warnings

**Figure 10.1** ■ Problem-Solving Form

Choose to Be Responsible

Name _____

Date _____

*Rules we agreed on:*

1. Speak politely to others.
2. Treat each other kindly.
3. Follow teacher requests.
4. Be prepared for class.
5. Make a good effort at your work and request help if you need it.
6. Obey all school rules.

*Please answer the following questions:*

1. What rule did you violate? _____
   _____

2. What did you do that violated this rule? _____
   _____

3. What problem did this cause for you, your teacher, or classmates? _____
   _____

4. What plan can you develop that will help you be more responsible and follow this classroom rule? _____
   _____

5. How can the teacher or other students help you? _____
   _____

I, _____, will try my best to follow the plan I have written and to follow all other rules and procedures that we created to make the classroom a good place to learn.

From *Comprehensive Classroom Management: Creating Communities of Support and Solving Problems* (9th ed.) by V. F. Jones and L. S. Jones, 2010, Boston: Pearson. Copyright © 2010 by Pearson Education. Reprinted by permission of the publisher.

and reprimands, the Think Time strategy removes a noncompliant student to another teacher's classroom to provide time for the student to regain focus and reenter the classroom after making a commitment to change the problem behavior (Nelson & Carr, 2000). Using the Think Time strategy requires the cooperation of another teacher whose classroom is in close proximity. The partner teacher reserves a location in the room that is not in a high-traffic area and that will minimize attention to the entering student. After arriving at the receiving classroom, the student is to wait quietly in the designated area and think about what happened. As soon as is practicable (e.g., 3 to 5 minutes), the receiving teacher makes contact with the student and gives him or her a debriefing form to fill out that asks, "What was your behavior?" and, "What behavior do you need to display when you go back to your classroom?" The student is asked if he or she can do it, or if a conference is needed with the teacher. If the student completes the form acceptably, the receiving teacher sends the student back to the original class.

If you use this strategy, you will need to partner with another teacher. After preparing a location in your rooms to receive Think Time students, you each need to teach your students about Think Time. Nelson recommends treating this task as you would any other complex procedure: Explain the purpose of the strategy (e.g., to help students learn self-control and to minimize disruption to learning) and what behaviors might result in Think Time. You also need to describe the signal you will use to send someone to Think Time (e.g., hand them a pass card) and model how students will be expected to leave the room and enter the other teacher's room. The students should also be shown an example of the debriefing form with examples of appropriate responses. Repeated use of Think Time with the same student would indicate the need to join this strategy with parent contact, office referral, and/or in-school suspension (ISS).

Think Time gives the teacher a way to manage students who don't respond to simpler desist techniques, and at the same time it short-circuits the reciprocal escalation of hostile interaction that can develop when a student resists a teacher's attempt to stop misbehavior. Another advantage is that Think Time provides a "cease fire" opportunity in which students acknowledge their part in the problem and identify a solution. In this respect, it is similar to other problem-solving strategies. Limitations of the strategy are that it takes the cooperation and commitment of another teacher, and it requires planning and systematic application to be successful.

*Use the Reality Therapy Model.*   William Glasser's (1975, 1977, www.glasser.com) ideas about reality therapy have been widely applied in education. The essential features when working with an individual student include establishing a caring relationship with the student, focusing on present behaviors, getting the student to accept responsibility, developing a plan for change, obtaining a commitment to follow the plan, and following up. Glasser believes strongly that students choose behavior depending on their perceptions of its consequences. Most students choose appropriate behaviors when they believe these will lead to desirable outcomes, and they avoid behaviors that they perceive will lead to undesirable consequences. Glasser's plan can be put into effect using the following steps:

**STEP 1: Establish involvement with the students.** If students believe the teacher cares for them and has their best interests in mind, they will be more likely to follow the teacher's guidance when evaluating and changing their behavior. A teacher can show commitment to and caring for students in numerous ways: smiling with them, commenting favorably to the students about their work, being friendly, and showing an interest in student activities, families, likes and dislikes, and hobbies. A teacher can also get involved by demonstrating school spirit, having a sense of humor, being a good listener, and taking time to talk with students about their concerns. The best time to establish involvement is before a student becomes disruptive, but even if a student has begun to exhibit problem behavior, it is not too late to begin. When a teacher makes a special effort to have two or three friendly contacts a day with such a student, it can be helpful in creating a more positive climate for change.

**STEP 2: Focus on behavior.** When a problem has occurred, Glasser recommends that a brief conference be held with the student. The initial concern should be to determine what the problem is. To this end, the teacher should ask questions only about "what happened" or "what's going on" and avoid trying to fix blame. Even if the teacher knows exactly what the problem is, it is wise to obtain the student's perspective.

**STEP 3: The student must accept responsibility for the behavior.** This means the student acknowledges that he or she did engage in the behavior. No excuses are accepted. Admitting responsibility is difficult, especially when there are so many other handy things to blame, but in the end, it is a form of denial to try to assign responsibility elsewhere when it was the student who engaged in the behavior. Of course, it is possible that more than one individual is responsible for the problem, but the specific student should still acknowledge ownership of his or her portion.

**STEP 4: The student should evaluate the behavior.** If students have difficulty perceiving their part or they minimize it, Glasser suggests asking, "Has the behavior helped or hurt you? Has it helped or hurt others?" The teacher may have to point out the negative consequences of continuing to misbehave. Unless the student sees that the behavior leads to negative consequences and that changing it will produce desirable consequences, there isn't much reason to expect a change.

**STEP 5: Develop a plan.** The teacher and the student identify ways to prevent the problem from recurring and determine the new behaviors needed. The plan can be written as a contract.

**STEP 6: The student must make a commitment to follow the plan.** Progress will be limited at best if students do not seriously intend to make a change. It may help if the teacher makes clear the positive and negative consequences of following or not following the plan. The plan should be doable in a reasonable time.

**STEP 7: Follow up and follow through.** If the plan works, the teacher should acknowledge the student's success and the resulting desirable behavior(s). If the plan doesn't work, it should be modified with the student; if a negative consequence was called for in the plan, it should be used. Glasser also proposes several additional steps beyond the classroom if a student continues to be a problem. For example, use of in-school suspension could be a consequence of continuing misbehavior; before the student is allowed to return to the classroom, an acceptable plan must be agreed on. Only after several failed attempts to obtain a behavioral change should the teacher refer the student to the principal.

The reality therapy approach to dealing with individual discipline problems has several positive aspects. It is a systematic way for teachers to deal with many kinds of individual problems, and it provides a simple yet effective process for getting right at the issues and avoiding being sidetracked by fault finding, conning, or excuse making. Research on the effects of this aspect of reality therapy is generally supportive for applications to individual students (Emmer & Aussiker, 1990).

*Use Time Away*   Time Away is a three-step strategy that is used to help students whose problem behaviors have become chronic or who escalate their conflicts with the teacher or fellow students (Albrecht, 2008). Use of this strategy requires a trained professional (i.e., facilitator) to work with the student outside of the classroom. The three steps in the Time Away process are these:

STEP 1: **Time-out.** The teacher sends the student to a designated area in the school where the facilitator supervises a brief time-out period. The purpose of the time-out is to remove social reinforcement that maintains the problem behavior and to give the student time to calm down.

STEP 2: **Redirection.** At the end of the time-out period and after the student has regained self-control, the facilitator works with the student on an academic task. Doing so provides an opportunity for the facilitator to establish rapport with the student; it also provides an activity that redirects the student's cognitive process to be more rational and cooperative.

STEP 3: **Conflict resolution.** The facilitator works nonjudgmentally with the student to develop an understanding of what led up to the problem or event and what consequences ensued. The process is similar to the steps described for problem solving in Chapter 9 and earlier in this chapter in the Jones model or reality therapy. The facilitator and the student summarize the understanding of the problem and plans for addressing it on a conflict-resolution worksheet.

At the end of this process, the student is returned to the classroom. The Time Away strategy has several advantages. It provides a way to target specific problems in an efficient and timely manner, and it allows the teacher to continue teaching the rest of the class. It also de-escalates rather than exacerbates conflict. An obvious limitation of the approach is the requirement to use a trained facilitator. Also, the teacher is not directly involved in the problem-solving process, so follow-up with the teacher might be needed to enact changes that would help the student address the classroom issues that instigated the process.

**Confer with a Parent.**   Sometimes a telephone call or an email to a parent can have a marked effect on a student's behavior, signaling to the child that accountability for behavior extends beyond the classroom. This approach assumes you have established with parents how they wish to be contacted. Parents react best if they don't feel they are being held responsible for their child's behavior in school (after all, they aren't there), so don't put the parent on the defensive. Describe the situation briefly, and say that you would appreciate whatever support the parent can give in helping you understand and resolve the problem. Acknowledge the challenge in rearing children as well as in teaching them. Be sure to use listening skills (see Chapter 9) during the conversation, and be alert for information that might help you determine an appropriate strategy for dealing with the student. Have your grade book handy so you can give the parent specific information about the student's progress if that information is requested or needed.

Rather than a phone conference, you might choose to schedule a face-to-face conference with a parent. Sometimes, but by no means always, when such conferences are arranged, it is because a problem has become severe, and other school personnel (e.g., a counselor or principal) may have to be present. If you have initiated the meeting, brief the others, and plan your approach ahead of time; inform parents and other staff members of who will be attending the meeting.

The chief drawback to parent conferences is the time and energy they require. However, the effort is frequently worth it. Although not every conference is successful, many times the student's behavior improves. Another potential problem is identifying beforehand the strategy that is best to follow with the parent. Occasionally parents underreact and condone the misbehavior by default or overreact and punish children excessively. As the year progresses, you will get to know parents better and will be able to gauge the probable effects of your call or conference.

**Create an Individual Contract with the Student.**   When a student's inappropriate behavior has become chronic or a problem is severe and must stop immediately, try an individual contract. You should first discuss the nature of the problem with the student, including the student's perspective on it. Then you and the student can identify appropriate solutions and agree on which course of action to take. Typically, a contract specifies changes the student will make, but it might also call for the teacher to alter some behavior or activity. You should make clear the consequences that will occur if the plan is not followed, and you can also identify an incentive to encourage the student to follow through with the contract. The plan and consequences are then written down and signed by the student. Contracts can also be used with other strategies (see the five-step plan and reality therapy sections).

# ■ Special Problems

Children sometimes behave in ways that require stronger measures than those described in the preceding sections. These behaviors include rudeness, chronic avoidance of work, fighting, bullying, and defiance or hostility toward the teacher.

Although these behaviors are not pleasant to contemplate, they are an inevitable result of close contact with up to 30 students for long periods of time. Fortunately, few teachers encounter these behaviors in large numbers. Regardless of their frequency, it is wise to be aware of ways to cope with them if they occur.

Before discussing each type of problem, we present general guidelines applicable to aggressive behaviors. Consider coping with these behaviors in two phases: the immediate response and a long-range strategy. At the time the behavior occurs, your immediate concern is to bring it to a halt with the least disruption possible. Because these behaviors are annoying or dangerous and can arouse your anxiety or anger, be careful not to exacerbate the problem. By staying calm and avoiding overreaction, rather than becoming overbearing or dictatorial, you are more likely to bring the situation to a successful conclusion. You may tell the student how you feel, but by avoiding an argument or an emotional confrontation you will be in a better position to deal with the student and the problem. Thinking about ways to handle disruptive behavior ahead of time and consulting with more experienced teachers will help you to act rather than react.

Long-range goals are to prevent a recurrence of the behavior and to help the student learn a more constructive means of dealing with others. Preventing a recurrence of the behavior is best accomplished by (1) finding out what triggered the incident and resolving the cause if possible and (2) having a predictable classroom environment with reasonable and consistently used rules, procedures, and consequences. Aggressive behavior rarely occurs in such classrooms. Helping these students acquire better behavior may require much individual attention from you over a period of time. The extent to which this goal is feasible is, of course, affected by many factors, including your time constraints and the severity of the student's problem. In dealing with students who have chronic problems, you may need consultation and assistance from the student's parents, the school counselor, a special education resource teacher, or the principal. You will need to document the student's behavior, your responses to the behavior, and the outcomes. Suggestions for handling specific types of behavior follow.

## Bullying

Bullying refers to repeated acts of aggression by one or more students directed toward a victim who often appears weak or isolated and thus is more vulnerable. The bully's intention is to receive peer approval and to assert power by dominating the victim. Bullying behaviors can take several forms: direct physical aggression (e.g., hitting, shoving), verbal and nonverbal aggression (e.g., name calling, threats, intimidation), relational aggression (e.g., ostracizing, isolating, spreading rumors about the victim), and cyberbullying. Cyberbullying utilizes the anonymity of technology (via email, social networks, etc.) to attack, expose, steal the identity of, or hurtfully entice another person. When these events occur in a school setting or among schoolmates, the results can be devastating, even deadly. Secretary of the U.S. Department of Education Arne Duncan opened the first federal summit on bullying in 2010 by noting that cyberbullying is "especially insidious" and, along with all other forms of bullying, indicative of a school that is not safe (U.S. DOE, 2010). Male students are more likely to engage in physical bullying, and female students are more likely to engage in relational aggression.

Bullying has been identified as a serious problem in many schools and communities. It is certainly contrary to a climate of respect and caring and can lead to serious and long-term emotional consequences for both the victim and the bully. For these reasons, schoolwide programs to address bullying are often adopted, and strategies for dealing with it are incorporated into school and district discipline codes. A widely used schoolwide program is the Olweus Bullying Prevention Program (see www.clemson.edu/olweus for information on this approach). This and other programs' treatment components may include development of a school (or community) antibullying policy, consequences for bullying behaviors, education of all students about the problem, social skills training, and more monitoring by adults of locations and activities in which bullying occurs (Hyman, Bryony, Tabori, Weber, Mahon, & Cohen, 2006).

If your school has adopted a special program to address bullying, it is likely that you will receive materials for classroom use, and you may participate in a workshop for teachers so that you are able to implement the program. Even if your school does not follow a specific program, there are actions you can take. First, make yourself familiar with your legal responsibility concerning student safety (cf. U.S. Office for Civil Rights, 2010). Realize that teachers are often unaware of bullying because they may not be present where it occurs (e.g., hallways, lunch room, bathrooms). When it occurs in the classroom, teachers may not notice subtler forms—gestures, staring down, threatening notes—unless the victim complains. So one action that can be taken is to do your part in monitoring student behavior in hallways and other nonclassroom spaces during transition times. Cooperate with other teachers and building administrators to cover the building so that there is an adult presence throughout.

If you become aware of bullying behavior that involves students in your class(es), you should talk with the affected class about the problem. Lead a discussion of the causes and effects of bullying, and be sure to emphasize the crucial role of the audience. Tell students you admire student onlookers who have the courage to give support to the victim, and say that bullies who seek to assert their power need to find constructive ways to gain the approval of peers. In general, a problem-solving approach can be used when speaking privately with the bully and the victim. However, if the bullying involves physical contact, your school's discipline code will likely require a referral of the aggressor to an assistant principal and a prescribed consequence. A school counselor may get involved in working with both students to develop appropriate behaviors.

Teaching students social skills is a strategy that can be used to help prevent bullying or to keep it from escalating. Role-playing appropriate interactions is particularly helpful for elementary students. Social skills, which help students communicate and resolve conflicts more effectively and also promote friendship and working together, include learning about and respecting other students' perspectives, active listening, negotiation and problem solving, asking for and giving help, taking turns and waiting, and dealing with disagreement. Students with pronounced social skills deficits can be referred to a school counselor, who may schedule group counseling sessions to work on skill development. Another possibility is to incorporate social skills training into selected classroom activities throughout the year. For example, when students engage in small-group activities or in whole-class discussions, various social skills are needed, and you can identify a set of group skills for students to practice. Depending on the age and skill level of your students, one or more skills might be selected for emphasis on different occasions.

## Tattling

Although tattling is often not disruptive, it can be a problem when it becomes a common practice. Most teachers in the early grades develop standard practices for dealing with tattling and apply them when it happens. To prevent tattling from occurring in the first place, let students know what kinds of information they should and should not report to you. For example, you need to be told about situations in which students are hurt or in danger. This includes bullying as previously described. You do not need to be told when students are whispering in class or are not doing their work. If you move around the classroom and monitor well, you will see such behavior occur, and students will not have to call your attention to it.

If it appears that several of your students are tattling frequently, it may be an indicator that students do not see you responding consistently or fairly to misbehavior. Plan a brief lesson with the class to clarify the difference between tattling and being socially responsible. Provide examples of tattling, such as (1) trying to get someone else in trouble, (2) trying to get someone else to solve a problem you could handle, or (3) trying to get help for someone else who is actually capable of solving the problem alone. One way to illustrate the differences is to draw a chart on the board with the headings "Tattling" and "Social Responsibility" and help students think of examples to write under each one. For example, under the Tattling heading you would include "Someone called me a name" or "Someone put their math paper in the spelling basket." Under the Social Responsibility heading you would include "Someone pushed me down and hurt me, and my elbow is bleeding" or "Someone is in the restroom crying and won't come out."

In deciding how you will handle tattling if it should occur, keep in mind that students who tattle are usually seeking attention from the teacher. If tattlers are successful in getting you to intervene with the alleged misbehavior, other students are likely to follow suit. It is usually sufficient to remind tattlers of what they are supposed to be doing at that moment and have them return to it.

Do be sensitive to situations in which a student may really need your support. If you discuss other options for the student to try, encourage the student to tell you how the other strategy worked if the situation recurs. Another response to the tattler may be, "I'm glad you know not to behave that way. I'll deal with Jimmy (or whoever the other student is) if I see him do that." Do not pull the accused student in for a "You did, too/No, I didn't" confrontation with the tattler. While you typically do not apply consequences to another child based on one student's report, it is prudent for you to follow up and check out the situation for yourself. If other students report similar problems with the same student, you will need to monitor that student more closely.

Other interventions that may be useful for persistent tattlers include pointing out the natural consequences of tattling (e.g., peers are likely to shun a tattler); coaching the student in strategies for handling situations without tattling (e.g., walking away); and teaching specific problem-solving techniques for students to use themselves (e.g., identify the problem, decide on a goal, develop a strategy and plan for action, carry out the plan).

## Chronic Avoidance of Work

You may have students who frequently do not complete assigned work. Sometimes they do not complete assignments early in the school year; more often, a student begins to skip assignments occasionally and then does so with increasing regularity until he or she is habitually not completing them. This behavior can be minimized by a carefully planned accountability system (review Chapter 4 for details). However, even in classrooms with a strong accountability system, some students may still avoid work.

It is much easier and better for the teacher to correct this problem before the student gets so far behind that failure is almost certain. To take early action, you must collect and check student work frequently and maintain good records. When a student has begun to miss assignments, talk with the student, seek information to help identify the underlying problem, and then take corrective action. If the student is simply unable to do the assigned work, you should provide appropriate assistance or modify the assignments. If the student feels overwhelmed by the assignments, break them up into parts whenever possible. Have the student complete the first part of the assignment within a specific time (perhaps 5 or 10 minutes); then check to see that it has been done. A bonus of a few minutes of free time at the end of the period can be offered for completion of the portion within the time limit or for working steadily without prodding. Sometimes you can provide a list of assignments for the student to check off. This can serve as a self-monitoring device and can provide a sense of accomplishment.

If ability is not the problem, the following procedures can be used in addition to talking with the student. Call the student's parents, and discuss the situation with them. Often they can supply the extra support needed to help motivate the student. A simple penalty of requiring that the student remain after school until assignments have been completed can prove effective. If the student rides a bus, you won't be able to use this procedure, of course, without making special arrangements with the parents. Any time a child is likely to be detained for more than a few minutes, alert the parents ahead of time. Another procedure that can be used when the parents are cooperative is for the child to take home daily a list of incomplete assignments and all books or materials needed to complete the work. Be cautious about using this procedure lest the student waste time, thinking all work may be done at home.

Be sure not to soften the negative consequences of repeated failure to complete work by giving students higher grades than they have earned. Doing so teaches them to avoid responsibility. Instead, provide added incentives for good effort and promptly completed work. Set up a reward system (see Chapter 8) that encourages students to do their best.

## Fighting

Fighting is less likely to occur in classrooms than on the playground, in the cafeteria, or in some other area of the school. In the elementary grades, you can often stop a fight without undue risk of injury. (If for some reason you cannot intervene directly, alert other teachers and administrators so that action can be taken.) When you do intervene, first give a loud verbal command to stop. This alone may stop the fight; it at least alerts the combatants that a referee has arrived. Instruct a student in the group of onlookers to go immediately for help; be specific about where the student should go. If you feel it is safe for you to do so, separate the fighters; as you keep them separate, instruct the other students to leave, to return to their play, or to go to their classes. Without an audience before which the fighters need to save face, you are more likely to be able to keep them apart until help arrives or until you can get them to a different location.

Your school will undoubtedly have a procedure for dealing with fighting; you should carry it out. Students may be questioned by the principal, who may call the students' homes, arrange a conference, and determine the next step.

If school policy leaves the teacher with the responsibility and wide discretion for following up on such incidents, decide on your procedures. Unless the fighting was very mild or stopped immediately, you will have to talk with the children's parents before the children go home. In any case, it is generally best to arrange a cooling-off period. If you cannot find someone to supervise your class, let the fighters wait in separate areas of your classroom or in the school office. Older children can cool

"... and suddenly there were teachers all over the place!"

© 1968 by Bill Knowlton. Reprinted from *Classroom Chuckles*, published by Scholastic Book Services.

off by writing their versions of how the fight started. If you do not know what started the fight, try to find out from uninvolved students. As soon as you have an opportunity, meet with the offenders, and get each one's point of view. The conference should focus on the inappropriateness of fighting and the need to resolve problems in ways other than physical aggression, accusations, or personal criticism. Help each student understand the other's point of view so they have a basis for better communication. Finally, stress the importance and your expectations of cooperativeness and friendliness toward one another or, at the least, the need to stay away from each other for the time being.

During the next day or two, watch for any indications of residual hostility. If the issue seems not to have been resolved, follow up by contacting the children's parents, discussing the matter with your principal, or talking with the students again.

## Power Struggles

Dealing effectively with power struggles requires understanding what motivates this behavior and using techniques that de-escalate any negative emotions. What drives people to attack others generally arises from needs for power, belonging, and/or respect. For students who act out hostile and aggressive feelings, one or more of these needs is unmet in their lives. Mendler (1997) has a number of suggested strategies for handling this problem.

Defiance or hostility is understandably threatening to teachers. They feel, and rightfully so, that if students are allowed to get away with it, the behavior may continue, and other students will be more likely to react in the same way. A student who has provoked a confrontation, usually publicly, feels that backing down would cause a loss of face in front of peers. The best way to deal with such an event is to try to defuse it by keeping it private and handling it individually with the student.

If an incident occurs during a lesson and is not extreme, deal with it by trying to depersonalize the event and avoid a power struggle: "This is taking time away from the lesson. I will discuss it with you in a few minutes when I have time." If the student does not accept the opportunity you have provided and presses the confrontation further, instruct the student to leave the group and wait at a preestablished time-out location. After the student has had time to cool off, give your class something to do, and discuss the problem with the student.

When discussing the incident, remain objective. Remember—act; don't react. Listen to the student's point of view, and respond to it, but do not engage in an argument. Separate the student's reason or excuse from the behavior itself, and point out that the behavior was not acceptable. State the consequence clearly, and implement it. If you are not sure how to respond, give yourself time by saying that you will think about it and discuss it later. However, you should still administer the penalty.

In an extreme (and rare) case, the student may be totally uncooperative and refuse to keep quiet or leave the room. If this happens, you can escort the student from the room yourself or, when dealing with a student who is older or larger, call or send another student to the office for assistance. In most cases, however, as long as you stay calm and refuse to get into a power struggle with the student, the student will accept the opportunity to cool down.

Although large-scale school violence is still extremely rare, heightened concern over isolated events in recent years has led many districts and schools to develop emergency plans similar to those for fires or natural disasters. You will need to familiarize yourself with these plans, which probably include steps such as remaining calm, moving students quickly to a safe area, and contacting administration and emergency personnel.

# ■ A Final Reminder: Think and Act Positively

In this chapter, many of the strategies presented for dealing with problem behaviors involve some form of punishment. This is especially the case for the strategies in the moderate and extensive categories. A drawback to punishment is that, by itself, it doesn't teach the student what behaviors should be practiced, so it may not help change a student's behavior in the way you intend. Consequently, it is important for teachers using one of these approaches also to communicate clearly about the desired behaviors. That is, the focus should remain on teaching the appropriate behaviors. Furthermore, a classroom in which the main consequences are negative does not have a good climate. Thus, teachers using strategies in the moderate and extensive categories more than occasionally should try to incorporate additional incentives or a reward system into their overall classroom management to help mitigate the effects of using punishment. After correcting student behavior, a teacher who supplies a generous helping of warmth and affection, offers ways to earn back points, and so on reassures the corrected students that all is not lost and that they have been restored to good grace.

Teachers should also be aware that sometimes the source of the problem lies in frustration with content that the student does not grasp or with tasks that the student lacks skills to perform. When the problem is one of a poor fit between a student's capabilities and academic requirements, the source must also be addressed by developing more appropriate class activities and assignments or by giving the student more assistance. In the implementation of any and all interventions, it is imperative to think and act positively. Of the multiple interventions possible, an effective classroom manager selects the ones to implement that can help teach students the appropriate behavior, that allow the classroom to retain a positive climate, and that maximize students' opportunity to learn.

If you have a special needs student whose behavior is causing a problem, you may find it helpful to discuss the situation with a special education teacher and ask for suggestions. In particular, find out whether the student has a special discipline plan as part of an individualized education program (IEP). Sometimes such a plan specifies particular ways to respond to the student or gives useful alternative strategies. Even if no specific discipline plan is included in the IEP, you may be able to obtain helpful ideas for working with the student. Working with special needs students is covered in detail in Chapter 11.

# Chapter Summary

When more serious, lengthy, or chronic misbehaviors present themselves, teachers employing effective classroom management skills respond to redirect the student(s) to appropriate behaviors and to teach the student(s) to make appropriate choices in the future. Management strategies that help teachers respond to minor misbehaviors (e.g., talking out of turn, off-task distraction) include such simple interventions as using nonverbal cues, giving the instructional activity momentum to avoid a lengthy transition, using proximity, calling the group to attention, redirecting the behavior, providing needed instruction, issuing brief desists, and providing the student alternative choices. If moderate interventions are required, these include withholding a student privilege, isolating/removing the student, applying a penalty, assigning a detention, and referring the student to the office. More extensive interventions may include completing a five-step intervention procedure, using the Think Time strategy, and using the reality therapy model. In addition, teachers utilize both parent conferences and individual student contracts.

Certain special situations require more distinct or immediate responses. These situations include bullying, tattling, chronic work avoidance, fighting, and power struggles. In the implementation of any and all interventions, it is imperative to think and act positively. Of the multiple interventions possible, the effective classroom manager selects the one that can help teach students to select the appropriate behavior and that allows the classroom to retain a positive climate.

# Further Reading

Brophy, J. E. (1996). *Teaching problem students*. New York: Guilford Press.

*This is a comprehensive text written with the perspective of how teachers can cope with and effectively teach students who have behavior and adjustment problems such as underachievement, aggression, defiance, immature behavior, and excessive shyness. The author presents research-based strategies to help these students succeed in school.*

Damiani, V. B. (2006). *Crisis prevention and intervention in the classroom: What teachers should know*. Lanham, MD: Rowman & Littlefield.

*Schools and teachers must deal with extreme problems and crisis events that occur either in the schools or in the community at large, such as violence, suicide, and natural catastrophes. This book explains how teachers can work with students to help them cope when a crisis occurs. It also provides information about how crisis-response teams work in schools and communities.*

Davis, S. (2004). *Schools where everyone belongs: Practical strategies for reducing bullying*. Wayne, ME: Stop Bullying Now.

*This book outlines research on effective bullying prevention and interventions and presents specific practices and skills that help schools implement that research.*

Emmer, E. T., & Stough, L. M. (2008). Responsive classroom management. In T. Good (Ed.), *21st century education: A reference handbook* (Vol. 1, pp. 140–148).

*This entry describes the research behind and use of interventions for student misbehavior.*

Harrist, A. W., & Bradley, K. D. (2003). "You can't say you can't play": Intervening in the process of social exclusion in the kindergarten classroom. *Early Childhood Quarterly, 18*, 185–205.

*This article presents research on an intervention with kindergarten students that taught social skills through nonexclusion.*

Hyman, I., Bryony, K., Tabori, A., Weber, M., Mahon, M., & Cohen, I. (2006). Bullying: Theory, research, and interventions. In C. Evertson & C. Weinstein (Eds.), *Handbook of research on classroom management: Research, practice, and contemporary issues* (pp. 855–884). Mahwah, NJ: Erlbaum.

*This chapter provides a comprehensive overview of bullying, including characteristics of bullies and victims, conditions conducive to bullying, its effects, the role of onlookers, and intervention strategies.*

Mendler, A. (1997). *Power struggles: Successful techniques for educators.* Rochester, NY: Discipline Associates.

*This short, easy-to-read book outlines specific steps teachers and other school staff can take to de-escalate the cycle of hostility that can occur when students are confrontational. It includes checklists and other aids to help identify causes of power struggles and other hostile behavior.*

Myles, B. S., & Simpson, R. L. (1994). Prevention and management considerations for aggressive and violent children and youth. *Education and Treatment of Children, 17,* 370–384.

*Aggression is typically preceded by warning signs and follows a sequence of stages. This article describes prevention and intervention strategies keyed to these stages. Many of the suggested strategies are also useful for nonaggressive inappropriate behaviors.*

Sprick, R. (1995). *The teacher's encyclopedia of behavior management: 100 problems/500 plans.* Longmont, CO: Sopris West.

*This book addresses individual and classwide problems common to schools. It includes model plans along with specific interventions.*

cecp.air.org/

*This is the Web site for the Center for Effective Collaboration and Practice, whose goal is improving services for children and youth with emotional-behavioral problems.*

www.apa.org/education/k12/bullying.aspx www.clemson.edu/olweus www.nasponline.org/resources/factsheets/

*These Web sites offer strategies for bullying prevention and social skills training programs to help students recognize and counter occurrences of social, emotional, and mental abuse.*

www.apa.org/ed/schools/cpse/activities/class-management.aspx

> *This Web site offers a set of modules to assist teachers with practical strategies for helping students behave individually and as a class, as well as interventions for emotional and behavioral problems.*

www.cfchildren.org

> *Committee for Children is an international organization committed to social, emotional, and academic learning. Special topics include bullying, youth violence, and emergent literacy. "Second Step" is an award-winning curriculum for teaching skills for social and academic success at the K–5 level. "Steps to Respect" is an award-winning program to combat bullying.*

www.state.ky.us/agencies/behave/homepage.html

> *The Behavior Home Page is an interactive Web site that is working to make a difference for children with challenging behavior.*

www.stopbullyingnow.com

> *This site presents practical research-based strategies to reduce bullying in schools. The PowerPoint presentation summarizing the basics of bullying prevention is very informative (www.stopbullyingnow.com/Davisbullyingprevpresentation.pdf).*

# ■ Suggested Activities

1. Teachers' reactions to the problem behaviors described in this chapter are often affected by the adult models they have observed and the type of discipline they received as children, both at home and at school. Recall your early experiences in this area, and consider their implications. To what extent do these earlier models provide a positive guide for managing problems of varying severity? Would the strategies that were effective for you be equally appropriate or effective for the varied kinds of students you may teach? Are there current behaviors or environmental problems that you did not experience (e.g., drug culture, poverty, single-parent/guardian homes, bullying)? Where should you add to or modify your approach? How do your responses reflect or inform your developing philosophy of education?

2. Review the descriptions of problem types presented at the beginning of the chapter. Decide which interventions would be best suited for each type. Given several alternative interventions for any type of problem, how would you decide which to use?

3. Within each type of intervention—simple, moderate, or extensive—are there any strategies that you distinctly prefer? Do you reject any? Discuss your reasons for liking or disliking particular approaches. How do these reactions reflect your philosophy of teaching and learning?

4. In the following situations involving problem behaviors, decide on a strategy for dealing with each and an alternative response if your first approach does not produce good

results. Indicate any assumptions you make about the teaching context as you choose your strategy. (See the key for this activity in the Appendix.)

*Situation 1.* Ardyth and Melissa talk and pass notes as you conduct a class discussion. Several other students whisper or daydream.

*Situation 2.* Desi and Bryce talk constantly. They refuse to get to work, and they argue with you when you ask them to open their books.

*Situation 3.* Dwayne manages to get most of his work done, but in the process he is constantly disruptive. He teases the girls sitting around him, keeping them constantly laughing and competing for his attention. Dwayne makes wisecracks in response to almost anything you say. When confronted, he grins charmingly and responds with exaggerated courtesy, much to the delight of the rest of the class.

*Situation 4.* When someone bumped into Marc at the drinking fountain, he turned around and spit water at the other child. Later Marc ordered a boy who was standing near his desk to get away, and he then shoved the boy. On the way back from the cafeteria, Marc got into a name-calling contest with another boy.

5. Make a list of student behaviors—including defiance, rudeness, aggression, and unresponsiveness—that are the most likely to embarrass you or make you uncomfortable. Think in advance about how you might handle each one.

6. Interview a practicing teacher to determine whether the teacher's school has a policy regarding bullying and how that policy is communicated to students and parents. What is the teacher's role in implementing the policy or program?

7. Obtain a current media description (e.g., newspaper or ezine article) of classroom misbehavior that grew out of hand. Discuss with a partner what may have initiated the incident, what actions a teacher could take to prevent and/or respond to a similar situation, and what repercussions there are for not preparing for this type of situation.

---

**MyEducationLab**

Now go to www.myeducationlab.com to:

- Take a Quiz to test your mastery of chapter objectives.
- Study chapter content with an individualized Study Plan.
- Deepen your understanding of particular concepts and principles with Classroom Management Simulations.
- Apply what you have learned in the chapter to your work with children in Building Teaching Skills exercises.

## CHAPTER 11

# Managing Special Groups

Although the classroom management principles and guidelines discussed so far in this book apply to most classroom settings, classroom management is also affected by the students' characteristics. The ages, academic ability levels, goals, interests, culture, and home backgrounds of students influence their classroom behavior. Some of your students may be English language learners whose parents may not speak English and whose home culture may vary significantly from the prevalent culture in the classroom. When your students make eye contact with you, they can be showing you respect in some cultures and disrespect in others. Consequently, adjustments in management and instructional practices are sometimes needed to meet the needs of different groups. Among the students who present special challenges are those who are working below or well above grade level and those who are academically or physically challenged, as well as those whose predominant language is not English. Classrooms can include all of these types of students, presenting a special teaching challenge. Effectively working with students having such diverse needs and abilities requires special effort.

This chapter presents information and suggestions that, combined with the principles described in previous chapters, will help you organize and manage classes with a range of student achievement or ability levels, students with below-level skills, and students with special needs.

# ■ Assessing Entering Achievement

To identify the extent of differences in needs and ability levels (i.e., the degree of heterogeneity) in your classroom, you should use several sources of information. These sources include your tests, your own observation of each student, and indicators of performance available in each student's file, including assessments from prior teachers, samples of the student's work, and standardized achievement test information. If one of your students is identified as having special needs, you will certainly consult with the resource teacher. Be cautious about forming a hasty impression of a student's abilities based on any single source of information. Forming and communicating low expectations to students can cause them to achieve below their potential.

Because of the importance of reading, language arts, and mathematics skills in the elementary school curriculum, these subjects will be the major focus of your initial assessment. As you evaluate your students, be alert to study and work habits such as following directions and maintaining attention on a task. Children with poor work and study skills or who are highly distractible may require special consideration in your room arrangement, in planning for instructional activities, and in monitoring.

When obtaining information about entering reading and math skill levels, give special attention to students for whom you lack information. Typically, these are students who have transferred from another school district. You must also be careful about an assessment when existing information is not consistent. Therefore, assess such children individually by listening to them read, checking their vocabulary and word-attack strategies, and testing their math skills. Consult with other teachers, other professionals, or both for help in selecting suitable assessment procedures if you do not already have them.

Often departmental chairpersons or curriculum coordinators have a file of classroom assessment materials, including checklists that can be used to keep a record of participation or other observable behaviors. In some academic areas, students build a portfolio of performance on a variety of tasks that carries forward

"I'm an underachiever.... What's your racket?"

© 1968 by Bill Knowlton. Reprinted from *Classroom Chuckles*, published by Scholastic Book Services.

from one year to the next. Additional information can be gleaned from careful observation of your students while they are working on initial assignments, participating in class or interacting in groups. The availability of such records and information will help identify students who need review, extra assistance, or enrichment in particular areas.

If possible, delay individual student assessment until several days after the beginning of school. During such testing it will be difficult to monitor your class, and you may have to leave students too long in independent work. By delaying testing, you can observe the students first, and the students will become better acquainted and more comfortable with you before they are tested. If you do individual testing, plan enough work to keep your class busy. When several students must be assessed individually, space the testing over several days.

# ■ Identifying Special Groups

In planning your classroom instruction, determine the range of entering achievement in basic skill subjects and the degree to which individual students are unable to work effectively with the grade-level curriculum. Other characteristics such as students' interests and backgrounds can affect learning and should be considered as you plan activities and set goals.

Sometimes information on student ability levels can help identify small groups for instruction, pair students for peer tutoring, and create cooperative groups for learning activities. Each of these types of activity requires special planning and management considerations.

# ■ Strategies for Individual Differences

In the next sections we describe strategies frequently used to adjust for individual differences, and we examine management concerns associated with them.

## Team Teaching

Teachers at the same grade level frequently form teams to deal with heterogeneous student populations. Students can then be reassigned to different teachers on the team for instruction in one or more subjects. This allows teachers to form relatively more homogeneous subgroups than would be possible using only students initially assigned to their individual classrooms. For example, two or three students whose entering reading skills are extremely low might be grouped for reading instruction with similar students from other classrooms. At the same time, students at the highest level in the classes might be combined into a single group and taught by another teacher on the team. This arrangement permits instruction for these students to be targeted closer to their skill levels than would be possible if they remained in their original classes. Still, it is important that these students participate in groups with mixed ability levels in other activities.

Team approaches to heterogeneity can be applied to a variety of subjects but are most common in reading and mathematics instruction. If ability grouping is used, teaming should be considered whenever the range of abilities is too great to be accommodated by three groups in reading and two groups in mathematics. Although extreme heterogeneity within a class could theoretically be accommodated by forming more groups, doing so is usually not practical because of the excessive demands on teacher planning and the reduction of time each group would receive for instruction. Because teaming requires careful planning and cooperation, the following items are important.

**Coordination of Schedules.**   The teachers on the team must establish compatible schedules for the subjects being team taught. If teachers deviate from the schedule without warning, children from other classrooms may be kept waiting with nothing to do, and everyone will be thrown off schedule.

**Movement.**   Because some students will be going from one room to another, they must know what procedures and behavior to use during transitions. A teacher should accompany children in transit between rooms until they have learned the routine and then can monitor students' movement if the destination is within sight.

**Needed Materials.**   Sometimes children have trouble remembering their materials. When they do not bring the appropriate materials, they may be sent back to their classrooms, thereby losing valuable time and sometimes disturbing students in both rooms. If students need different sets of materials on different days, all teachers involved should be notified so they can prompt students to remember what is needed and when, perhaps by posting a list of materials to take or by reminding students as they prepare to leave the room.

**Rules and Procedures.**   Students coming to you from another teacher's class may not know your expectations for their behavior. Therefore, discuss with them the rules for conduct in your room and the procedures needed for small-group work and independent work. Do this when you first meet with your new students, and then monitor them carefully until good behavior becomes established. If possible, plan rules and procedures with other members of the team to establish a common set of expectations. Consistency across settings simplifies the task of teaching students to behave correctly.

**Responsibility for Work.**   In addition to rules for conduct and procedures for behavior, be sure to keep students responsible for their work. This may be more difficult to do in a team-teaching situation than with the students in your regular class because the full range of incentives, penalties, and parental contact may be limited. Also, you will not be able to supervise the students at other times of the day when they might have an opportunity to work on assignments (and when, ideally, you would check work and provide supplementary instruction). Here are several steps for keeping students accountable:

1. When you meet with students each day, check their work before you dismiss them, and give students whatever feedback they need to complete the work successfully.
2. Be clear about your expectations for work, other requirements, and your grading criteria.
3. Return checked papers promptly. Timely feedback is one of the strongest predictors of academic success, so don't let classwork accumulate.
4. Be certain that students, especially younger children, realize that you are responsible for checking their work and assigning a report card grade.
5. Contact parents if children begin to miss assignments in your class. Don't rely on the homeroom teacher to do this.

## Modifying Whole-Class Instruction

In some subjects, the use of small groups for instruction is not feasible or even desirable. Limited time, the problem of ascertaining individual differences on relevant entering skills, and greater procedural complexity may make small-group instruction less efficient than whole-class instruction. When used for subjects such as science or social studies, whole-class instruction can be modified to accommodate extremes in abilities and interests. A number of simple modifications and cautions should be considered.

**Interactive Instruction.**   Try to involve all students in presentations, discussions, and recitations by making a conscious effort to call on everyone, not only those who are eager to respond. Sometimes using individual cards to select respondents at random can help you be inclusive. Allow children who have limited access to the content because of reading difficulty the opportunity to restate the main idea or summarize another student's response. Students with a special ability or an obvious interest in a topic can be encouraged to complete special projects and to organize their ideas in oral reports to the class. These opportunities allow the students to advance their understanding and receive recognition.

**Seating Arrangements.**   Students who need closer supervision or more than the usual amount of explanation should be seated near the front of the room (or wherever you usually conduct whole-class presentations). Their proximity to you will enable you to check for understanding more readily and make it easier to monitor their behavior and progress.

**Directions.**   Require all students' attention, and provide both oral and written directions when feasible. Some students have difficulty remembering and following a long series of verbal directions, so break them into manageable chunks, and use visual cues. Also consider asking students to repeat or rephrase the directions to check what was heard. Verify that they understand, help them practice the steps, and monitor carefully to provide corrective feedback. Be sure to check in regularly with students who have problems following directions. If you have seated them near you, you will be able to provide them with quick assistance.

**Assignments.**   If you give the same assignments to all students in a highly hetero-geneous class, the work may be much too easy for some students and much too dif-ficult for others. One size will not fit all. Consider giving assignments in two parts: a basic assignment for all students to complete and a second, more difficult part that is assigned to some students or that can be completed for extra credit. When assign-ments are the same for everyone, the students complete them with different degrees of proficiency and speed. In such cases, use a grading or credit system that, at least in part, emphasizes individual progress rather than competition among students. Enrichment or extra-credit material for students who finish classwork early should be work related and not distracting to other students, so avoid free-time activities that are so attractive that slower-working students feel deprived or attempt to quit or rush through their work. Set up a system for giving credit, feedback, or recogni-tion for completion of enrichment activities. If you allow students to read when they finish their work, be sure to provide supplementary reading materials at a variety of reading levels.

## Supplementary Instruction

Sometimes student needs in some subject areas cannot be adequately met in the regular education classroom. For example, a student's skills may be so deficient in reading or math that the student cannot profit from small-group instruction; even the lowest group may be far beyond the student's current level. Or a student may be so overstimulated by 25 or 30 students in a regular classroom that he or she cannot focus on assignments long enough to complete them. Such students may fall behind in their performance even though they possess average or above-average ability. Also, students whose first language is not English may need intensive help that can-not be provided in the regular instructional program. Finally, some students may possess special talents that programs for the gifted can more fully develop. In all of these cases, supplementary programs may be available. The term *pull-out* is some-times applied to these programs because the students are taken out of the regular classroom for part of the school day to receive special instruction. Check to see whether a student is enrolled in a pull-out program intended to supplement or to replace his or her regular classroom instruction. This will have important implica-tions for your planning. Examples of pull-out programs include these:

- **Special education.** This is usually available in a resource room. Students with learning disabilities and other conditions that interfere with learning or adjust-ment in a regular classroom receive instruction (usually reading or math or both) for part of the day. These students return to the regular classroom for other instruction.

- **Title I programs.** These are special programs established in schools that serve students from lower-income families. Students with deficits in academic skills receive supplementary instruction from special teachers.
- **Enrichment programs.** Programs that provide enrichment in particular subjects are often established for students who have special talent in these areas. These programs frequently use community resources, parents, or other volunteers as well as the regular teaching staff to provide programs during or after school hours.
- **English language learning programs** (ELL). These programs assist students with limited proficiency to learn English and also provide support for the students, their regular classroom teachers, and the students' families.

The aspect of supplementary programs that can have a major impact on your classroom management plan is the removal of students from your class during the time that regular instruction is proceeding. Thus, scheduling must be carefully planned so that the students being pulled out do not miss essential instruction and so that the other students' instructional program is not interrupted. Transitions out of and back into your classroom can become a headache if they are not handled well.

**Coordinating Times with Other Teachers.**   As soon as schoolwide schedules are set for lunch periods and activities such as music, art, and physical education classes, plan a schedule with the other teachers that will be as convenient as possible for everyone. If a number of students leave for special reading instruction, arrange with the reading teacher to have these students leave in a group at a time when you will be meeting with a reading group in your class. If several students are pulled out for special instruction in a subject such as mathematics, you will probably want to schedule your math instruction for the rest of the class at that time.

**Staying on Schedule.**   When class schedules involve pull-outs and drop-ins, staying on schedule is vital so that students can be where they need to be at appropriate times. Display a large clock where everyone can see it. If you have trouble remembering to look at the clock, enlist the aid of the students in prompting you. Older students should eventually assume responsibility for their own schedules. You may want to post a list of times at which students are supposed to leave in order to remind both you and the students. You can also set a timer as a reminder.

**Interim Activities for Drop-In Students.**   Sometimes you may not quite be finished with one group when it is time for another group to meet. Students working at their desks in the teacher's room should have enough activities to keep them busy. However, drop-in students sometimes arrive early and have nowhere specific to sit other than in the small group. Develop a procedure for incorporating these students so that small groups and independent workers are not distracted. Some teachers tell students to take an empty seat while waiting; others set aside a waiting area on a small rug or at a table. While there, students can begin reading the next lesson in their textbook or workbook or do other constructive activities.

**Reinvolving Returning Students.** After receiving instruction outside the room, some pull-out students may dawdle or seem confused about what they are supposed to do when they return to the room. To avoid confusion, establish routines so students always know what to do when they return. Post assignments or give students a list of assignments to help them remember. If you are working with a small group when students return, give the small group something to do, and go to the returning students to be sure they get back on task. Student helpers can take responsibility for explaining the assignment or activity to individual returning students.

**When Supplementary Instruction Is Cancelled.** Sometimes the special teacher is absent, or for some reason the special class is not conducted. When this occurs, it is important to have students at work while you carry on with regular instruction. In some cases, students may be included in regular class activities. In other cases, you must provide special activities. If possible, meet regularly with the other teachers so you will know what the students are working on and will be able to assign something appropriate. Have free-time or enrichment activities set aside to accommodate varying levels of ability. It is important to monitor these students and give them something meaningful to do; otherwise, valuable learning time is lost, and students may become bored or disruptive.

**In-Class Aides.** Sometimes teachers are fortunate enough to have parents or other adult volunteers, teacher aides, or university education students who help out in their classrooms. These assistants may help with one particular subject or with all subjects. Other aides may help with materials and administrative tasks and have little contact with the children. If you have one or more aides, there are several things you can do to promote smooth functioning in your classroom. You should be specific in informing the aide of his or her responsibilities for teaching or working with students and for disciplining students. You will want aides to enforce your rules consistently when they are in charge of students. If you must leave the room, inform students that the aide will be in charge of the class and will enforce the rules as you do. If the aide will be working with individual students or small groups, create a space that will not cause distractions for the rest of the class, particularly if you are instructing simultaneously. Students should be told whether and when they may go to the aide for help.

**Content Mastery Classroom.** A special form of supplementary (pull-out) program that has become widely used is the Content Mastery Classroom (CMC), which designates one or more teachers, at least one of whom is trained in special education, to work with students identified for supplemental instruction. Students may go to the CMC for extra help on assignments or new material or to have extra time to spend on tests. In many school districts, both a general education and a special education teacher are available in the CMC to help students, but in some places this is solely a special education option. An advantage of the CMC, compared to a resource room or self-contained class, is that it allows the integration of special education students in regular education classrooms but provides support for them when they need more help. Also, the regular education teacher, who may have 30 other students, does not have to provide as much supplemental instruction. Another advantage is that students may either be sent by the general education teacher or go on their own initiative when they feel the need for extra help.

It is important to coordinate with the CMC teachers about which students may go to the CMC and when and what kind of information and materials they will need to take with them. For younger students, a laminated assignment card may be helpful, with your name and grade level printed on it; when a student is to go to the CMC, you might write on the card a brief description of the help the student needs, page numbers in the text the student will take, and the time the student leaves your room. It is also possible, however, that the CMC teacher will have other routines for getting information about student assignments and that you can use them.

When you have one or more special-needs students who use the CMC regularly, you should provide assignments ahead of time (e.g., weekly) so that appropriate planning can be done by the CMC teacher. When students take your tests in the CMC, be sure you have discussed ahead of time your expectations for assistance. Because the CMC teacher works with your students individually, he or she may have suggestions for adapting instruction or management that can help you in teaching the student. Because CMC teachers have had substantial training and experience in working with students with special needs, you may be able to benefit from their suggestions. The CMC teacher may be reluctant to give unsolicited advice, so be sure to ask if you have questions about how best to work with particular students.

**Inclusion.**    Inclusion programs for special needs students provide support to enable them to participate in as many regular education activities as possible. Typically, a special education teacher works with regular education teachers of designated students, both to help modify assignments and written material as specified on the students' individualized education programs (IEPs) and to provide assistance within the classroom itself. Scheduled planning meetings for the special education and the regular education teachers are crucial to the success of any inclusion program. Only by knowing exactly what activities are planned by the regular education teacher can the special education teacher know how to provide relevant support for the student.

On some occasions, the special education teacher may be in the regular classroom, as when students are working on assignments or class projects. At other times, the special education teacher may provide copies of modified assignments. Both the timing and the nature of the special education teacher's participation in class, as well as the extent of lesson modifications, can be specified during planning sessions. Case Studies 11.1 and 11.2 at the end of this chapter illustrate how regular education teachers can accommodate students with special needs in the classroom.

## Individualized Instruction

When each student receives instruction, is given assignments at a level established by a careful assessment of entering skills, and is encouraged to progress at whatever pace his or her abilities and motivation allow, the instructional program is said to be individualized. Some educators consider individualized instruction the best means of coping with heterogeneity because it offers, at least in principle, instruction tailored to the needs of each child. However, individualized instruction can be difficult to implement. It requires (1) careful and continuous assessment of individuals' progress, (2) management of time so that all students receive adequate interactive instruction from the teacher, (3) sufficient resources that include materials suitable for all ability levels in the class, and (4) time for the teacher to plan and develop appropriate activities. The absence of one or more of these features limits individualized instruction as an effective program. Therefore, such programs should be implemented gradually, allowing adequate time to develop the necessary resources. Because of these difficulties, we regard the first strategies for coping with heterogeneity and low-achieving students to be the modification of whole-class instruction, supplementary instruction, and team teaching. Only when these strategies are not adequate should individualized instruction be employed.

Sometimes the teacher's role in individualization diminishes to the point that almost all of the time is devoted to making assessments, giving assignments, keeping records, and checking. When this occurs, students receive little interactive instruction from the teacher and do little except complete worksheets, and they begin to equate learning with finishing. The teacher's diminished instructional role may be partly due to the incorrect perception that because instruction is individualized, the teacher can instruct only one student at a time. In fact, it is far more efficient if the teacher presents information to and conducts recitations with groups of students, supplementing the group lessons with individual instruction for students who require extra help.

When individualization of instruction is used for one or more subjects, you should anticipate a number of management problems and take action to prevent them or at least minimize their impact.

**Transitions.**   Students engaged in individual rather than group activities generally finish their work at different rates. If the next activity is also individually based, many transitions will occur throughout the period of instruction, causing confusion and lost time. Some students may not know what to do next; others may delay starting the next activity. More efficient transitions can be effected if you are alert to helping students who are between activities. Post written assignments somewhere to move students to the next task. You can also have students bring completed work to be checked in order to provide structure during the transition and to be certain that students know how to get started on the next activity.

**Monitoring Behavior.**   Different expectations for students doing different activities, along with a variety of simultaneous activities, make monitoring student behavior during individualized instruction difficult. Because the teacher often instructs individual students or performs other tasks associated with individualized instruction (such as assessment), monitoring becomes complex. To overcome these problems, consider the following key behaviors:

- Know what all students are supposed to be doing at any given time so that you can support their efforts and prevent problems.
- Be sure students know what they are expected to do and what conduct is appropriate in different activities.
- Be alert for students who are having trouble getting started or finishing an activity so that you can provide help. Don't be engrossed in helping one or a few students, and don't wait until students quit working or become disruptive before providing assistance.
- Circulate among the students, and look at their work periodically. Scan the room frequently to detect early signs of frustration or task avoidance.
- Usually a few students require more supervision than others. When possible, be sure these students are seated where you can observe and assist them readily.

**Encouraging Student Responsibility for Work.**    Using an individualized instruction program does not guarantee that students will accept responsibility for completing assignments and participating in learning activities. In fact, some students take advantage of the more complex instructional arrangements and limitations on the teacher's monitoring capability to avoid responsibility and to expend minimal effort. To avoid these problems, make sure directions for assignments and other activities are clear. Many teachers prefer to review directions with students at the beginning of the period devoted to individualized instruction. List a basic set of activities on the board, and review them; or give students activity or assignment folders that list what is to be done, and check off completed work. This system helps both you and the students keep track of progress. Setting time limits for work on one activity before students proceed to the next will help them pace their efforts.

Students should expect their work to be checked frequently. If they become accustomed to simply completing one activity and starting a new one without feedback, they may practice errors, and their performance will deteriorate. Develop monitoring procedures that include periodic progress checks and evaluation, as well as feedback on completed assignments and other work. It is also important to review overall student progress and decide whether the pace and scope of work are adequate. Some teachers prefer to do this in weekly or every-other-week reviews and a short conference with individual students.

**Contracts.**    Contracts are often used with individual instruction. Contracts usually include a list of assignments or activities to be completed by a student during a fixed period of time, such as a day or a week. Contracts may also specify the goals or objectives, materials, and incentives associated with completing the contract. Use of a contract has a number of advantages: It is a good way to communicate assignments and objectives, it enables students to suggest modifications they would find helpful or interesting, and the student's signature on the contract can increase motivation for completion within the agreed-on time period.

## Additional Strategies

**Student Cooperation: Help from Peers.** Another method for coping with extreme heterogeneity and for dealing with low achievers is to use students to help other students. Examples of such peer-helping arrangements include the following:

- Students work in pairs, reading and listening to each other read. "Reading with a buddy" can be part of contract work.
- When the teacher is busy with small-group or individualized instruction, students who need help are encouraged to get assistance from another student before interrupting the teacher. Students can be assigned the role of monitor to assist peers.
- Group leaders are assigned to each learning station to answer questions and set up materials.
- A capable, mature student is assigned as a helper for another student who needs frequent assistance. The helper's responsibilities are to answer questions and explain directions.
- Students may be permitted to help or seek help from a neighbor on some independent work activities.
- A student from an upper grade may tutor a younger student.

When using student helpers, recognize the potential for excessive noise, poor attention to the task, or excessive reliance on the helper by the helpee. Also, not all students are amenable to this type of arrangement or will work well together. Negative effects can be averted by communicating clearly what is and is not permitted and by monitoring the helping arrangements and relationships to prevent undesirable side effects. For all of these variations from regular instruction patterns, gradual introduction of new arrangements gives the best opportunity for managing their implementation and for correcting problems.

**Cooperative Groups** For many activities, using small groups with mixed ability levels, diverse backgrounds, or both provides a good opportunity for all students to help and to learn from each other. Researchers such as Slavin (1995) and Gillies (2007) have shown that working in mixed-ability teams can benefit both higher- and lower-achieving students in many subject areas. Benefits of cooperative groups include increased achievement, positive cultural relations, mutual concern among students, and increased self-esteem. Refer to Chapter 7 for details on managing cooperative groups.

**Peer Tutoring** Peer tutoring provides an opportunity for each student to have one-on-one assistance, particularly when the teacher is unavailable. It can be done during class by pairing students at similar levels to work together or by asking a student who has achieved a certain level or learned a concept to work with another student who has not. The student who receives assistance benefits from individualized instruction. The helper, or peer tutor, benefits from planning for and explaining the concept.

To use peer tutoring effectively, certain management issues must be addressed. First, decide when tutoring is and is not acceptable. There may be some subjects or concepts for which peer tutoring is not appropriate. For instance, you may not be assured that the potential peer tutors have sufficiently learned a concept to be able to provide assistance.

Second, decide where tutoring will occur. Some teachers provide a special location within the classroom where peer interactions are less likely to interrupt other classroom activities or disturb students who are working unassisted. Other teachers may allow students to work quietly side by side at their desks.

Third, if you do use peer tutors, be prepared to teach students how to do tutoring. Potential tutors should be shown how to model behaviors, instructed in how to ask questions to assess the other student's understanding, and counseled on interpersonal behaviors. For long-term peer tutors, you may want to provide a brief training during class or after school. Other directions can be given as part of the overall instructions for an activity.

# ■ Working with Students with Special Needs

This section deals with students who have special needs, either because they are physically or mentally challenged or because they have background characteristics such as language proficiency that affect their classroom performance.

Research on students with special physical, mental, or emotional disabilities supports the benefits of providing instruction in the least restrictive environment (LRE), meaning among their nondisabled peers to the extent possible. Further, it is legally mandated that special education students be served in the LRE. As a result, more and more students with special needs are being served in the regular education classroom with some outside help from specialized teachers. Meeting these students' needs presents special challenges to teachers with a classroom full of children. Fortunately, research has provided specific guidelines to help teachers work with these students in ways that promote their peer acceptance and their self-esteem as well as their academic achievement. Following are suggestions for planning instruction for students with different types of special needs.

## Students with Learning Disabilities

Although there is still no consensus on a concise definition of *learning disability*, certain characteristics are commonly seen. One primary feature is more difficulty with and lower achievement in certain academic areas than would otherwise be expected, based on these students' overall ability levels. Other common problems experienced by these students are disorganization and a disconcerting tendency to forget something they seemed to understand thoroughly just a short time earlier. Often accompanying these difficulties are the students' natural sense of frustration and the potential for anger or hopelessness, along with a negative view of themselves.

Students with learning disabilities generally respond well to a positive and structured approach with predictable routines. They may forget steps even in familiar routines, however, and require much patience and repetition. These students need more help than others in learning to identify and pay attention to relevant cues. Point out cues and relevant directions, and have students repeat directions out loud to be sure they understand what to do. Emphasize what is correct rather than what they are doing wrong. Model the appropriate behavior or actions to ensure that they are transferring positive learning rather than reinforcing negative learning. Avoid trial-and-error activities in which students may spend too much time doing the wrong thing, thus adding to their confusion. Overlearning is important for these students, especially because of their retention problems. It is more helpful to distribute numerous short practices of tasks over a period of time than to have fewer but longer practices.

Students with learning challenges benefit from a wide range of multisensory experiences to assist them in learning concepts and to help them overcome problems of inexperience. Be aware that although social praise may help motivate, it may also interfere with the development of independent decision-making skills. Use praise sparingly, and articulate specifically what was praiseworthy. Avoid generalized, nonspecific praise, which may only direct attention elsewhere and miss getting the desired result.

A learning disability by itself does not make behavior problems more likely. However, children with a learning disability who do not receive effective intervention for their learning problems are apt to experience frustration with their schoolwork and lower performance, which may contribute to a variety of behavior problems. Such problems may be addressed by strategies that have been presented elsewhere in this book, in addition to interventions directed at the children's specific learning problems.

## Students with Emotional or Behavioral Problems

Remembering that students with a diagnosed emotional disturbance are often different from others merely in their degree of emotionality rather than in the types of feelings they have may relieve some potential anxiety in working with these students. Any psychological report available, treated confidentially, can be helpful both in shedding light on why students are having such problems and in providing recommendations for working with the students successfully. The school psychologist and special education teacher can also help you understand and support these students. It is likely that a behavior management plan has been developed through special education services, so being familiar with the plan and clear on how to follow it may prevent problems. If behavior is a serious issue, adjust your expectations: Overlook minor inappropriate behavior, but reinforce acceptable behavior, and reduce known stressors. A positive, supportive, structured, and predictable environment helps these students feel safe and accepted.

If you have students who tend to have temper outbursts or become easily or violently frustrated and angry, reinforce all attempts they make toward self-control. Learn to recognize any behavioral cues that precede an outburst so that you can anticipate and intervene to prevent any loss of control. Maintain a balanced perspective, remembering that it is more important that these students get through the day without an outburst than that they follow instructions exactly or complete assignments errorlessly. Sometimes, if you think problems are developing but have not escalated yet, allow the students to change their activity momentarily to defuse the situation (e.g., "Would you be willing to take this note to the office for me?" or "Why don't you get a drink of water, and then we'll work this out together?"). Offering structured choices can also be helpful, especially with students who have a strong need to control and who often appear noncompliant and oppositional (e.g., "Would you prefer to do the odd-numbered problems or the even-numbered?" or "Would it be helpful for you to work a while in the study carrel, or do you think you can concentrate well enough at your own desk?").

Work with your principal, counselor, other teachers, and the child's parent(s) to devise a plan if a student with emotional problems has a tantrum or explodes in your classroom. When these students have to be removed from the classroom to a safe time-out place, they should be supervised as they cool down. Students with emotional or behavioral problems often do not know why they lose control and are frequently embarrassed and remorseful afterward. These students generally do not understand how their feelings relate to what has happened and have not learned to discern the subtle changes that trigger outbursts. Learning impulse control and the ability to anticipate and divert these feelings in an acceptable manner is often their greatest need.

After any kind of violent outburst, when both you and the student have regained your composure (it may take longer for one than for the other), it is important that you reestablish your relationship with the student. Other than attempting to learn from each incident to prevent future occurrences, leave each incident behind, and do not focus on past failures.

One crucial reminder: When students lose rational control and are verbally or physically abusive or violent, it is rarely personal, even though it may sound and feel that way. If you have learned about the backgrounds and histories of these students, logic will tell you that you have merely been a handy target, not the root cause of their pain or rage. Logic and feelings do not always coincide, however. Having someone listen to you and give you support and feedback when dealing with extremely volatile students is essential to your ability to continue to be supportive for these students.

## Students with Serious Social Deficits (Autism Spectrum Disorders)

Within the past few years, increasing numbers of students with severe social skills problems are being diagnosed as having autism spectrum disorders (ASD), also known as pervasive developmental disorder (PDD). A milder form of the disorder is called Asperger's syndrome (Hodgdon, 1995, 1999; www.nimh.nih.gov/publicat/autism.cfm). As very young children, many of these individuals appear to be especially bright because of their ability to learn, remember, and recite facts. As they grow older, however, it becomes apparent that they have limited understanding of these facts and cannot generalize or apply the things they relate so accurately. Another severe deficiency becomes apparent: Although highly verbal, they have extremely poor communication skills. They tend to stand too close, avoid eye contact, talk too long and loudly in a preaching or robotic manner, and talk in great detail about factual matters that do not interest their peers.

Further, ASD individuals are quite rigid in their outlook and develop set ways of doing things. They escalate quickly into extreme and visible anxiety when a routine is changed or when their expectations are not met. They may also have an acute sensitivity to sounds, with loud noises causing pain to their ears. Frequently they have concomitant learning disabilities and poor gross and fine motor skills. Strong emotion may cause them to engage in repetitive, stereotyped movements such as hand flapping.

When students have had such problems to a severe degree, it is likely that they have already been referred for special education services. Some attempt has probably been made to teach them adaptive ways to cope with their strong need for regularity and predictability and skills for preventing escalating aggressive behavior. Because most of these students have at least average intellectual abilities, they can usually succeed in regular education classes and can thrive on the intellectual stimulation. However, their unique reactions and behavioral responses, despite the coping mechanisms that they have learned, require that you understand their difficulties and use strategies to help them tolerate anxiety-provoking situations, such as unanticipated change, movement, or noise. The following teaching strategies can help support these students in the regular classroom:

1. Use visual cues and prompts. Because students with ASD are visual rather than verbal learners, physically demonstrate how you want things done, and use manipulatives and cues whenever possible.

2. Avoid giving both an auditory and a visual task at one time. Often these students cannot process both inputs simultaneously—they cannot look and listen at the same time.

3. Make instructions brief. Students with ASD often have trouble remembering sequences, especially in terms of how they are to apply these instructions. Write instructions for them, or check to be sure they have written them correctly. Focus on giving only one or two instructions at a time.

4. Do not insist that these students maintain direct eye contact with you. Eye contact is extremely difficult and produces anxiety for them, but you may insist on their attention in other ways.

5. Use "social stories" or "social scripting" techniques, which can be highly effective in helping these students prepare for new events, experiences, or changes in routine and prevent an escalation of anxiety. The teacher can write out a story or work with the student to do so before the event and help the student become familiar

with it before the time for change to occur. Example: "On Thursday I am not going to math class from homeroom. I am going with my homeroom class to an assembly in the auditorium. After the assembly, I will go to math class."

6. Capitalize on students' strengths and interests. Students with ASD may be skilled at computer work or drawing; or they may become absorbed in a particular topic such as maps, weather, trains, or electronics. Reward them for completing assignments, and provide ways for them to develop their talents and contribute positively in class.

7. Give these students specific social feedback and step-by-step instructions. They do not learn social skills readily by observing others, so be alert to awkward situations, and be ready to step in. If you cannot provide needed instruction in the social areas, ask the special education teacher or counselor about any problems you see. Consider using the social scripting technique to help these students when they are in extensive peer interactions.

## Students with Attention Deficit and Hyperactivity

Broad characteristics of students with attention deficit and hyperactivity include distractibility, a short attention span, impulsiveness, an inability to organize, and a high level of physical movement. As distracting as these behaviors are, it is important to remember that they are not deliberate. Even for the most highly motivated children, it is difficult and takes a long time to learn ways to compensate for or control these problems. A low-key approach with much predictability and structure is almost essential to enable these students to function successfully. Frequent, often daily, communication with parents is necessary to ensure that school and home techniques and expectations are compatible.

Techniques that have had the greatest degree of success in working with these children include the following:

- Be sure you have their attention before giving oral instructions.
- Give brief and clear instructions, preferably one step at a time.
- If instructions involve a series of steps, have them written in sequence; teach students to complete one step before going on to the next. Having students mark off each step as they complete it helps them to keep track and see progress.
- Monitor these students closely as they begin a new assignment or activity; be willing to explain directions again.
- Adjust the amount of work required within a time period to be compatible with the attention span of these students. The amount may be increased gradually as their ability to concentrate increases.
- Remind these students that accuracy is more important than speed and that they need not be the first to finish or to speak up. Reinforce neatness and accuracy; when feasible, do not penalize messiness or errors. When accuracy is an issue, reinforce effort.
- Collect completed assignments; these students will often lose completed work before turning it in.

- Show them how to use window cards as frames to help focus attention on a specific area, problem, line of print, or paragraph. Teach them to use their fingers as pointers so that they stay focused on the page or line.
- Organize the daily schedule so that stimulating or exciting activities come after, rather than before, activities requiring concentration.
- Develop a plan for these students to move around every few minutes—for example, by bringing up their papers after they have completed part of the assignment, perhaps a few math problems or a paragraph.
- Find a spot with few distractions, and offer these students the option of doing independent work there.
- Prepare several low-pressure, low-risk activities for times when they need to spend a few minutes regaining control or relaxing.
- Teach students relaxation techniques such as deep breathing, tensing and relaxing muscles, and so on to relieve tension during long periods or tests.
- If students receive medication at school, establish a cue or routine to help them remember to go to the nurse at the proper time. Monitor this until they have assumed the responsibility successfully.
- Express your confidence in these students and their ability to learn new concepts and skills.

## Students Who Are Deaf or Hearing Impaired

Students with serious hearing loss may be able to function in regular classes if some crucial modifications are made. If you have one or more students who are deaf or hearing impaired, consult regularly with a teacher specializing in auditory handicaps in order to learn about students' needs and techniques that benefit. If assistive devices are available (e.g., FM auditory systems, caption decoders for videos), the specialist can show you how to use them.

It is usually best to seat these students near the center of the room and close to the front. Face the students when speaking, and use a doc-cam when presenting so that students can see your face while you are writing. Have the room well lighted so these students can see your lips and face to lip-read. Take care not to stand in front of windows or a bright doorway while talking; the glare behind you makes your face difficult to see.

Students with hearing loss often miss important information, being able to catch only portions of words or phrases. Because understanding is more complex than just hearing or responding and because these students are often reluctant to ask you to repeat, plan to repeat and rephrase important information or instructions. When possible, provide written backup as well. The amount of new content vocabulary introduced routinely may be overwhelming, so the support of an auditory specialist in introducing vocabulary may be necessary for these students to succeed in the regular classroom. Content Mastery, a special form of supplementary program described earlier in this chapter, may be utilized to reteach, especially for written language assignments.

During classroom discussions, these students need to have you restate other students' questions and responses because deaf or hearing impaired students are probably not able to lip-read them. Also check for understanding frequently during guided practice. These students require close monitoring as they begin written work. If note taking is required, ask a student with legible handwriting to take notes, using carbon paper, or to provide a copy to students needing help; students who are deaf or hearing impaired cannot take notes and lip-read at the same time. Utilize captioning for online videos or movies; the narration and placement of actors may make it impossible to lip-read at all. You might also assign a buddy to cue deaf or hearing impaired students when it is important to watch the teacher, to locate information in the text being discussed, and so on.

Increasingly, students who are deaf or hearing impaired are assigned interpreters to accompany them to regular classes. Again, consultation with the specialist on your campus is helpful to make clear what the role of the interpreter is to be. Interpreters may assist with oral or sign language interpretation and provide a "communication bridge" between teacher and student. As such, they relay information from the teacher to the student and vice versa, but they do not typically function as a teacher's assistant in the classroom. Their role is to devote their skills to supporting their assigned student in order to ensure this student's success.

## Students Who Have Visual Impairments

Students who are blind or who have severe visual impairments may be able to function well in regular classes with your help. Suggestions for adaptations of teaching methods and materials should be available in the student's functional visual assessment, written by a teacher of these students. The following suggestions may provide direction in accommodating their needs.

- Remember to read aloud anything that is displayed on the board, screen, or wall.
- Allow these students to record the lesson or to have fellow students make copies of their notes, which can be read aloud to the visually impaired students at home. Large type, dark print, and good contrast are easier to see.
- When possible, use tactile models and hands-on activities along with verbal descriptions to demonstrate concepts; these students often miss gestures, facial expressions, and details in demonstrations.
- Encourage visually impaired students to ask for help; if in doubt about how you can help them, ask them directly, and do not hesitate to discuss their vision problems with them.
- Remember that students with partial vision may tire more quickly, in part because of the concentration and effort required to perceive material close to their eyes. Frequent changes in the focus of activities may alleviate this.
- Seat these students with their backs to the windows. Glare on materials, on someone who is speaking, or on the board or other displays seriously impedes their ability to see at all.
- Allow these students to walk up to the board or other displays as needed.
- Students with visual impairments may have limited knowledge of spatial relationships and directionality and may miss social cues. Assist these students in peer interactions and personal adjustment.

## Students with Limited English Proficiency

Many students in our schools have a first language other than English. Some of these students have acquired sufficient English language skills to perform successfully in English-only classes. Others have not acquired a sufficient level of skill in speaking, understanding, reading, or writing English and need additional assistance to participate successfully.

Some students need bilingual classes in which content is presented in their predominant language, with a specified amount of time daily spent learning English. Other children know English well enough to benefit from being in a class with a bilingual teacher; here the content is presented in English, but the teacher is able to explain in the students' primary language when necessary. For many students, English language learning occurs in conjunction with content learning in a regular classroom, ideally with the aid of an English-as-a-Second-Language (ESL) certified classroom teacher and with instruction in English for a portion of the day.

Although children who speak virtually no English probably have a bilingual or an ESL teacher for most of the day, they often attend such subjects as P.E., music, and art without the support of the bilingual teacher. If you find that you have students who speak little or no English in your class, here are suggestions for communicating with them:

- Find out from the bilingual or ESL teacher which children understand some English and which ones understand none, so that your expectations will be fair and realistic. If there is no bilingual or ESL teacher on your campus, find out who the specialist is and how to contact that person to evaluate the student(s) and make suggestions.
- Learn what these children prefer to be called, and be sure to pronounce their names correctly.
- Learn key words in the children's native language, such as *listen*, *yes*, *no*, *please*, *good*, *stop*, *look*, and *thank you*.
- Help these students learn basic vocabulary words needed for your class. These are the instructional words you use regularly, along with words needed to understand the content of your class. Provide the bilingual or ESL teacher with an ongoing list of these words to reinforce with the students.
- Rather than rely on someone to translate for you, use your creativity in communicating, speaking naturally, and using phrases, gestures, and drawings or pictures.
- Reinforce key points with visual aids and demonstration when possible and by repeating in clear and concise words.
- Because these children are not accustomed to processing English and assume that they will not understand what is said, ask the bilingual or ESL teacher to encourage them to pay close attention when they are with you to see whether there are words or phrases they can understand or learn.
- Consider assigning peer "buddies" who are outgoing and warm to communicate what you cannot and to let you know when the students need your help and are reluctant to ask.

- Keep in mind that a long receptive period, during which individuals respond with gestures or nods before they feel confident enough to speak any English words, is normal for students with limited English proficiency.
- Be careful not to ignore or marginalize these students; include them in class activities as much as possible. For example, assign them to cooperative small groups with their peers. They may not be able to participate fully at first, but the interactions with their peers are important.
- Provide opportunities for these students to share with the class information about their language and culture. Demonstrations of clothing or foods and the introduction of a few simple words can help to integrate these children into the life of the classroom.
- Note variations in the cultures of home and school, and demonstrate respect in handling these differences (see Weinstein, Tomlinson-Clarke, & Curran, 2004).

## Students Living in Extreme Poverty

Many schools have increasing numbers of students who live in significant poverty, which requires understanding and adjustments from school staff. A key to success for these children is a strong, trusting relationship with the teacher in an environment in which they can feel safe, not threatened or stressed. You will probably be their primary motivator and the one who must help them understand how school can ultimately benefit them and why it will be worth it for them to attend regularly and to work hard. You will also be the one to help them learn how to negotiate what, for them, are the "hidden" rules and expectations of the school, many of which are taken for granted by their classmates.

When young children from an impoverished background come to school for the first time, they are unlikely to have the "going-to-school" skills that many other children already have. They may talk louder than other children or physically defend themselves against perceived threats. They are generally more sensitive to nonverbal than to verbal messages and are often not skilled at processing verbal explanations. Rather, they tune in to tone of voice, volume and inflections, gestures, and facial expressions because they may have learned hypervigilance and sensitivity to cues as vital survival skills. These children will need the most basic expectations demonstrated before they can adhere to your classroom rules and procedures.

In making explicit the school rules, explain that those rules and the rules of their neighborhood may be different, just like rules in various games are different (e.g., there's no tackling in basketball, but it's expected in football; there's no hitting at school even when you're called a name, though it may occur in your neighborhood). You must make explicit each specific step—for example, what they are to do when they first arrive in the morning: where to go; how to walk, not run, in the halls; how to walk in line properly; whether or how to talk (quietly or in a whisper); what to bring or not to bring to school; what to do with anything they do bring; and so on. These students may have difficulty with the new requirements and will depend on you to be encouraging and supportive even as you redirect, remind, and correct them.

In impoverished neighborhoods, cultural references and practices can be significantly different from mainstream school traditions. For example, great emphasis may be placed on saving face. Thus, when being disciplined, these children may try to imitate adults they have observed by grinning or laughing off your reprimand or correction. Take great care not to overreact or to humiliate these students, and whenever possible, discipline them in private. This protects their dignity, reduces their need for defiance, and shows your sensitivity to their well-being even while requiring that they follow the rules.

Practical approaches to working with these students can be found in Payne (1998). Because such students are often at risk for educational disadvantage, strategies suitable for this population are applicable (cf. Hargis, 1997). The following strategies may be useful for work with students from impoverished backgrounds:

1. Have extra supplies and materials on hand in case they don't have them. Determine whether the school or district has a fund for such items or whether there are community organizations that can provide help.
2. Teach procedures step by step. Encourage self-talk that focuses on the steps.
3. Because these students need a guide to and rationale for the school's expectations, use a three-step approach: (a) point out what they are supposed to do, (b) give meaning (i.e., reasons why), and (c) provide a strategy (i.e., how to do it).
4. Because these students are often preoccupied with problems at home, help them "bracket" their worries, to put off worrying about something until a specific later time. Obviously, you will not do this if the problem needs to be addressed immediately.
5. Assign them a peer buddy, and encourage them to discuss problems and solutions together.
6. Emotions affect children's ability to learn, and fear is a common feeling for these children. Allow them to write a letter or make a drawing expressing strong feelings; offer to keep it in a safe place or even in a sealed envelope for them.
7. Encourage positive self-talk that will enhance their feelings of self-control: "I do the task for myself—not for the teacher, not for my parents, but for myself."
8. Teach goal setting: Have them write down a concrete plan for class one day, and at the end of the day see what goals were met.
9. Allow them to help another student with something they do well.
10. When you meet with a parent of the student, demonstrate your enjoyment of and caring for his or her child. This goes a long way toward establishing a cooperative and mutually supportive relationship. Even if the focus of the meeting is to discuss a problem, you should set a pleasant and cordial tone. Keep the focus on positive steps to be taken to address any problems.

# ■ Teaching Lower-Achieving Students

Many teachers feel they need help to organize instruction to successfully teach students who are on a low academic level. Whether you have a class with only a few low achievers or one with many students whose entering skills are far below grade level, give special attention to the instructional needs of these students. Good instructional practices for all student populations are especially important when teaching low-achieving students.

## Active Instruction

Students performing at a low academic level make more progress in basic skills when their teachers provide structured classroom activities with close supervision and active, teacher-led instruction. Large amounts of class time spent in unstructured or free-time activities should be avoided, as should situations calling for frequent self-direction and self-pacing. It is especially important for lower-achieving students to have many opportunities to interact with the teacher during instruction, to answer the teacher's questions and receive feedback about their work. Low-achieving students should be seated where they can easily be monitored and given assistance (Brophy & Evertson, 1976; Good & Brophy, 2008; Good, Grouws, & Ebmeier, 1983).

## Organizing and Pacing Instruction

When teaching lower-achieving students, you encourage more learning and better classroom behavior when you break instruction into small segments or short activities with frequent assessments of understanding. Avoid activity plans that require students to attend to a presentation or to work for 25 or 30 minutes at a stretch on the same independent work assignment. Instead, use two or more shorter cycles of content development and work samples in each lesson, as described in Chapter 6. Advantages to using several cycles instead of one when teaching lower-ability students are numerous: Because of limited attention spans it is easier to maintain student involvement, and by carefully monitoring the first independent work/classwork exercise, you can quickly see whether the students are able to complete the assignments, which in turn allows you to pace instruction appropriately and give ample feedback.

In planning lessons for lower-ability students, it is more effective to cover material very thoroughly than to cover a lot of material quickly. Plan for plenty of practice and repetition, and keep lesson plans flexible enough to allow for reteaching. This does not mean, however, that assignments for lower-level students should be limited to routine, repetitious, and uninteresting work. On the contrary, assignments and class discussion should provide opportunities for all students to think, be creative, and organize and apply what they know. At least some of the questions lower-ability students encounter in written and oral work should give them practice with these higher-level operations.

Clear communication is important for everyone, but especially for lower-achieving students. Therefore, plan introductions of new content carefully. Disjointed or overly complex communication is likely to result in confusion, frustration, and misbehavior. The guidelines for clarity discussed in Chapter 9 emphasize paying careful attention to the amount of information presented at one time, appropriate vocabulary, and the use of concrete or specific examples to illustrate new concepts. Check for student understanding frequently, and avoid overlapping many procedural directions. Once you get students' attention, present directions in a step-by-step fashion, waiting for them to complete each step before going to the next.

## Remedial Instruction

For learning to occur, all students (and especially lower-achieving students) must be provided with instructional materials and tasks at which they can succeed. Therefore, lower-achieving students often require remedial instruction. When beginning a new unit, you may find that some students do not have the prerequisite skills. Or after teaching a lesson, you may see that several students have not mastered the new material. Both situations require that you provide remedial instruction. Two considerations are crucial: First, build time for remediation into your classroom activity plans; second, get instructional materials matched to the students who need remediation. Talk with your instructional supervisor, a resource teacher, or other colleagues to obtain instructional materials that your low-ability students will be able to complete successfully.

## Building Positive Attitudes

Even in lower elementary grades, lower-achieving students are more likely to have developed a poor self-image or poor attitude toward school. By the upper elementary grades, lower-academic-level students have often fallen two or more grade levels below average for their grade and age group. Some may have failed one or more grades in previous years. Because of their frequent failure in school in the past, some of these students will have become very discouraged and may react by giving up easily or by fighting back. These reactions may be seen in the extreme in apathy, shyness, belligerence, or clowning in class. Especially in earlier grades, these students may perceive classroom events as arbitrary or mysterious and may not expect to understand or to succeed in schoolwork.

As a teacher of lower-achieving students, your task is to improve these students' self-images and expectations of accomplishment. You can take several steps. First, it is important that these students finish their work and not give up, and this may require that you shorten assignments for some or provide extra time and encouragement to finish. However, the extra time lower-achieving students are given to finish assignments should not prevent them from participating in interesting and worthwhile activities with the rest of the class. Consistently being denied participation in show-and-tell, art activities, interest centers, and recess does not contribute to an improved self-image. Rather, you need to provide materials and assignments that lower-achieving students are able to finish in the time available.

To create opportunities for all children to be successful, keep in mind that some students who have difficulty with reading or mathematics are gifted in drawing, technology, or strategy. Try to vary your instruction in ways that bring these strengths to light.

Because class discussions are opportunities for students to display their knowledge, teachers' questions and students' answers are public, and therefore your handling of discussions often communicates expectations about student performance. How lower-achieving students are treated during class discussions can affect their attitude and achievement. Staying with students until they answer a question, giving them time to answer without being interrupted, providing constructive feedback for wrong answers, and helping students improve their answers are all ways that you can help low-achieving students succeed (Brophy & Evertson, 1976; Good & Brophy, 2008).

A warm, supporting, and accepting classroom climate benefits lower-achieving students. But be thoughtful in your use of praise; research suggests that praise is more helpful when it is specific and contingent on good work, good behavior, or both. Frequently rewarding lower-achieving students with vague or general praise, with praise for wrong answers, or for sloppy, incomplete work may convey the message that you don't expect much from them. Be alert for opportunities to give lower-achieving students deserved and specific praise.

# ■ Teaching Higher-Achieving Students

Higher-ability students may present special challenges in heterogeneous classes. The need to keep these students productively involved in learning activities requires that they be challenged at the appropriate level and given sufficient activities to avoid boredom or disruption of the rest of the class.

Research has shown that higher-ability students learn more when they are challenged. The level of success on activities can sometimes be lower than that needed for students with less ability; that is, they may not become as frustrated if they do not perform with an extremely high level of success. Effective teachers of higher-ability students tend to work at a faster pace than normal with these students and introduce more variety in their teaching methods and materials.

It bears noting that not all of your high-ability students will function in your classroom in the same way. Some high-ability students are high achievers; these students are often a joy to work with. High achievers may be well-socialized, independent workers who have developed positive attitudes toward school and learning. Some high-ability students, however, appear very different. They may be highly creative, highly divergent, gifted thinkers who approach every problem you present in your classroom differently from their peers, or they may create behavior problems. You must be careful not to confuse compliant behavior with academic ability.

The ability, creativity, and divergence of students who are gifted should be nurtured and encouraged, which may be difficult in a heterogeneous classroom. Classrooms with more open-ended assignments, where each student pursues a project or a problem to the extent of his or her ability, may provide more support for divergent thinkers and may help to avoid behavior problems that arise out of boredom or frustration with the limitations of highly structured assignments.

Have resource materials available for these students to use for bonus questions or extra projects. Develop a file with a variety of ideas for projects. Include extra or bonus questions on all assignments and tests, and encourage these students to attempt them. If your classroom has a computer, create a home page with links that provide enrichment for areas you cover in class. Involve these students in activities that can benefit others, such as peer tutoring, peer counseling, and school improvement projects. Encourage your higher-ability students to keep up with current events (as appropriate for their age) and to send their written questions or opinions to the newspaper or to people in the news.

Higher-ability students can contribute greatly to the learning environment in your classroom. Their contributions to class discussions and activities may encourage creativity and divergent thought in your other students. Your positive response to the special groups that make up your class signals to all students that their range of abilities, interests, and skills is welcomed and appreciated.

# ■ Models for Identification

The instruction of children with special needs in the United States is covered under federal law: the Individuals with Disabilities Education Improvement Act, 2004 (IDEA 2004). This law includes two models for determining student eligibility for special education services: IQ–achievement discrepancy and response to intervention. School districts and states vary in their designation of which model(s) to use. The IQ–discrepancy model utilizes standardized testing to determine if a student has a discrepancy between his or her ability to succeed in a subject (IQ) and his or her performance in that subject (achievement). The classroom teacher serves as the catalyst for a student's testing when that teacher suspects that a learning disability is preventing a student from learning and hence refers that child for testing. Tests are primarily administered by a school psychologist. Criticisms of this model include these: The range of discrepancy that qualifies a student for services is arbitrary, even standardized tests can have unreliable results, and identification of students for special services does not consider the possibility of poor instruction as the cause of a student's learning difficulties.

The *response to intervention* (RTI) model is a "multi-tiered method for delivering instruction to learners through increasingly intensive and individualized interventions" (iris.peabody.vanderbilt.edu, Online Dictionary, accessed 1/26/11). Inherent in RTI is the classroom teacher's collection and analysis of data on students' academic progress on a consistent and frequent basis. Within Tier 1 the classroom teacher provides high-quality instruction (defined by IDEA 2004 as research validated) and assesses all students (i.e., universal screening) to see if any are at risk for failure. In Tier 2 the classroom teacher and/or another educational professional (e.g., Title I teacher, classroom aide) provides interventions for alternative or additional support to the students at risk (individually or within small groups) and monitors their progress. When a student is still at risk for failure after the Tier 2 interventions, Tier 3 is designed to provide more intensive instruction (which may still involve the classroom teacher) and to utilize the collected data to identify if and what special education services are needed. The qualification for services depends on a district's or state's policies as well as the results from any evaluations requested to identify specific learning disabilities. (See iris.peabody.vanderbilt.edu for a number of instructional modules on RTI.)

Criticisms of the RTI model include these: There is no specific timing, number, or type of interventions designated as sufficient; and the time and expertise required of the classroom teacher can be prohibitive, considering the teacher's other instructional responsibilities. In particular, the classroom teacher must rule out poor instruction (or a poor instructional environment) as the cause of a student's learning difficulties (Kauffman, 2008).

The multitiered approach of RTI has also been applied to student difficulties with classroom behavior. Positive behavioral interventions and supports (PBIS) involves a universal Tier 1 in which all students are provided high-quality instruction on behavioral expectations. Classroom teacher monitoring (including the collection of data) identifies students at risk for failure to meet these expectations. In Tier 2 classroom teachers provide interventions for these students and continue to monitor. Students still struggling to meet expectations are recommended for additional assistance through Tier 3. The Office of Special Education Programs of the U.S. Department of Education hosts a Web site to provide information and assistance to schools concerning PBIS (www.pbis.org).

# ■ Chapter Summary

Effective classroom managers, while orchestrating groups, also are attentive to individuals. Knowledge of each student's needs, abilities, and dispositions can give a teacher the appropriate context within which to make instructional choices. Student characteristics that can influence choices include a student's entering achievement levels, eligibility for special services, and the availability of additional teaching resources. Interpreting the numerical data on a student's entering achievement in light of your observations will give you additional information.

Specific student classifications that require specialized classroom management include learning disabilities, emotional/behavioral problems, autism spectrum disorders, attention deficit and hyperactivity, hearing impairment, visual impairment, limited English proficiency, extreme poverty, and giftedness. Some of the unique teaching strategies available to support both the whole class and individual students include team teaching, modifying the whole-class instruction, individualizing instruction, and utilizing cooperative groups and peer tutoring. When additional teachers are involved in classroom instruction, coordinating schedules, timely completion of lessons, and mutual implementation of rules, procedures, and consequences are important areas for collaboration.

A strategy that can assist individual students who struggle with learning in a specific area is response to intervention (RTI). RTI has implications for classroom management, as does positive behavior interventions and supports (PBIS), in an attempt to meet the needs of individual students. These programs can assist teachers in achieving student self-regulation, maintaining an organized and well-paced instructional flow, helping students participate actively, and providing remediation and/or enrichment as needed.

# ■ Further Reading

Albrecht, S. F. (2008). Time away: A skill-building alternative to discipline. *Preventing School Failure, 53*(1), 49–55.

*As an overall approach to PBIS, this article describes an intervention to teach students appropriate behavior through three steps: time-out, redirection, and conflict resolution. The final phase includes a problem-solving worksheet.*

Buzzell, J. G., & Piazza, R. (1994). *Case studies for teaching special needs and at-risk students.* Albany, NY: Delmar.

*This book contains more than 20 cases written by teachers chronicling their experiences with students with special needs. The cases cover the full range of physical, mental, and emotional disabilities and provide grounding for analysis and problem solving.*

Kauffman, J. M. (2008). Special education. In T. Good (Ed.), *21st Century education: A reference handbook* (Vol. 1, pp. 405–413).

*This author provides an overview of the history, terms, responsibilities, challenges, and critiques of special education.*

Kronberg, R., Jackson, L., Sheets, G., & Rogers-Connolly, T. (1995). A toolbox for supporting integrated education. *Teaching Exceptional Children, 27*(4), 54–58.

*Including students with special needs in the regular education classroom requires that special educators, regular educators, and administrators work together to develop new conceptions about roles and responsibilities. This article suggests a framework for thinking about how all participants should cooperate, and it describes numerous activities and strategies to further this goal.*

Lane, K., Falk, K., & Wehby, J. (2006). Classroom management in special education classrooms and resource rooms. In C. Evertson & C. Weinstein (Eds.), *Handbook of research on classroom management: Research, practice, and contemporary issues* (pp. 439–460). Mahwah, NJ: Erlbaum.

*This chapter explains the acting-out cycle common in behavior problems and suggests research-based strategies for prevention in both more and less restrictive special education settings. The authors describe three strategies: differential reinforcement (rewarding the nonoccurrence of the targeted behavior), choice making (reducing aversive tasks by including preferred activities), and high-probability requests (matching low-preferred with highly preferred tasks).*

Lotan, R. A. (2006). Managing group work in the heterogeneous classroom. In C. Evertson & C. Weinstein (Eds.), *Handbook of research on classroom management: Research, practice, and contemporary issues* (pp. 525–539). Mahwah, NJ: Erlbaum.

> *This chapter explores the effective use of groups in classrooms having students who are academically and linguistically diverse. The emphasis is on redefining the teacher's role and creating conditions for broadened participation among students.*

Sandomierski, T., Kincaid, D., & Algozzine, B. (2007). Response to intervention and positive behavior support: Brothers from different mothers or sisters with different misters? *PBIS Newsletter 4*(2). Accessed January 26, 2011, at www.pbis.org/pbis_newsletter/volume_4/issue2.aspx

> *This article describes RTI and PBIS through a comparison of their key components.*

Soodak, L., & McCarthy, M. R. (2006). Classroom management in inclusive settings. In C. Evertson & C. Weinstein (Eds.), *Handbook of research on classroom management: Research, practice, and contemporary issues* (pp. 461–489). Mahwah, NJ: Erlbaum.

> *The authors review the research on effective instruction in inclusive settings and provide helpful charts of three broad classifications of strategies: teacher-directed, peer-mediated, and self-directed. They include findings and implications and research support for each.*

Students with special needs [Special issue]. (1996). *Educational Leadership, 53*(5), 42–74.

> *This theme issue contains helpful articles about the challenges in educating students with special needs. The authors deal with such issues as preventing learning disabilities through early intervention programs (Slavin), teaching English language learners (Gersten), holistic approaches to teaching students with attention deficit disorder (Armstrong), and identifying and developing special talents (Feldhusen).*

iris.peabody.vanderbilt.edu

> *The home site of the Iris Center at Peabody College, Vanderbilt, supported by the U.S. Department of Education's Office of Special Education Programs, promotes better awareness and understanding of the needs of special learners. Course enhancement materials, interactive training modules (including a series on RTI), case studies, activities, a dictionary, and an extensive resource library are available at this site.*

www.ccbd.net

> *This Web site of the Council for Children with Behavioral Disorders includes up-to-date information concerning issues and research related to behavioral disorders.*

www.nagc.org

> *The National Association for Gifted Children provides links to a number of resources for higher-ability students.*

www.nichcy.org/

> *Organized by the National Information Center for Children and Youth with Disabilities, this is a comprehensive site with in-depth coverage of issues including learning disorders and behavioral problems. Fact sheets for specific disabilities are provided at www.nichcy.org/disability/specific.*

www.nimh.nih.gov/publicat/autism.cfm

> *This Web site for the National Institutes of Mental Health provides current information about diagnoses, treatment, and therapy for children with autism spectrum disorders.*

# ■ Suggested Activities

1. Discuss your responses to the following prompts with a peer: What moments in your schooling left you feeling isolated, rejected, alienated, bored, and/or incapable? How did you move beyond this? In what ways were teachers involved in helping you? How will you identify students with similar feelings in your classroom? In what ways do your responses inform your philosophy of education?

2. Read Case Studies 11.1 and 11.2, which describe two teachers' strategies for working with students with special needs. Identify 10 strategies Mr. Bartolo and Ms. Chin are using to help the special needs students in their classrooms. How are they also meeting the needs of their other students?

3. Read Case Study 11.3. Respond in writing to these questions: What modifications does Mrs. Laskey make to meet the needs of her inclusion students? How would these modifications benefit the students involved? Why do you think she has the class arranged in groups? What does this mean for her inclusion students?

4. Problems 11.A and 11.B describe two situations that elementary teachers frequently encounter. Use ideas presented in this chapter to identify strategies that could be used in these situations. Check your ideas with the suggestions in the Appendix.

# ■ Case Study 11.1

## ORGANIZING READING INSTRUCTION FOR LOW-ACADEMIC-LEVEL STUDENTS

Mr. Bartolo is beginning his second year as a first-grade teacher in an urban elementary school that serves a predominantly Latino population. His 26 students present a variety of challenges: a wide range of reading levels, several students with limited English proficiency, students who receive supplemental instruction from the resource teacher, and one student who has been diagnosed with attention-deficit/hyperactivity disorder.

In his first year of teaching, Mr. Bartolo used the recommended basal reading series with small, homogeneous groups of students. He has followed this format for the first 6 weeks of his second year, but he is especially concerned with the progress of two students in the classroom. Jason is one of four students in the highest reading group; he has above-average academic abilities but has difficulty getting along with his classmates. Juan is one of five students in the lowest reading group; his family immigrated from Puerto Rico at the beginning of the school year, and he speaks limited English.

Mr. Bartolo is familiar with peer tutoring, and he knows that several colleagues utilize it in their classrooms. After discussing peer tutoring with another colleague and with the boys' parents, he decides to implement this strategy with Jason and Juan. Mr. Bartolo hopes that the tutoring arrangement can strengthen Jason's social skills and help Juan's reading.

Before the peer tutoring begins, Mr. Bartolo knows that he must work with Jason and Juan to teach them strategies for comprehension and decoding unknown words during their small-group reading instruction. Other skills necessary for peer tutoring—such as listening, sharing, and problem solving—have been emphasized during the first 6 weeks of school. In addition to these skills, Mr. Bartolo schedules extra time to practice the peer tutoring with Jason and Juan. After several practice sessions, Jason and Juan begin the tutoring without Mr. Bartolo's assistance. He continues to monitor and intervene as necessary, and he sees signs of improvement in the boys.

Along with the small-group instruction and limited implementation of peer tutoring, Mr. Bartolo modifies student assignments as necessary. This includes making audiotapes of books, shortening assignments, providing one-on-one instruction, and designing literacy projects for heterogeneous cooperative groups. Mr. Bartolo is confident that his students' reading comprehension will improve this year. He is thinking of expanding the peer tutoring to include every student in his class next year. What things should he consider?

# ■ Case Study 11.2

## SUPPORTING STUDENTS WITH AUDITORY DISABILITIES IN THE CLASSROOM

Ms. Chin has a lively class of 24 second graders, two of whom have severe auditory impairments. Bobby wears hearing aids that require Ms. Chin to wear an FM power pack so he can hear what she is saying. Sally has a cochlear implant but has virtually no hearing. Both children use sign language, although Bobby speaks to some extent. An interpreter follows the two throughout the day, sitting or standing near the teacher during instruction and signing. The interpreter stays near them during independent work periods to translate and sign any instructions that may be out of the children's line of vision.

During the first week of school, and before Bobby and Sally began attending Ms. Chin's class full time, she explained hearing impairments to the class so that they would understand. A specialist for auditorily impaired persons showed the students the FM equipment, let them hear through it, and played a sound file to demonstrate what sounds were like for those with hearing loss. Ms. Chin also spoke with the class about the interpreter's role, emphasizing that all other students were to look at the teacher, not the interpreter. She marked a place on the carpet with masking tape as "Sally's spot," because Sally needed to be at the front and center of the room to see the teacher and the interpreter during rug time.

Ms. Chin learned basic signs herself and began using them while speaking to the class. Above the alphabet letters at the top of the board, she posted hand signs for each letter. The school also began a Sign Club, through which the entire student body learned five new signs a week. Ms. Chin found that several children quickly picked up signing and began communicating with Sally and Bobby with signs, words, and gestures once they arrived.

Now during center time, Ms. Chin usually places the FM power pack in the middle of the table for Bobby. She has taken care to let both Bobby and Sally sit near children with whom they have become friends in order to ease their problems with communication. Many activities are already structured to be hands-on, a preferred means of learning for auditorily impaired students. Ms. Chin does not use phonics approaches with Sally and Bobby because even with Bobby's partial hearing he misses distinctions among "ch," "sh," "th," and some other sounds. Ms. Chin works closely with the special education teacher, who also teaches Bobby and Sally for part of the day, to coordinate and reinforce what they are learning. In addition, Ms. Chin communicates often with Bobby's and Sally's parents so that they, too, can reinforce what the children are learning in school.

Ms. Chin keeps a signing manual in her classroom, and when she starts a new unit, she sends vocabulary words home along with the signs for any words that are unusual so that she, the interpreter, the special education teacher, and the parents will be consistent in using the same signs. Bobby and Sally learn vocabulary words both orally and through signs. Several other manipulatives are available to help these students learn, such as a number line, shapes, and puzzle boards.

---

## ■ Case Study 11.3

### TEACHING STUDENTS IN A THIRD-GRADE INCLUSION CLASS

Mrs. Laskey has 22 energetic third graders, including four who qualify for special education support. She has student desks arranged in groups of five or six, with only one special student in any one cluster. She does not single out the four students, but she does make sure to check with them frequently for understanding. During discussion periods she calls on the four students often, sometimes just to have them repeat instructions; she says this helps her know they are keeping up and also provides them with easy success. When students are doing written work or taking tests, she makes sure to walk by the desks of the four students, helping them when she sees a problem rather than waiting for them to raise their hands for help. Based on recommendations from each child's IEP, Mrs. Laskey gives directions in small and distinct steps, shortens written assignments, clearly defines limits (physical/behavioral), extends time requirements, reads tests aloud, allows use of math manipulatives during math tests, and has the students repeat directions. One of the students has a history of behavior problems, and she engages him frequently, allowing him some extra movement around the classroom when it will not be disruptive.

During tests and during certain instructional periods such as language arts, Ms. Bonner, the special education teacher, comes into Mrs. Laskey's classroom. Ms. Bonner is there specifically to work with the four students in the special education program, in accordance with their IEPs; at times she may also help other students when the four seem to be understanding and working well. This way, the four students are provided the extra support they need but are not singled out. On occasion, especially just after a new concept has been introduced, Ms. Bonner may take one or more of the four students to a corner of the room for additional instruction.

When Mrs. Laskey has her class gather on the rug for story time or instruction, the four children sit among their peers, wherever they choose. The child who has difficulty with behavior often chooses to sit in back of the other students so he can stand up and move around. Mrs. Laskey may motion or speak to him if he is becoming too active. If his movement becomes disruptive, she gives him the option of controlling his own behavior and becoming quieter in the back; she asks him whether he can do that or whether it would help him to sit next to her. His choice varies, and he seems to understand that she knows he must work harder than other students to control his behavior. When he does opt to move up next to her, she touches his shoulder now and then for additional support and reminders. This also helps him focus on the material she is presenting, because he is closer to her.

# PROBLEM 11.A

## Team Teaching

Mr. Miller and two other fourth-grade teachers use team teaching for math instruction. Shortly after lunch each day, some students from the other teachers' classes come to Mr. Miller's room, and some of his students go to the other two teachers' rooms. Mr. Miller has grown dissatisfied with the arrangement because he feels that too much of his teaching time is wasted while groups change rooms, reorganize, and get ready to work. Sometimes students arriving early disrupt lessons. At other times, stragglers hold up the rest of the class. Students frequently arrive without the materials they need for that day. While Mr. Miller answers questions and deals with problems, students begin chatting and wandering around. When Mr. Miller is ready to start the lesson, he has trouble getting students settled down to work. What can Mr. Miller do to make teaming work more smoothly?

# PROBLEM 11.B

## A Heterogeneous Class

Ms. Ortiz feels that her class this year is more difficult to teach than any she has had in her four years of teaching third grade. Of 26 students in her class, seven are beginning the school year functioning at first-grade level or below in reading. Five of the seven are also far behind in mathematics concepts; the other two are on grade level. Three students in the class have advanced reading and mathematics skills, whereas others are nearer to grade level. Ms. Ortiz is frustrated in her attempts to meet the needs of the lowest-achieving students while challenging the highest-achieving students. She now conducts four reading groups. What strategies might Ms. Ortiz consider?

---

## MyEducationLab

Now go to www.myeducationlab.com to:

- Take a Quiz to test your mastery of chapter objectives.
- Study chapter content with an individualized Study Plan.
- Deepen your understanding of particular concepts and principles with Classroom Management Simulations.
- Apply what you have learned in the chapter to your work with children in Building Teaching Skills exercises.

# APPENDIX

## Answer Keys for Selected Chapter Activities

### CHAPTER 2

### Activity 1

The room arrangement shown in Figure 2-3 could contribute to classroom management problems in a number of ways (suggestions for improvement are provided in italics):

- When the teacher presents information from the area near the main board, several students at the back table have their backs to the teacher and the displays, making it difficult for them to see the material. Those at the back table who face the board are quite a distance from it and may struggle to see as well. It is more difficult for the teacher to monitor students at a distance. *Move student seating toward the main board, and arrange it in ways that will allow all students to see the presentation.*
- Traffic lanes are clogged or blocked, especially near the bookshelves, the computer, and en route to the bathrooms and the pencil sharpener. *Make sure sufficient room is available for travel throughout the room.*
- The small-group table in the center of the room near the student desks might cause distractions for students seated at their desks. There is no place at the table where the teacher can sit and easily see everybody in the room. *Move the small-group table to the periphery, and make sure the teacher has a seat that allows all students to be viewed.*
- The teacher should consider using a low bookcase near the door to avoid blocking the view of the center. Because of the location of the bookcase, the center may be difficult to monitor. *Move the bookshelf to a less blocking position (e.g., where the pencil sharpener is now).*
- When the teacher assists individual students at their desks, he or she will have difficulty monitoring students in several places in the room. *Follow the suggestions in the first two items in this list.*
- The isolated desk near the girls' restroom door could be a source of potential problems. It blocks the path to the door and the computer, so a student seated there would be distracted by the traffic to and from these two areas. The location of the desk makes it difficult for the teacher to monitor a student seated there. *Incorporate this desk into the larger arrangement.*
- The student sitting at the desk against the teacher's desk might be distracted if the teacher worked with other students at the teacher's desk. Also, this student desk is far from the main instructional area. *Incorporate this desk into the*

*larger arrangement. Use the small-group table if a student needs a separate location to focus temporarily.*

- The location of the computer workstation may be a distraction to students using the station as others move to and from the restroom. There may also be an electrical hazard with water from the restrooms or water fountain entering the computer workstation. *Move the computer station to a less congested location (another Internet connection exists).*
- Storing books between the water fountain and the sink may lead to book damage. *Move the bookshelf to a more appropriate location (e.g., where the wastebasket is now).*

## CHAPTER 3

### Activity 4

Some of the potential procedures Ms. Smith could put in place include these:

- Entering the classroom (e.g., promptness, placement of materials, seating)
- Daily bell work (i.e., activity for students to complete while she takes care of administrative issues such as attendance)
- Group attention signal to alert the class to focus on her
- Schedule for instruction (i.e., knowing in advance the day's plan)
- Passing out papers (e.g., timing, helper)
- Student requests for assistance (how, when, where)
- Pencil sharpener/wastebasket/restroom/water fountain use
- Listening
- Following directions
- Obtaining needed materials

## CHAPTER 4

### Activity 4

#### Diagnosis

The continuing confusion of Mr. Ambrose's students about due dates, directions, and completion of work suggests that although he may have planned plenty of activities for the students, he may not be explaining requirements clearly or checking for understanding frequently enough. In addition, students are not receiving feedback about their progress or the quality of their work, nor are there any apparent rewards or penalties connected with work completion or lack of it. Having students hold their papers until the next day may result in many papers being misplaced and in further delaying feedback about the correctness of the work.

## Suggestions

Mr. Ambrose can begin to improve his situation by trying the following strategies:

- Each assignment should be explained carefully and in detail in addition to being posted on the board. Students can be encouraged to keep an assignment book or some other record of daily assignments in particular subjects. Mr. Ambrose can also keep a record of the assignments in a folder so that students can refer to it if needed or can check on assignments they missed while they were absent. Keeping several days' assignments posted on the board may be confusing unless these are clearly marked.
- While giving directions and explanations, Mr. Ambrose should be aware of signs of confusion or inattention. He should also be sure to go over sample questions, problems, or exercises with the class; use a standard format for headings on papers; and use routines whenever possible to avoid constantly having to reexplain or give new directions.
- Mr. Ambrose should have students begin assignments under his direction. He can do a small part of an assignment orally, then question students to check their understanding until he is sure they can work independently.
- He should circulate around the class and monitor student progress rather than sit at his desk doing paperwork. He should allow students to come to his desk for help only after they have tried the assignment. Then he should allow only one student at a time to come up. When several students need help, he should circulate around the class again rather than encouraging come-ups.
- Assignments should be checked and collected as they are completed. If they are too complex to be checked immediately, Mr. Ambrose should check for completeness and return incomplete work to the students to finish. It may be helpful to set aside one or two specific times each day to review each student's progress on assignments. That way, students will know they are accountable, and Mr. Ambrose can more easily identify problems that students are having with their work. In addition, he will be able to identify students who are having difficulty and need extra help before they get too far behind. Students who fail to turn in assignments should be given assistance and direction promptly.
- Mr. Ambrose can encourage students to set goals by helping them keep records of their scores on assignments in particular subjects. He may be able to boost motivation by encouraging the students to set a class goal of improved completion rates or overall student averages and may then provide a treat or a special activity as a reward.

## CHAPTER 5

### Activity 1

Ms. Stevens has a blend of authority types in her presentation. She seems to demonstrate bureaucratic authority with the consequence of having to repeat the procedures and the praise for the second effort having success, professional authority in that she explains the procedure specifically (e.g., what it will include, will not include, time allowed), and charismatic authority in her positive interactions and clear communication. Ms. Stevens may also lean on her traditional authority as a teacher at the beginning of the year to help her establish helpful procedures such as this one.

After developing this procedure, Ms. Stevens would be able to continue to practice it and provide feedback as needed to help the class make quick transitions between other tasks and the Spanish lesson (or another rug-time activity). Quick transitions would eliminate the potential for disruptions and distractions as well as increase the time available for teaching.

## CHAPTER 6

### Activity 4

Examples of Kounin's concepts in the description:

As Mr. Case is about to begin class after lunch, he makes eye contact with two students who are exchanging notes; the students quickly get out their class materials. (Withitness) "Let's begin by working some of the exercises at the end of the chapter; you will need a piece of paper with a heading." As students begin to get out their materials, Mr. Case calls out, "Oops, I forgot to tell you to bring money for tomorrow for the field trip. How many of you will be going?" (**Lack of smoothness**) After a brief discussion, students finish getting out their materials. Mr. Case says, "We'll go through these exercises orally, but I also want you to write the answers on your papers as part of today's classwork. I'll come around later and check your answers. (**High-participation format and accountability**) Now, who can answer the first question? Hands please. Tyrone?" Mr. Case conducts the lesson by calling on various students, some with hands up, others seemingly at random from the nonvolunteers. (**Group alerting**) About halfway through the exercises, a student enters the room and says that he is new to the school and has been assigned to the class. Mr. Case goes to his desk, sits down, and says, "OK, come here. I'll check out some of your books to you. (**Lack of overlapping**) I wish the school office wouldn't send children in the middle of the period. Where are you from anyway? That's a nice shirt you are wearing." (**Lack of smoothness**) After finishing with the student and sending him to a seat, Mr. Case leaves his desk and says to the class, "Now where were we? Oh, yes, question 7. Say, where did Kim and Lee go? I didn't give them permission to leave." (**Lack of withitness**) After several more minutes, Mr. Case calls a halt to the activity and says, "Now, I'd like us to discuss the test coming up this Thursday. Let's make sure that you are all clear on what will be on the exam and what you will need to do to get ready for it." After a pause he adds, "I almost forgot. Get your questions from before, and look at the next to the last one. We have to add an important point that was left out...." After finishing the item, Mr. Case turns the topic back to the upcoming test. (**Lack of momentum**) "Now, where were we? Oh, yes. I want to show you some items that will be similar to those on the test. Here's one." He writes it on the board, then pauses: "Well, I don't want to give away the test, do I?" Without discussing the test further, he turns to another topic. (**Lack of smoothness**) "Just wait until you hear about the video we will be viewing tomorrow. I saw it on another teacher's Web posting during lunch, and she said that her students thought it was one of the most interesting, exciting stories they had ever seen!" (**Group alerting**).

## Activity 5

### Diagnosis

Although Ms. Lake has planned interesting presentations, her students seem to be floundering during the follow-up activities. A large part of Ms. Lake's problem lies with poor instructional clarity, poor sequencing of activities, and unclear directions. Students' poor showing on the five-item test suggests that related content from the previous week was not understood. The 20-minute presentation contains several indicators of poor clarity, including presenting information out of sequence, backtracking, inserting extraneous information, and moving from one topic to another without warning. In addition, the assignment does not support the content development activity. The assignment is made without checking for understanding, and the directions are vague and indefinite.

### Suggestions

Ms. Lake would achieve more success with her class if she concentrated on the following items:

- Information should be presented systematically. Ms. Lake should plan the lesson sequence and stick to it; state major goals and objectives; pace the lesson so that adequate time is available to cover major points; and avoid vagueness by being specific and using familiar words.
- Ms. Lake should review her procedures for keeping students responsible for work, especially communicating work requirements and giving directions clearly. She should be sure that step-by-step directions are given for complex assignments, and she should ask students to repeat directions if they think they do not understand them.
- During content development activities, frequent work samples should be obtained and other checks on comprehension used. With this information, available instruction can be adjusted as needed.
- Ms. Lake should consider carefully the amount of information being presented in any one lesson. It might be better to present less information and leave sufficient time to check classwork before assigning homework.
- Complex lessons should be broken down into smaller parts, and later concepts should not be presented until primary ones are mastered.
- If some students still do not seem to understand after a presentation and discussion, Ms. Lake can meet with them in a small group to review the

presentation and answer questions. If one or two students consistently have difficulty, they can be seated near her desk so that it is easier to work with them.

- During the independent work portion of lessons, Ms. Lake should circulate to check student progress and to make sure that assignment directions are being followed.

## CHAPTER 7

### Activity 5

### Case Study 5.2

a. Note concepts described in this chapter that are evident in Ms. James's procedures and strategies. *What functions do the associated procedures and strategies serve?*

**Room arrangement**—desks clustered, purpose described, seating assignment to be made with variety across the year / *Clarity in expectations, security in anticipating future tasks*

**Student materials/storage**—yellow folder prepared and placed with each group, serves as storage until students have required notebook, different color used with each class / *Organization and preparation maximizes teaching time, color-coding limits confusion*

**Procedures and routines**

Communication—hands to be raised: stated, practiced, and reinforced; group conversation at appropriate volume: modeled and reviewed / *Importance given through initial emphasis, feedback provided to promote compliance, establishes path for respectful communication*

Movement—sharpen pencils/get materials as needed but not during instruction; student role for getting textbooks / *Reduces distractions and superfluous movement*

Transitions—return materials to folder; turn diagnostic test over; new seating announced in advance / *Prepares students for next task, identifies when students have completed previous task*

**Group attention signals**—asks for attention / *Indicates plan to speak to the entire class*

**Forming groups**—initially as students choose, teacher assignment explained; assignment made after observation; groups identified in writing; movement from pairs to larger group / *Explicitly states how groups formed, forethought possible for assigning groups, practice provided for pairs and then larger groups*

Interdependence

Roles—gives chair assignments and uses them for registration tasks/procedures instruction/materials distribution; reviews prior to larger task / *All students given opportunity to assist, prevents confusion/domination/abdication*

Joint responsibility—explains benefit of group learning; makes group responsible for new member as needed; must work together to solve task; can help one another on individual assignment / *Builds tasks that promote group emphasis, continues to validate group ties in individual assignment*

Individual accountability

Expectations—learning to work with a variety of peers; group reporter selected after task completed / *Makes all students potential reporters*

Tasks—will have individual notebooks and test independently; individual assignment completed showing work; completed as homework if not finished in class / *Notebooks/tests/assignments require students to demonstrate own learning*

Group tasks

Initial—begins with registration/procedures/diagnostic test/grading policies; television-watching analysis of own age group; paired problem solving / *Reinforces expectations/procedures, age appropriate, helps with group assignments/future planning*

Group work skills

Social—sharing, helping, listening, encouraging, working hard on television task: noted but not necessarily taught / *Highlights the importance of these skills*

Explanatory—practiced on Day 3 but not taught / *Could be touchstone for later lesson*

Leadership (not mentioned)

**Monitoring**—observes group tasks even while working on attendance; monitors diagnostic test; monitors while obtaining textbook numbers / *Helps maintain expectations/gets to know students/identifies potential problems/completes administrative tasks*

**Interventions**—gives feedback on raising hands / *Reinforces importance of procedure*

Student goals/participation—bulletin board of math applications with opening discussion, learning to work in groups, importance of trying, emphasis on estimating, necessity of explanations, acceptance of mistakes / *Emphasizes key instructional themes for the year, helps students acclimate to this learning environment*

**b. Are there any areas discussed in this chapter in Ms. James's classroom during the first three days? Would you suggest introducing them? Why or why not?**

Ms. James does not cover group attention signals. Her charisma may be enough with this specific class that she will be able to "ask" for their attention; however, it is likely she will need to have alternative methods. If the class has not worked in groups before/is talkative/does not meet the expectation of acceptable noise, she has not taught them a way to be called back for further instruction. If she could teach this on Day 1 and reinforce on Days 2 and 3, it would be helpful. Additionally, group work skills are not explicitly taught in Ms. James's first three days; however, she implies the need for social and explanatory skills. Specific instruction, practice, and feedback in group work skills will be required for the learning environment she is establishing—but need not be crammed into her already-full first three days. While many of the areas are covered in her first three days, Ms. James will need to continue teaching, practicing, and providing feedback to her students in these areas to establish the environment she has set as a goal.

**c. Ms. James teaches in a departmentalized fifth-grade math class. What changes might be appropriate for earlier grades? For different content areas?**

Responses will differ according to the grades/content areas selected.

## CHAPTER 8

### Activity 6

### Problem 8.1

### Diagnosis

Ms. Greene has failed to communicate and reinforce her expectations for classroom behavior and to establish rules and procedures that deal with the problem areas in her classroom. She apparently did not stop inappropriate behavior when it first began occurring; as a result, what could have been a good start during the first weeks of school has deteriorated into a difficult situation. At this point, even the well-behaved students are misbehaving, and her only deterrent has lost its effect.

### Suggestions

Ms. Greene should decide what kinds of behavior she expects of her students with regard to general conduct, as well as procedures they should follow in particular activities. She should then develop new rules and procedures where they are needed and clarify and reteach those that were part of her original plan but are no longer effective. For example, she could set aside specific times for students to get drinks, use the restroom, sharpen pencils, or visit the class pets.

She should select a time—perhaps a Monday or the day after a school vacation—to introduce or to review and reteach the rules and procedures to her class. She should also explain to the students the rationales for the desired behaviors and perhaps rehearse complex ones so she can give students feedback about especially important behaviors. She will certainly want to remind the students about when they are allowed to whisper quietly. Because students have acquired poor classroom talk habits, they may need visual cues such as stop or go signs to remind them about when they must work quietly and when they may whisper or talk in classroom voices. She can also help students learn when it is appropriate to talk quietly and when it is not by alerting them about class noise levels and encouraging them to monitor it themselves.

Ms. Greene should review with the students the procedures for working in small groups. She may have to adopt these practices:

- Use shorter independent work periods, breaking up activities in the groups more often.
- Help students pace themselves by setting a timer to signal when work should be completed.
- Tell students ahead of time what work will be checked and when. Remind them that they will be questioned about their assignment when they come to the reading circle.
- Make sure that students in the first group understand their assignment by having them do an example or two before calling for the second group.
- Monitor the out-of-group students for appropriate behavior while working with the reading group.
- After sending one group back to independent work, wait to call the second group until the work of the other students has been checked and help has been given when needed.

After the rules and procedures are introduced—or reintroduced—to the class, Ms. Greene should do the following:

- Monitor the class with the goal of anticipating and preventing misbehavior before it occurs and noting appropriate behavior.
- Make sure that students have enough work to do and that they understand and are able to complete the activities. Students should also know what specific things they can do when they have finished their assigned work.
- Structure time for movement and activity.
- Make statements that pace students through their work, such as, "You should now be working on problems 2 through 5, and no one should be talking," or "After I've checked your paper, you may go to the listening center."
- Reward academic performance and other desirable classroom behavior regularly, using stars, happy faces, displays of student work, pats on the back, smiles, and so on.

- Be certain that stated consequences for inappropriate behavior are related to the misbehavior and that they can be carried out consistently. Positive consequences as well as negative ones should be communicated to students.

## CHAPTER 9

### Activity 9.3

1. b
2. c
3. d
4. a
5. c

## CHAPTER 10

### Activity 4

In the situations provided, the following strategies might resolve the problems.

**Situation 1:** Assuming that this is not a common occurrence and that the students are generally participating in the discussion, try proximity (specifically with Ardyth, Melissa, and those students whispering). If that doesn't work, try group focus or redirecting the behavior.

**Situation 2:** Assuming that simple interventions have not worked with Desi and Bryce, try removing the student (i.e., separating them from one another, but perhaps not from the class). If that doesn't work, use a penalty or withhold a privilege.

**Situation 3:** Assuming Dwayne is seeking attention, provide that through other avenues (e.g., class helper, teaching assistant) while simultaneously giving the student a choice (e.g., "Allow your peers to focus on their work, OR you will have a new assigned seat that is separate from them"). If that doesn't work, use problem solving (see Chapter 9) to help Dwayne channel his charming behavior into more appropriate venues (e.g., reading the morning announcements with flair).

**Situation 4:** Assuming that these incidents are being responded to one at a time in a progressive fashion, in response to the spitting, issue a brief desist along with using a penalty (e.g., cleaning up the mess/apologizing). Following the shoving, respond with isolating the student, discuss the behavior and its cause/effect, withhold a privilege (e.g., a missed opportunity to interact with peers), and include a means to apologize to the peer. (Note: Shoving may fall under a school's zero-tolerance policy, which would result in an immediate referral to the school office and, typically, a suspension of Marc.) After the name-calling, use the Think Time strategy (to give him time away from classmates) along with conferring with a parent (sharing the day's pattern of aggressive behavior, working together to identify potential causes and preventative actions, and discussing the penalty that will be implemented).

## CHAPTER 11

### Activity 4

### Problem 11.A

These approaches would help the team operate more smoothly:

- Strive for good cooperation and group planning among unit or team teachers. Each teacher must try to maintain the schedule. Have students watch the time. Post times for students to leave, and list the materials they should take with them. Use a timer if necessary.
- Use established routines as much as possible for beginning and ending lessons; monitor the class to be sure that students follow them.
- Teach students exactly what behaviors are expected during transitions; include expectations for voice level, use of the pencil sharpener, procedures for passing between classes, getting ready for the lesson, and so on.
- If early-arriving students are a problem, establish a waiting area where these students must wait quietly until the teacher can speak with them without interrupting the class.
- Use a short review activity with the group while waiting for stragglers to arrive. Make sure students know what they are supposed to do when they return to their class. If they return while the teacher is conducting a lesson, the group or the class can be given a brief activity to do while the teacher makes sure that students coming in get settled.

### Problem 11.B

Here are specific suggestions for Ms. Ortiz:

- Each day, plan assignments that all students can complete; then provide supplementary assignments at different levels—enrichment and extension for students who have demonstrated mastery, review and practice assignments for students who are still practicing the content.
- Find out whether any students in the class qualify for special assistance such as special education, resource room, or bilingual tutoring.
- Use some small-group instruction in both reading and (at least temporarily) mathematics. Be sure to keep groups flexible, changing membership according to achievement.

- Consider whether it might be possible to team with one or more teachers so that students on similar levels can be grouped for basic skills instruction.
- Consider the use of peer tutoring for certain activities and assignments.
- Share materials with other teachers to build a collection of supplementary materials above and below your grade level.
- Arrange student seating so that you have easy access to lower-ability students and can monitor and help them readily during whole-class instruction.
- Be sure to include all students in class discussions and recitations. Seek students of varying ability levels to answer questions.
- After giving assignment directions to the whole class, check the lower-ability students first to make sure that they understand the directions and are beginning work. If more than two or three students need further directions, meet with them immediately as a small group.
- When instructing the lower-level students, break assignments and lessons into small segments, and check frequently for understanding. Follow the suggestions for basic skill instruction presented in Chapter 11 in the section on teaching lower-achieving students.
- Consider using heterogeneous cooperative groups for activities and long-term projects.
- Consider using supportive, remedial, or enrichment software programs.

# REFERENCES

Akin-Little, K. A., Eckert, T. L., Lovett, B. J., & Little, S. G. (2004). Extrinsic reinforcement in the classroom: Bribery or best practice. *School Psychology Review, 33*, 344–362.

Alberti, R. L. (Ed.). (1977). *Assertiveness: Innovations, applications, issues*. San Luis Obispo, CA: Impact.

Albrecht, S. F. (2008). Time away: A skill-building alternative to discipline. *Preventing School Failure, 53*(1), 49–55.

Battistich, V., Solomon, D., Watson, M., & Schaps, E. (1997). Caring school communities. *Educational Psychologist, 32*, 137–151.

Berger, E. H., & Rojas-Cortez, M. R. (2011). *Parents as partners in education: Families and schools working together* (8th ed.). Englewood Cliffs, NJ: Prentice Hall.

Bitter, G. G., & Legacy, J. (2008). *Using technology in the classroom* (7th ed.). New York: Pearson Education.

Borich, G. (2006). *Effective teaching methods* (6th ed.). Upper Saddle River, NJ: Prentice Hall.

Brophy, J. (1981). Teacher praise: A functional analysis. *Review of Educational Research, 51*, 5–32.

Brophy, J. E. (1996). *Teaching problem students*. New York: Guilford Press.

Brophy, J. E. (2000). Teaching. In H. J. Walberg (Series Ed.), *Educational practices*. Brussels, Belgium: International Academy of Education.

Brophy, J. E. (2004). *Motivating students to learn* (2nd ed.). Hillsdale, NJ: Erlbaum.

Brophy, J. E. (2006). History of research on classroom management. In C. Evertson & C. Weinstein (Eds.), *Handbook of research on classroom management: Research, practice, and contemporary issues* (pp. 17–43). Mahwah, NJ: Erlbaum.

Brophy, J. E. (2009). Connecting with the big picture. *Educational Psychologist, 44*, 147–157.

Brophy, J. E., & Evertson, C. M. (1976). *Learning from teaching: A developmental perspective*. Boston: Allyn & Bacon.

Burns, M. (1995). The 8 most important lessons I've learned about organizing my teaching year. *Instructor, 105*(2), 86–88.

Butin, D. (2000). *Classrooms*. Washington, DC: National Center for Educational Facilities (ERIC Report No. ED446421). Available at www.edfacilities.org/ir/irpubs.html

Buzzell, J. G., & Piazza, R. (1994). *Case studies for teaching special needs and at-risk students*. Albany, NY: Delmar.

Cameron, J. (2001). Negative effects of reward on intrinsic motivation—a limited phenomenon: Comment on Deci, Koestner, and Ryan (2001). *Review of Educational Research, 71*, 29–42.

Carifio, J., & Carey, T. (2009). A critical examination of current minimum grading policy recommendations. *High School Journal, 93*(1), 23–37.

Castle, K., & Rogers, K. (1994). Rule-creating in a constructivist classroom community. *Childhood Education, 70*(2), 77–80.

Cohen, E. G. (1994). Restructuring the classroom: Conditions for productive small groups. *Review of Educational Research, 64*, 1–36.

Cohen, E. G. (1998). Making cooperative learning equitable. *Educational Leadership, 56*, 18–21.

Damiani, V. B. (2006). *Crisis prevention and intervention in the classroom: What teachers should know*. Lanham, MD: Rowman & Littlefield.

Davis, (2004). *Schools where everyone belongs: Practical strategies for reducing bullying*. Wayne, ME: Stop Bullying Now.

Deci, E. L., Koestner, R., & Ryan, R. M. (2001). Extrinsic rewards and intrinsic motivation in education: Reconsidered once again. *Review of Educational Research, 71*, 1–27.

Delgado-Gaitan, C. (2004). *Involving Latino families in schools: Raising student achievement through home-school partnerships*. Thousand Oaks, CA: Corwin Press.

Diller, D. (2008). *Designing classrooms for literacy: Spaces and places*. Portland, ME: Stenhouse.

Doyle, W. (1986). Classroom organization and management. In M. Wittrock (Ed.), *Handbook of research on teaching* (3rd ed., pp.392–431). New York: Macmillan.

Doyle, W. (2006). Ecological approaches to classroom management. In C. Evertson &

C. Weinstein (Eds.), *Handbook of research on classroom management: Research, practice, and contemporary issues* (pp. 97–125). Mahwah, NJ: Erlbaum.

Drummond, K. V., & Stipek, D. (2004). Low-income parents' beliefs about their role in children's academic learning. *Elementary School Journal, 104*(3), 197–213.

Emmer, E. T. (1988). Praise and the instructional process. *Journal of Classroom Interaction, 23*, 32–39.

Emmer, E. T., & Aussiker, A. (1990). School and classroom discipline programs: How well do they work? In O. Moles (Ed.), *Student discipline strategies: Research and practice* (pp. 129–165). Albany, NY: SUNY Press.

Emmer, E. T., & Gerwels, M. C. (2002). Cooperative learning in elementary classrooms: Teaching practices and lesson characteristics. *Elementary School Journal, 103*, 75–91.

Emmer, E. T., & Stough, L. (2008). Responsive classroom management. In T. Good (Ed.), *21st Century education: A reference handbook* (Vol. 1., pp. 140–148). Los Angeles: Sage.

Erwin, J. C. (2003). Giving students what they need. *Educational Leadership, 61*(1), 19–23.

Evertson, C. M. (2010). *Creating conditions for learning: A comprehensive program for creating an effective learning environment* (8th ed.). Nashville, TN: Vanderbilt University, Peabody College.

Evertson, C. M., & Poole, I. R. (2004a). *Effective room arrangement*. Nashville, TN: Vanderbilt University, Peabody College, IRIS Center. Available at iris.peabody.vanderbilt.edu

Evertson, C. M., & Poole, I. R. (2004b). *Fostering student accountability for classroom work*. Nashville, TN: Vanderbilt University, Peabody College, IRIS Center. Available at iris.peabody.vanderbilt.edu

Evertson, C. M., & Poole, I. R. (2004c). *Norms and expectations*. Nashville, TN: Vanderbilt University, Peabody College, IRIS Center. Available at iris.peabody.vanderbilt.edu

Evertson, C. M., & Poole, I. R. (2008). Proactive classroom management. In T. Good (Ed.), *21st Century education: A reference handbook*. Thousand Oaks, CA: Sage.

Evertson, C. M., & Weinstein, C. S. (Eds.). (2006). *Handbook of research on classroom management: Research, practice, and contemporary issues*. Mahwah, NJ: Erlbaum.

Fenning, P. A., & Bohanon, H. (2006). Schoolwide discipline policies: An analysis of discipline codes of conduct. In C. Evertson & C. Weinstein (Eds.), *Handbook of research on classroom management: Research, practice, and contemporary issues* (pp. 1021–1039). Mahwah, NJ: Erlbaum.

Finders, M., & Lewis, C. (1994). Why some parents don't come to school. *Educational Leadership, 51*, 50–54.

Fraser, B. J., & Walberg, H. J. (Eds.). (1991). *Educational environments: Evaluation, antecedents and consequences*. Oxford, England: Pergamon.

Fuchs, D., Fuchs, L. S., Mathes, P. G., & Simmons, D. G. (1997). Peer-assisted learning strategies: Making classrooms more responsive to diversity. *American Educational Research Journal, 34*(1), 174–206.

Gavin, K. M., & Greenfield, D. B. (1998). A comparison of levels of involvement for parents with at-risk African American kindergarten children in classrooms with high versus low teacher encouragement. *Journal of Black Psychology, 24*, 403–417.

Gay, G. (2006). Connections between classroom management and culturally responsive teaching. In C. Evertson & C. Weinstein (Eds.), *Handbook of research on classroom management: Research, practice, and contemporary issues* (pp. 343–370). Mahwah, NJ: Erlbaum.

Gillies, R. M. (2007). *Cooperative learning: Integrating theory and practice*. Los Angeles: Sage.

Glasser, W. (1975). *Reality therapy: A new approach to psychiatry*. New York: Harper & Row.

Glasser, W. (1977). 10 steps to good discipline. *Today's Education, 66*, 60–63.

Good, T. L., & Brophy, J. E. (2008). *Looking in classrooms* (10th ed.). Boston: Allyn & Bacon.

Good, T. L., Grouws, D., & Ebmeier, H. (1983). *Active mathematics teaching*. New York: Longman.

Greene, J. O., & Burleson, B. R. (Eds.). (2003). *Handbook of communication and social interaction skills*. Mahwah, NJ: Erlbaum.

Hansen, J. (2010). Teaching without talking. *Phi Delta Kappan, 92*(1), 35–40.

Hargis, C. H. (1997). *Teaching low achieving and disadvantaged students* (2nd ed.). Springfield, IL: Charles C. Thomas.

Harrist, A. W., & Bradley, K. D. (2003). "You can't say you can't play": Intervening in the process of social exclusion in the kindergarten classroom. *Early Childhood Quarterly, 18*, 185–205.

Hattie, J. (2009). *Visible learning: A synthesis of over 800 meta-analyses relating to achievement.* New York: Routledge.

Hill, C. E. (2009). *Helping skills: Facilitating exploration, insight, and action* (3rd ed.). Washington, DC: American Psychological Association.

Hodgdon, L. A. (1995). *Visual strategies for improving communication: Practical supports for school and home* (Vol. 1). Troy, MI: Quirk Roberts.

Hodgdon, L. A. (1999). *Solving behavior problems in autism* (Vol. 2). Troy, MI: Quirk Roberts.

Hoover-Dempsey, K. V., Walker, J. M. T., Sandler, H. M., Whetsel, D. R., Green, C. L., Wilkins, A. S., & Clossen, K. (2005). Why do parents become involved? Research findings and implications. *Elementary School Journal, 106*, 105–130.

Hoy, A. W., & Weinstein, C. S. (2006). Students' and teachers' knowledge, beliefs, and perceptions about classroom management. In C. M. Evertson & C. S. Weinstein (Eds.), *Handbook of research on classroom management: Research, practice, and contemporary issues.* Mahwah, NJ: Erlbaum.

Huffman, H., Jernstedt, G., Reed, V., Reber, E., Burns, M., Oostenink, R., et al. (2003). Optimizing the design of computer classrooms: The physical environment. *Educational Technology, 43*(4), 913.

Hyman, I., Bryony, K., Tabori, A., Weber, M., Mahon, M., & Cohen, I. (2006). Bullying: Theory, research, and interventions. In C. Evertson & C. Weinstein (Eds.), *Handbook of research on classroom management: Research, practice, and contemporary issues* (pp. 855–884). Mahwah, NJ: Erlbaum.

Jackson, P. (1968). *Life in classrooms.* New York: Holt, Rinehart & Winston.

Jennings, P. A., & Greenberg, M. T. (2009). The prosocial classroom: Teacher social and emotional competence in relation to student and classroom outcomes. *Review of Educational Research, 79*, 491–525.

Jeynes, W. H. (2005). A meta-analysis of the relation of parental involvement to urban elementary school student academic achievement. *Urban Education, 40*, 237–269.

Johnson, D. W., & Johnson, F. P. (2005). *Joining together: Group theory and group skills* (9th ed.). Boston: Allyn & Bacon.

Johnson, D. W., & Johnson, R. T. (1994). *Learning together and alone: Cooperative, competitive, and individualistic learning* (4th ed.). Boston: Allyn & Bacon.

Jones, R. A. (1995). *The child–school interface: Environment and behavior.* London: Cassell.

Jones, V. F., & Jones, L. S. (2010). *Comprehensive classroom management: Creating communities of support and solving problems* (9th ed.). Boston: Pearson.

Kauffman, J. M. (2008). Special education. In T. Good (Ed.), *21st Century education: A reference handbook* (Vol. 1., pp. 405–413). Thousand Oaks, CA: Sage.

Kottler, J. A. (2002). *Students who drive you crazy: Succeeding with resistant, unmotivated, and otherwise difficult young people.* Thousand Oaks, CA: Sage/Corwin Press.

Kounin, J. S. (1970). *Discipline and group management in classrooms.* New York: Holt, Rinehart & Winston.

Kounin, J. S., & Gump, P. (1974). Signal systems of lesson settings and the task related behavior of preschool children. *Journal of Educational Psychology, 66*, 554–562.

Kronberg, R., Jackson, L., Sheets, G., & Rogers-Connolly, T. (1995). A toolbox for supporting integrated education. *Teaching Exceptional Children, 27*(4), 54–58.

Kuhn, D. (2007, June). How to produce a high-achieving child. *Phi Delta Kappan, 88*(10), 757–763.

Lane, K., Falk, K., & Wehby, J. (2006). Classroom management in special education classrooms and resource rooms. In C. Evertson & C. Weinstein (Eds.), *Handbook of research on classroom management: Research, practice, and contemporary issues* (pp. 439–460). Mahwah, NJ: Erlbaum.

Le Maistre, C., & Paré, A. (2010). Whatever it takes: How beginning teachers learn to survive. *Teaching and Teacher Education, 26*, 559–564.

Leahy, S., Lyon, C., Thompson, M., & Wiliam, D. (2005, November). Classroom assessment: Minute by minute, day by day. *Educational Leadership, 63*(3), 19–24.

Lotan, R. A. (2006). Managing group work in the heterogeneous classroom. In C. Evertson & C. Weinstein (Eds.), *Handbook of research on classroom management: Research, practice, and contemporary issues* (pp. 525–539). Mahwah, NJ: Erlbaum.

McNally, J., I'Anson, J., Whewell, C., & Wilson, G. (2005). "They think that swearing is okay": First lessons in behaviour management. *Journal of Education for Teaching, 3*(3), 169–185.

Meager, J. (1996). Classroom design that works every time. *Instructor, 106*, 70–73.

Mendler, A. (1997). *Power struggles: Successful techniques for educators*. Rochester, NY: Discipline Associates.

Mergendoller, J. R., Markham, T., Revitz, J., & Larmer, J. (2006). Pervasive management of project-based learning. In C. Evertson & C. Weinstein (Eds.), *Handbook of research on classroom management: Research, practice, and contemporary issues* (pp. 583–615). Mahwah, NJ: Erlbaum.

Mueller, C. M., & Dweck, C. S. (1998). Praise for intelligence can undermine children's motivation for performance. *Journal of Personality and Social Psychology, 75*(1), 33–52.

Myles, B. S., & Simpson, R. L. (1994). Prevention and management considerations for aggressive and violent children and youth. *Education and Treatment of Children, 17*, 370–384.

Nastasi, B. K., & Clements, D. H. (1991). Research on cooperative learning: Implications for practice. *School Psychology Review, 20*, 110–131.

Nelson, J. R., & Carr, B. A. (2000). *The think time strategy for schools*. Longmont, CO: Sopris West.

Pace, J. L. (2003). Revisiting classroom authority: Theory and ideology meets practice. *Teachers College Record, 105*, 1559–1585.

Payne, R. K. (1998). *A framework for understanding poverty*. Highlands, TX: RFT.

Pianta, R. C. (2006). Classroom management and relationships between children and teachers: Implications for research and practice. In C. Evertson & C. Weinstein (Eds.), *Handbook of*

research on classroom management: Research, practice, and contemporary issues (pp. 685–709). Mahwah, NJ: Erlbaum.

Poland, S., & McCormick, J. S. (1999). *Coping with crisis: Lessons learned*. Longmont, CO: Sopris West.

Price, K. M., & Nelson, K. L. (2007). *Planning effective instruction* (3rd ed.). Belmont, CA: Thomson Wadsworth.

Randolph, C. H., & Evertson, C. M. (1995). Managing for learning: Rules, roles, and meanings in a writing class. *Journal of Classroom Interaction, 30*(2), 17–25.

Reeve, J. (2006). Extrinsic rewards and inner motivation. In C. Evertson & C. Weinstein (Eds.), *Handbook of research on classroom management: Research, practice, and contemporary issues* (pp. 645–664). Mahwah, NJ: Erlbaum.

Renninger, K. A. (2009). Interest and identity development. *Educational Psychologist, 44*, 105–118.

Ryan, R. M., & Deci, E. L. (2000). Self-determination theory and the facilitation of intrinsic motivation, social development, and well-being. *American Psychologist, 55*, 68–78.

Sandomierski, T., Kincaid, D., & Algozzine, B. (2007). Response to intervention and positive behavior support: Brothers from different mothers or sisters with different misters? *PBIS Newsletter, 4*(2). Accessed January 26, 2011, at www.pbis.org/pbis_newsletter/volume_4/issue2.aspx

Schussler, D. L., Poole, I. R., Whitlock, T. W., & Evertson, C. M. (2007). Layers and links: Learning to juggle 'one more thing' in the classroom. *Teaching and Teacher Education, 23*, 572–585.

Seiter, E. (2005). *The Internet playground: Children's access, entertainment, and mis-education*. New York: Peter Lang.

Shores, E., & Grace, C. (2005). *The portfolio book: A step-by-step guide for teachers*. Upper Saddle River, NJ: Merrill/Prentice Hall.

Shukla-Mehta, S., & Albin, R. W. (2003). Twelve practical strategies to prevent behavioral escalation in classroom settings. *Preventing School Failure, 47*, 156–172.

Simon, H. A. (1957). *Models of man: Social and rational*. New York: Wiley.

Skiba, R. J., & Rausch, M. K. (2006). Zero tolerance, suspension, and expulsion: Questions of equity and effectiveness. In C. Evertson & C. Weinstein (Eds.), *Handbook of research on classroom management: Research, practice, and contemporary issues* (pp. 1063–1089). Mahwah, NJ: Erlbaum.

Skinner, E. A., & Belmont, M. (1993). Motivation in the classroom: Reciprocal effects of teacher behavior and student engagement across the school year. *Journal of Educational Psychology, 85,* 571–581.

Slavin, R. (1995). *Cooperative learning: Theory, research, and practice* (2nd ed.). Boston: Allyn & Bacon.

Soodak, L., & McCarthy, M. R. (2006). Classroom management in inclusive settings. In C. Evertson & C. Weinstein (Eds.), *Handbook of research on classroom management: Research, practice, and contemporary issues* (pp. 461–489). Mahwah, NJ: Erlbaum.

Spady, W. G., & Mitchell, D. E. (1979). Authority and the management of classroom activities. In D. L. Duke (Ed.), *Classroom management: The 78th yearbook of the National Society for the Study of Education* (pp. 75–115). Chicago: University of Chicago Press.

Sprick, R. (1995). *The teacher's encyclopedia of behavior management: 100 problems/500 plans.* Longmont, CO: Sopris West.

Students with special needs [Special issue]. (1996). *Educational Leadership, 53*(5), 4–74.

U. S. Department of Education. (2010, August). The myths about bullying: Secretary Arne Duncan's remarks at the bullying prevention summit. Accessed January 26, 2011, at www.ed.gov/news/speeches/myths-about-bullying-secretary-arne-duncans-remarks-bullying-prevention-summit

U. S. Office for Civil Rights. (2010, October 26). Dear colleague letter. Accessed January 26, 2011, at www2.ed.gov/about/offices/list/ocr/letters/colleague-201010.html

Walker, J. M. T., & Hoover-Dempsey, K. V. (2006). Why research on parental involvement is important to classroom management. In C. Evertson & C. Weinstein (Eds.), *Handbook of research on classroom management: Research, practice, and contemporary issues* (pp. 665–684). Mahwah, NJ: Erlbaum.

Walker, J. M. T., & Hoover-Dempsey, K. V. (2008). Parent involvement. In T. L. Good (Ed.), *21st Century education: A reference handbook* (Vol. 2, pp. 382–391). Los Angeles: Sage.

Wang, M. C., Haertel, G. D., & Walberg, H. J. (1993). Toward a knowledge base for school learning. *Review of Educational Research, 63,* 249–294.

Weinstein, C. S., & David, T. G. (Eds.). (1987). *Spaces for children: The built environment and child development.* New York: Plenum Press.

Weinstein, C. S., Tomlinson-Clarke, S., & Curran, M. (2004). Toward a conception of culturally responsive classroom management. *Journal of Teacher Education, 55*(1), 25–38.

Wiggins, G., & McTighe, J. (2005). *Understanding by design* (Expanded 2nd ed.). Alexandria, VA: ASCD.

Wiske, M. S. (1994). How teaching for understanding changes the rules in the classroom. *Educational Leadership, 51*(5), 19–21.

Zuker, E. (1983). *Mastering assertiveness skills: Power and positive influence at work.* New York: AMACON.

# INDEX